OUR COLLECTION OF PRESTIGIOUS LISTEES

A LIFETIME OF ACHIEVEMENT

VOLUME I

Marquis Who's Who Ventures LLC
© 2024 Marquis Who's Who Ventures LLC
ISBN: 978-0-8379-7815-4
ISSN: 2769-1306

SERIES 4

For information, contact:
Marquis Who's Who
350 RXR Plaza
Uniondale, NY 11556

Manufactured in the United States of America.

MANAGEMENT TEAM

Erica Lee CHIEF EXECUTIVE OFFICER
Kristine McCarthy CHIEF MARKETING OFFICER
Deborah Morrissey EXECUTIVE VP OF HUMAN RESOURCES
Renée Dutcher-Pryer DIRECTOR OF EDITORIAL SERVICES
John Sartoris DIRECTOR OF DIGITAL AND PRINT PUBLICATIONS
Iris Cannetti DIRECTOR OF CUSTOMER SERVICE AND COMPLIANCE
Michael Swinarski MANAGING DIRECTOR OF SALES AND TRAINING
Nikki Masih SENIOR SALES MANAGER
Irmela Kastrat SALES MANAGER
Fran Bardio DIRECTOR OF RECRUITMENT

PRODUCTION STAFF

SENIOR EDITOR

Shaina Indovino

SENIOR PROOFREADER

Jason Ripple

PROOFREADER

Todd Oesterle

STAFF WRITERS

Lee Hamilton	Ryan Lazarus
Kenneth Hanley	Sean Levinson

GRAPHIC DESIGNER

Henry Monge

BRANDING SPECIALISTS

Gina Anselmo	Renee Molino	Elizabeth Venditto
Laura Curcio	Tina Ruggiero	Heather Villani
Roe Grossman	Jon Storey	Mykal White
Ilene Horowitz	Susan Tyson	Chaundra Woods

Table of Contents

Featured Members

ARCHITECTURE / CONSTRUCTION / DESIGN

ARTS

BUSINESS SERVICES

COMMUNITY / SOCIAL WORK / NONPROFIT

EDUCATION

Table of Contents

LAW / LEGAL SERVICES

MEDIA / ENTERTAINMENT

MEDICINE & HEALTH CARE

REAL ESTATE

RELIGION / SPIRITUAL SERVICES

RESEARCH & SCIENCE

TECHNOLOGY

OUR COLLECTION OF PRESTIGIOUS LISTEES

A LIFETIME OF ACHIEVEMENT

VOLUME I

Sean Dalle

Founder & Managing Partner (Retired)
Datum Commercial Contracting LLC

CEDAR PARK, TX UNITED STATES

From 2016 until his retirement in 2023, Sean Dalle thrived as a managing partner and as the founder of Datum Commercial Contracting LLC. With more than 30 years of construction experience to his credit, he specialized in overseeing the development of a broad range of commercial properties, including fitness centers, car washes, gasoline service stations, restaurants and indoor amusement centers. Mr. Dalle also focused on overseeing a team of more than 40 employees, establishing close relationships with his clients, recruiting new staff members and collaborating with subcontractors to ensure timely completion of complex projects.

Prior to the establishment of Datum Commercial Contracting, Mr. Dalle excelled as a superintendent, project manager and estimator with Drolette Construction Inc. between 2012 and 2016. During this period, he played an instrumental role in the development of myriad health care facilities and health care providers within the Central Texas region. Toward the end of his tenure with Drolette Construction, Mr. Dalle's leadership helped the aforementioned organization double its annual sales from $12 million in 2015 to more than $25 million in 2016.

Throughout his career with Datum Commercial Contracting, Mr. Dalle has spearheaded the building and remodeling of more than 150 Planet Fitness locations across multiple U.S. states, including Washington, Texas, New Mexico and Florida. Likewise, he has additionally overseen the construction of Love's Travel Stops and Country Stores in Colorado, South Carolina, Kentucky, Iowa and Louisiana. Moreover,

Mr. Dalle and his team have garnered further recognition for constructing locations of Altitude Trampoline Park in Pueblo, Colorado, and Lombard, Illinois.

Born in Rochester, New York, Mr. Dalle began his professional career at the age of 14, at which point he accepted a position with a local commercial construction company. Fueled by his entrepreneurial spirit, he eventually established his own construction organization, where he honed his leadership skills and learned the value of honesty, integrity and transparency in maintaining long-term business partnerships. Mr. Dalle also completed undergraduate coursework in accounting at a local college to expand his business acumen.

Thanks to his widespread reputation, Mr. Dalle has been featured in numerous local publications such as Austin Construction News. In addition to the support of his team and his renowned leadership skills, he attributes a great deal of his success to his firm understanding of his professional strengths and weaknesses. Mr. Dalle also credits his vast professional network to his ability to speak to his clients and colleagues with tremendous kindness and respect, which has influenced many former customers of Datum Commercial Contracting to recommend their services to respected industry peers.

Alongside his responsibilities with Datum Commercial Contracting, Mr. Dalle regularly contributes to multiple local charitable organizations that support impoverished families throughout his home state of Texas. In the coming years, he intends to prepare for his eventual retirement while gradually transitioning his responsibilities as a project manager and a superintendent to his younger colleagues. Mr. Dalle is extremely proud to have helped myriad members of his team improve their professional skill sets and create prosperous lifestyles for their families, particularly his lead estimator and his traveling superintendent. Since his transparent approach to his work has consistently contributed to his professional growth, he advises aspiring construction executives to communicate their reservations about upcoming projects with their colleagues before accepting opportunities requiring additional resources and highly specific expertise.

Jose G. Jimenez-Buquor

Owner & Principal Architect (Retired)
Jimenez Architects

SAN ANTONIO, TX UNITED STATES

For more than 30 years, Jose G. Jimenez-Buquor found success as an urban designer, owner and principal architect of Jimenez Architects. Prior to his retirement, he focused on designing medical facilities, schools and apartment buildings for public housing programs. Mr. Jimenez also specialized in preserving the condition of historic structures and local landmarks across his home state of Texas, particularly in the city of San Antonio.

Alongside his responsibilities with Jimenez Architects, Mr. Jimenez has additionally served as a professor at numerous academic institutions across the United States such as the University of Texas at San Antonio, Washington University in St. Louis, Missouri, and California Polytechnic State University. During the 1980s, he garnered further recognition as the author of numerous scholarly articles in relation to the influence of Hispanic architecture on modern architecture in the U.S., all of which were published by Oxford University Press. In order to stay up to date with the latest developments in his field, Mr. Jimenez continues to maintain active affiliations with the American Institute of Architecture and the Bexar County Historical Commission.

Thanks to his widespread reputation, Mr. Jimenez has been recruited to share his expertise in urban planning in major cities on multiple continents. For more than five years, he was appointed an architect and urban designer in Paris, France, on behalf of the United Nations Educational, Scientific and Cultural Organization (UNESCO). Mr. Jimenez had previously served as a city planner in Saudi Arabia on behalf of CH2M Hill, which has since been acquired by Jacobs Solutions Inc.

Born in San Antonio, Texas, Mr. Jimenez's decision to pursue a career as an architect was heavily influenced by his uncle, who enjoyed a prosperous career as the owner of an organization that specialized in engraving letters on monuments, gravestones and building facades. He was also inspired by the role of architecture in preserving the history of San Antonio. During the Civil War, Mr. Jimenez's great-great-grandfather served as the mayor of the aforementioned city.

In 1963, Mr. Jimenez obtained a Bachelor of Architecture at the University of Texas at Austin. He was subsequently selected for a scholarship to further his architectural prowess in Greece under the tutelage of Constantinos A. Doxiadis, who is widely recognized as a pioneer in the field of urban planning. During the 1970s, Mr. Jimenez furthered his skills while participating in the design of a public housing project in Saticoy, California. He eventually concluded his education in 1976, at which point he completed a master's degree in architecture and urban design at Washington University in St. Louis.

In recognition of his contributions to the restoration of Milam Park in San Antonio, Mr. Jimenez was presented with an accolade on behalf of the aforementioned city. In addition to his knowledge of architecture in myriad foreign nations, he attributes a great deal of his success to his education. Following the completion of a Bachelor of Architecture, Mr. Jimenez was deeply honored to become the first member of his family to obtain an undergraduate degree. To honor his professional achievements, he has been included in the 76th edition of Who's Who in America.

In the coming years, Mr. Jimenez intends to devote more attention to his passions for watercolor painting and international travel. He also aims to spend more time with his grandnephews. Since his tenures in France, Saudi Arabia and Greece played a central role in his professional growth, Mr. Jimenez advises aspiring architects to seek inspiration from renowned architects from all over the world.

Jeffrey M. Johnson

Senior Project Manager
Fenagh Engineering and Testing

HUNTINGTON BEACH, CA UNITED STATES

Drawing on more than 15 years of experience in the construction industry, Jeffrey M. Johnson currently excels as a senior project manager with Fenagh Engineering and Testing. In this capacity, he specializes in assessing the quality of various building materials such as steel, concrete, cement and asphalt. Mr. Johnson also focuses on overseeing a team of more than 75 building inspectors and evaluating the structural integrity of construction projects involving the development of hotels, apartment complexes, schools, hospitals and multifamily homes.

Prior to his recruitment at Fenagh Engineering and Testing, Mr. Johnson thrived as a senior project manager and as an operations manager for Twining Consulting, Inc. for more than five years. He had previously contributed to the aforementioned building inspection and materials testing agency as a deputy inspector between 2008 and 2017. During this period, Mr. Johnson was continuously appointed as the lead inspector for a broad range of structural elements for different construction processes such as steel welding, steel bolting, wood framing and structural masonry.

Alongside his primary responsibilities at Fenagh Engineering and Testing, Mr. Johnson regularly serves as a mentor to his younger colleagues. He also coordinates inspections and tests with steel fabrication organizations located all over the United States in order to establish close relationships with potential partners located outside of his home state of California. Due to the wide geographical range of Fenagh Engineering and Testing's customer base, Mr. Johnson frequently oversees projects in myriad major cities within California, including San Diego, Ventura and Irvine.

Born in Anaheim, California, Mr. Johnson's interests in construction and engineering emerged at a very young age. During his childhood, he garnered attention from his three brothers and his three sisters for his affinity for deconstructing and reconstructing numerous objects around their childhood home. Mr. Johnson eventually began his professional career in the early 1990s, at which point he accepted a position as an ironworker.

During his tenure as an ironworker, Mr. Johnson suffered a debilitating injury that inspired him to pursue further success as a building inspector. Mr. Johnson subsequently became a certified master of special inspections on behalf of the International Code Council. Likewise, Mr. Johnson additionally became a certified post-installed concrete anchor installation inspector on behalf of the American Concrete Institute. He was eventually recruited as an office administrator for a building inspection agency, where he gradually advanced to the position of operations manager over the course of just four months.

Throughout his career as a building inspector, Mr. Johnson notably oversaw a large project involving the development of nine buildings across 17 acres of land. In addition to his exceptional work ethic, he attributes a great deal of his success to his ability to exceed the expectations of his customers and secure their loyalty. Mr. Johnson also draws tremendous inspiration from his father, who demonstrated the importance of establishing documented protocols and procedures in order to simplify daily operations while building his own career as a business leader.

In the coming years, Mr. Johnson intends to pursue a position as a principal or vice president at Fenagh Engineering and Testing. He also aims to devote more time toward his passions for meditation, bicycling, reading and listening to music. Since his communication skills have played an instrumental role in his professional growth, Mr. Johnson advises aspiring construction executives to establish a strong professional network by forging meaningful relationships with their customers.

Edward Leftwich

Chief Executive Officer
RMI Designs

SMYRNA, GA UNITED STATES

A fter receiving a bachelor's degree in architecture in 1979 at the University of KwaZulu-Natal in his home country of South Africa, Edward Leftwich departed to see the world. Taking a job as a crewman on a yacht, he sailed up the coast of Africa for nine months, experiencing everything from pirate attacks to being thrown off the boat in Yemen. When the boat docked in Egypt, he left his position to travel to Greece and Israel. In 1980, he hitchhiked in an 18-wheeler behind the Iron Curtain, making his way through five communist countries until he reached Denmark. Afterward, he found his way to London and began working as an architect. Because of London's economic downturn in 1981, his position became precarious, and he decided to purchase a one-way ticket to America. He arrived without a job or contacts and immediately set about acquiring both. Eventually, he found employment in Charlotte, North Carolina, where he worked for a year before moving to Atlanta, Georgia, to work for John Portman & Associates International, Inc., in 1982. Corporate life didn't suit his adventurous, headstrong spirit, so he left the company to start his own architecture firm, RMI Designs, in late 1985.

As a child, Mr. Leftwich decided he would be an architect, inspired by his father's career as a portrait painter. He wanted to be an artist himself but strived to have a more reliable income. For Mr. Leftwich, architecture allowed him to express himself creatively while still maintaining career stability. After creating RMI Designs, Mr. Leftwich considers his most notable achievement to be opening an office in Dubai, a city in the United Arab Emirates, in 2006. Because of his unique decision as a small business owner to open a second office in a foreign country, he was featured in Fortune Small Business Magazine. He has also been featured in The Atlanta Journal-Constitution, Atlanta Business Chronicle, Entrepreneur magazine, Millenium Magazine and CNN. Previously, he has been featured in Marquis Who's Who Top Professionals and received the Albert Nelson Marquis Lifetime Achievement Award. Other awards he has received include the Joint Cost Saving Award and the Miliken Award for Best Supplier of the Year. Mr. Leftwich is an active member of the CCC, the American Institute of Architects (AIA) and the Circle of Trust, and he is a volunteer with Habitat for Humanity.

In 1989, Mr. Leftwich designed the Reebok Step, a compact home and studio workout system used in step aerobics, for which he was given part ownership in the Reebok corporation. Soon after, when he traveled to Hong Kong to oversee the production of another invention, he was pleasantly surprised to see his newly designed step at the hotel gym. To those looking to enter the architecture field, Mr. Leftwich would advise having patience and a positive attitude and to expect that things may not always turn out as well or as quickly as one might like.

Looking ahead, Mr. Leftwich plans to write a book about his journeys. His immediate goal is to continue to grow his business while stepping back to have more time for his interests and hobbies, like traveling and oil painting. When he leaves the field, he hopes to be remembered with great fondness as a kind and good person.

Charles R. Matschek, AIA

Senior Architect
AM Technical Solutions

Architectural Consultant
MYP Maquetas

PORTLAND, OR UNITED STATES

A n established and respected architect, Charles R. Matschek, AIA, celebrates 50 years of success in his field. After receiving a Bachelor of Architecture with a minor in film criticism from the University of Oregon, Mr. Matschek began his career as an architect in San Diego, California. Over a period of 15 years, Mr. Matschek worked abroad as an architect in places like Singapore and New Zealand. Throughout his time overseas, he cultivated professional and personal relationships within the Hispanic community and made frequent trips to Mexico. One of these connections introduced him to the proprietors of MYP Maquetas, an architecture firm in Zapopan, Mexico. Subsequently, he assumed the role of consultant and representative, serving as the face of the company's business prospects within the United States. His ties to the firm's owner have exceeded two decades, and the two continue to maintain a close professional relationship.

When Mr. Matschek returned to the U.S. in 1996, he served as an associate architect and then a consulting architect for Ankrom Moisan Architects, Inc., in Portland, Oregon, until 2011. Following his position with Ankrom Moisan Architects, he worked as an architect with MEC Engineering from 2011 to 2013, when he moved to AM Technical Solutions in Hillsboro, Oregon, as a construction project coordinator. In the realm of construction, Mr. Matschek takes considerable pride in his contributions to various commercial mixed-use buildings. Among these, his most distinguished accomplishment lies in his architectural oversight of the Evergreen Aviation Museum in McMinnville, Oregon. For his exceptional concrete work on the project, he was acknowledged by the American Concrete Institute.

Prior to the museum project, Mr. Matschek served as an architect for the air operations and training facilities at Portland International Airport on behalf of Horizon Airlines, a partner within the Alaska Air Group. The position provided him with invaluable insights into the operational intricacies of the airline industry, encompassing protocols for operations, training, regulatory compliance, security measures, supply chain logistics, critical aircraft components, and aircraft inspection and maintenance procedures. Mr. Matschek left AM Technical Solutions to explore other career opportunities but ultimately returned to the company in 2023 as a senior architect. Presently, he works with both AM Technical Solutions and MYP Maquetas.

In his spare time, Mr. Matschek is a motorsport enthusiast, having been a driving instructor and coach with the Cascade Sports Car Club since 2010. Additionally, he is a proud supporter of the Friends of PIR (Portland International Raceway), a 501(c)(3) nonprofit responsible for the raceway's preservation and care. He also enjoys mountaineering and skiing and has been a board member with the Friends of Timberline, a historical society in Portland, Oregon, that protects Portland's historic Timberline Lodge, since 2010.

A native of Oregon, Mr. Matschek proudly represents the fifth generation of a lineage deeply rooted in the region. His ancestral heritage traces back to his great-grandfather, who facilitated his grandfather's pursuit of higher education at the University of Oregon in 1910. This familial tradition continued as Mr. Matschek and his father are both University of Oregon alumni. Mr. Matschek keeps in mind the motto, "Hold no expectations," which has served him well over his long and vibrant career.

Jeff Couch

Photographer & Owner
Jeff Couch Food Images

PALM DESERT, CA UNITED STATES

Since 2017, Jeff Couch has thrived as a photographer and owner of Jeff Couch Food Images, a photography studio based in Palm Desert, California. With more than 35 years of experience in the food service industry to his credit, he specializes in capturing images of a broad range of food and beverage items as well as cooking tools and fully prepared meals. Mr. Couch also focuses on channeling his photographs into advertising materials for restaurants, hotels, catering companies and individual chefs.

Alongside his responsibilities as a photographer and as the owner of a photography studio, Mr. Couch excelled as the owner of an organization related to food service sales and marketing across the United States' West Coast between 2001 and 2021. He had previously found success as the vice president of sales and marketing for a manufacturer of commercial cooking equipment for the restaurant industry throughout the 1990s. Between 1985 and 1992, Mr. Couch honed his creative skills while working as a chef in his native country of Canada.

Throughout his career with Jeff Couch Food Images, Mr. Couch has captured images of menu items from myriad renowned restaurants throughout his home state of California, including Charcoal Venice, Osteria Mozza, and Republique Restaurant. Likewise, he has also photographed menu items from iconic food service outlets in Los Angeles, California, such as Canter's Deli and The Original Pantry Café.

Moreover, Mr. Couch's photographs have been featured in a host of popular attractions and bustling centers of activity, including the Santa Monica Pier, Los Angeles Union Station and El Pueblo de Los Ángeles Historical Monument.

Born in London, Ontario, Canada, Mr. Couch began his career in the food service industry as a cook in a hotel. Serving in this part-time capacity for a number of years eventually inspired him to pursue a career as a chef. Mr. Couch subsequently underwent culinary training at Fanshawe College in Ontario, Canada.

After finding success in the food service industry for several decades, Mr. Couch attended the University of California Los Angeles Extension, where he earned a Photography Certificate, with distinction, in commercial photography in 2016. He also became a certified professional photographer on behalf of the Professional Photographers of America. In order to stay up to date with the latest developments in his field, Mr. Couch continues to maintain active affiliations with the Professional Photographers of America as well as American Photographic Artists.

In 2022, Mr. Couch was selected for a Silver Award in the food category of the WPE International Photography Awards. He had previously been included in One Eyeland's list of the Top 100 Photographers of 2019. Moreover, Mr. Couch has additionally been celebrated with multiple accolades on behalf of American Photographic Artists and Foodelia.

Thanks to his widespread reputation, Mr. Couch has been featured in several digital and print publications such as LensCulture, Canvas-Rebel and Shoutout LA. In addition to his family's support, he attributes a great deal of his success to his firm commitment to his professional goals. Mr. Couch is particularly proud to have photographed menu items for numerous chefs who have been distinguished with a Michelin Star on behalf of the Michelin Guide. In the coming years, he intends to showcase his expertise in an array of cookbooks and major publications within the culinary community.

Nasreen Haroon

Artist
Nasreen Haroon Collections

LOS ANGELES, CA UNITED STATES

F or more than 30 years, Nasreen Haroon has thrived as a visual artist of abstract and impressionist oil paintings. In this capacity, she focuses on creating spiritual and celestial images containing unique color combinations and scattered arrangements of gold leaves. Ms. Haroon also specializes in composing landscapes depicting her childhood in Karachi, Pakistan, as well as natural scenes in France, Italy and her home state of California.

Throughout her career, Ms. Haroon's paintings have been exhibited at galleries in many nations, including the ARTA Gallery in Toronto, Ontario, Canada, the Schomburg Gallery at Bergamot Station in Santa Monica, California, and ArtChock the Gallery in Karachi, Pakistan. Thanks to her international reputation, her art has appeared in the United States Embassies in Pakistan, Senegal, Algeria, Nigeria, Saudi Arabia and Bangladesh. Widely renowned for her cultural diplomacy efforts in the United Arab Emirates, Ms. Haroon has additionally showcased her art at the Sharjah Cultural Palace and Dubai's MIRAJ Islamic Art Centre.

In 2007, Ms. Haroon was recruited as a cultural envoy to the United Arab Emirates, where she served as an art educator for students in the cities of Dubai, Abu Dhabi and Sharjah. Likewise, she has shared her expertise in lectures and workshops at myriad academic institutions, including the California Institute of Arts, the University of Southern

California, and the University of California, Los Angeles. Ms. Haroon has also been appointed as a guest lecturer and speaker at numerous museums and cultural centers in Algeria, including the National Museum of Fine Arts, the Palace of Culture and the National Library of Algeria. In 2008, she helped coordinate the development of a painted mural at a shelter for victims of domestic abuse in the aforementioned African nation.

Between 1999 and 2002, Ms. Haroon found further success as a board member for the Islamic Center of Southern California. She had previously excelled as the vice president of the Pakistan Arts Council of the University of Southern California Pacific Asia Museum between 1997 and 1999. During the beginning of this period, Ms. Haroon was simultaneously recruited as a founding board member of the Los Angeles chapter of Developments in Literacy, which provides educational services to underserved communities in Pakistan.

Born in Karachi, Pakistan, Ms. Haroon's artistic talents initially emerged at the age of 13. In 1972, she obtained a Bachelor of Arts in psychology, philosophy and history at St. Joseph's College for Women. Ms. Haroon eventually relocated to Santa Monica, California, in 1980. Between 1983 and 1994, she served as a design consultant for Hotel Shangri-La in Los Angeles, which is now known as the Beacon.

In 2023, the Pakistan Arts Council of the University of Southern California Pacific Asia Museum selected Ms. Haroon for a Distinguished Artist Award. She has been featured in the 76th edition of Who's Who in America and has also been honored with a Trailblazer Award on behalf of NewGround: A Muslim-Jewish Partnership for Change. Moreover, Ms. Haroon is particularly proud to have been featured on a popular Algerian talk show known as "Bonjour Algerie" for more than 30 minutes, which enabled her to showcase the diversity of the fine arts community of the United States.

Along with her father's support, Ms. Haroon attributes a great deal of her success to her selfless approach to her profession. In the coming years, she intends to compose more abstract paintings while continuing to advocate for global peace and unity. In her spare time, Ms. Haroon relaxes by reading, gardening and designing handmade jewelry.

Willette Murphy Klausner

Theater and Film Producer & Owner
WMK Productions, Inc.

LOS ANGELES, CA UNITED STATES

For more than 40 years, Willette Murphy Klausner has thrived as a producer of feature films and theatrical productions as well as the owner of WMK Productions, Inc. In these capacities, she focuses on securing funding to produce plays and musicals for New York City's Broadway theater district. Ms. Klausner also regularly collaborates with playwrights, performers and screenwriters to develop stories for original productions and revivals or sequels of iconic musicals.

Alongside her responsibilities with WMK Productions, Ms. Klausner found further success as the president and owner of a musical production known as "Three Mo' Tenors" between 2001 and 2013. She additionally contributes to the Coalition for African Americans in the Performing Arts as a board member of the development wing. Ms. Klausner had previously served as a board member for the Los Angeles Music Center and the Women in Film Foundation.

Throughout her career, Ms. Klausner has been appointed as a mentor for the Front Row Productions Fellowship, which is distributed on behalf of Columbia University, the American Cinema Foundation and the advisory board of Women in Film Los Angeles. In order to stay up to date with the latest developments in her field, she continues to maintain active affiliations with the League of Professional Theatre Women and the International Women's Forum. Outside of her professional circles, Ms. Klausner has garnered widespread recognition as a co-founder of the American Institute of Wine and Food, which was initially established by Julia Child, Robert Mondavi and several other iconic figures from the food industry.

Prior to the formation of WMK Productions in 1981, Ms. Klausner prospered as the vice president of the marketing research department for Universal City Studios LLC for more than five years. During this period, she played an instrumental role in the creation of the aforementioned department, which was among the first of its kind for a major film production company. Ms. Klausner notably conducted a series of marketing initiatives to promote the 1975 film "Jaws," which eventually became the first feature film to gross more than $1 million.

Born in Omaha, Nebraska, Ms. Klausner and her family relocated to California during her childhood. In 1981, she obtained a Bachelor of Science in economics at the University of California, Los Angeles. Ms. Klausner subsequently completed coursework at the Wood Tobé–Coburn School, which has since closed, before finding success as a fashion model for Bloomingdale's Inc. and MADELEINE Mode GmbH, which is owned by TriStyle Mode GmbH.

While completing her undergraduate degree, Ms. Klausner was elected the first female senior class president of the University of California, Los Angeles. She was also among the first African American fashion models to be featured in a major American fashion magazine and the first female vice president at University City Studios. In 2022, the Drama League honored Ms. Klausner with a Lifetime Achievement Award.

In addition to her determination and exceptional work ethic, Ms. Klausner attributes a great deal of her success to the support of her parents, who taught her the value of hard work at a very young age. In the coming years, she intends to further the development of a theatrical production known as "Cosette," which will be based on a primary character from the iconic musical, "Les Misérables." Likewise, Ms. Klausner also aims to develop an American version of Charles Dickens' "Oliver Twist" that will be titled "Twist."

Michael Lam

Art Consultant
Vision Art Media

NEW YORK, NY UNITED STATES

Since 2018, Michael Lam has thrived as an art consultant, art curator and the driving force behind Vision Art Media. His work involves orchestrating art exhibitions and promotional campaigns for visual artists globally, showcasing their creations in distinguished museums, galleries and nonprofit institutions thereby broadening their reach.

Leveraging his extensive professional network, Mr. Lam consistently creates avenues for abstract and figurative artists from Europe and Asia, especially cultivating a dedicated following for them through solo exhibitions in his native New York. Throughout his tenure at Vision Art Media, he has utilized his marketing acumen to propel the careers of visual artists hailing from Norway, Croatia, Italy, Germany and several Asian nations, including the Philippines, China and Singapore.

Beyond his contributions to Vision Art Media, Mr. Lam has previously garnered acclaim as an art professor in various countries. He has also made substantial contributions to the AEIOU Foundation and various humanitarian organizations, including the United Nations Children's Fund, advocating for early intervention services for children with autism spectrum disorders.

Hailing from China, Mr. Lam's artistic talent blossomed during his childhood, as he honed his skills in Chinese calligraphy and visual arts. Over time, he developed a distinctive single-stroke painting style, renowned for its harmonious blend of abstract and figurative elements. After achieving success in his home country, Mr. Lam relocated to New York over two decades ago. Over the subsequent years, his works were prominently displayed in esteemed galleries and museums such as the Agora Gallery and the Lower Eastside Tenement Museum.

In recognition of his contributions, Mr. Lam was honored with the Special Achievement Award by the International Council of Museums Asia-Pacific Alliance in 2019 and the Sandro Botticelli Prize in Florence, Italy, in 2014, acknowledging the originality of his artistic expression. In 2023, he was named the Top International Art Consultant of the Year by IAOTP.

Stephen Suber, MusD

Composer

Professor of Music

Southeastern Louisiana University

HAMMOND, LA UNITED STATES

With over four decades of practiced experience to his credit, Stephen Suber, MusD, has achieved professional success in the field of academia. Bearing particular expertise in composition, history and music theory, he has served as a professor at Southeastern Louisiana University (Southeastern) since 1982. Drawing consistent motivation from passing on his knowledge to others, he consistently strives to imbue his students with a passion for music that equals his own and has found immense gratification from hearing his ideas come to life through their efforts.

Outside of his work as a teacher, Dr. Suber has also distinguished himself as a composer with over 55 pieces to his credit. Much of his creative output dabbles in a variety of mediums, comprising symphonic pieces, choral works, accompanied songs, electronic tape, mixed ensembles with live performers and large orchestras. His older pieces are particularly dear to him, including a piano concerto titled "Enchantments: Concerto for Piano and Orchestra," which was largely sketched during his two-month residency at the Helene Wurlitzer Foundation Colony in Taos, New Mexico, in 1989. The piece, commissioned by the Louisiana Music Teachers Association, was ultimately performed by the Southeastern Louisiana University Chamber Orchestra, featuring Gerard Schwartz as conductor and David Evenson as pianist. In addition to "Enchantments," a great deal of Dr. Suber's work is available for listening via his website profile at the American Composers Alliance.

Dr. Suber came of age in a military family, which afforded him the unique opportunity to travel far and wide throughout the world. While living in Turkey, he took piano lessons from a Julliard graduate and later learned to play the clarinet, which became a long-abiding hobby. Though he initially saw a life for himself in foreign service as a diplomat, Dr. Suber had a life-changing epiphany while studying in college. During that time, he was involved in a traumatic car accident that led him to truly appreciate his talent for music. Having completed his undergraduate studies at Principia College, he went on to study music at Mills College, where he earned a Master of Arts in 1974. Following this accomplishment, he matriculated at Indiana University Bloomington and ultimately attained a Doctor of Music in 1982. Throughout his final two years there, he also shared his lessons as a visiting lecturer in composition at the School of Music.

Outside of his aforementioned accomplishment in composing "Enchantments," Dr. Suber is most proud to have been recognized for his talent in the form of "Symphony: Of Wind and Light," which he composed for the Indiana State University Orchestral Composition Contest and premiered in 1982 via the Indianapolis Symphony Orchestra. Additionally, as a teacher, he was thrilled to allow his class to be taught by American composer Leonard Bernstein, which lasted well into the wee hours of the morning. Well-regarded for his contributions to the field, Dr. Suber was named Composer of the Year by the National Music Teachers Association in 1993.

In accounting for his standout success, Dr. Suber credits the influence of the various mentors with whom he studied during his education, including Reinhart Ross, Robert Ashley and Terry Riley. Likewise, he attributes much of his prosperity to a sense of gratitude for having been chosen to excel at music. In offering his advice to those who may seek to follow his example, he would encourage burgeoning musicians to follow their dreams and always view things in a positive light. Looking toward the future, Dr. Suber plans to continue teaching and working in academia for as long as possible.

Martha Bond Branson

Owner & Manager
Stone Creek Farms
Stone Creek Hunting Club, LLC

MACON, GA UNITED STATES

F or more than 45 years, Martha Bond Branson has thrived as the owner and manager of Stone Creek Farms and the Stone Creek Hunting Club, LLC in Macon, Georgia. In these capacities, she specializes in overseeing several systematic conservation and reforestation programs for the continuous production of timber. Ms. Branson also focuses on facilitating the production of various crops and livestock while coordinating promotional initiatives to increase membership for the Stone Creek Hunting Club.

Alongside her responsibilities at Stone Creek Farms and the Stone Creek Hunting Club, Ms. Branson currently works as a Republican representative for the Jones County Board of Elections in Gray, Georgia. She simultaneously serves as the vice chairperson of the Jones County Republican Party, which had previously appointed her as the chairperson. Likewise, Ms. Branson contributes to the Georgia Republican Party as a member of numerous committees. She also excels as a board member of The Cannonball House in Macon, Georgia, a historically significant Greek revival home listed on the U.S. National Park Service's National Register of Historic Places.

Between 1967 and 1974, Ms. Branson established her political expertise while working for Ronald John Thompson, who is recognized as the first mayor of Macon, Georgia, to have been affiliated with the Republican Party. She subsequently accepted a position with John James Walker Flynt Jr., who served in the U.S. House of Representatives for two congressional districts in Georgia. Ms. Branson has also held clerical positions with numerous financial services organizations, including the Bank of America Corporation, H&R Block, Inc., and a mortgage banking company known as Bark and Brooks Inc., where she found success as a receptionist and secretary during the early 1980s.

Outside of her professional circles, Ms. Branson regularly supports multiple charitable and health care research organizations, including Samaritan's Purse and St. Jude Children's Research Hospital, through her affiliation with the Ingleside Baptist Church. She also maintains an active affiliation with the Tennessee Walking Horse Breeders' and Exhibitors' Association. Ms. Branson had previously contributed to the aforementioned organization as a board member for many years after participating in myriad Tennessee Walking Horse show competitions.

Born in Macon, Georgia, Ms. Branson was designated governor of Georgia Girls State, which is an educational program of the American Legion Auxiliary, while attending A.L. Miller Senior High School, which has since closed. During this period, she was selected to represent the state of Georgia at the American Legion Auxiliary Girls Nation event in Washington, D.C., where she was introduced to numerous members of the U.S. Congress. Toward the late 1950s, Ms. Branson completed undergraduate coursework at Mercer University. She subsequently completed additional coursework at Crandall Junior College, which has since closed. To celebrate her professional achievements, she has been included in the 76th edition of Who's Who in America.

In addition to her Baptist faith, Ms. Branson attributes a great deal of her success to the influence of her parents and her grandparents, particularly her grandfather, who is recognized as the original founder of Stone Creek Farms. She is extremely proud to have been celebrated with several accolades as a competitive Tennessee Walking Horse rider. Ms. Branson was also deeply honored to represent Ronald John Thompson at a charitable event to support children with leukemia. In the coming years, she intends to chronicle her diverse career and unique childhood experiences into a book.

Paul Frederick Burmeister

Farmer

Owner & Agriculturist
Paul Burmeister Farm

CLAFLIN, KS UNITED STATES

F or more than 60 years, Paul Frederick Burmeister has thrived as a farmer and an agriculturist. For 45 years, he has been the owner of Paul Burmeister Farm near Claflin, Kansas. In the former capacity, he specializes in the production of winter wheat, spring oats, smooth bromegrass and grain sorghum. Mr. Burmeister also focuses on maintaining the condition of the aforementioned farm's soil and providing local grain cooperatives and cattle farmers with a variety of wheat and grains.

Alongside his responsibilities with Paul Burmeister Farm, Mr. Burmeister has excelled as an active affiliate of the Kansas Natural Resource Council, Inc., as well as the Natural Resources Defense Council in New York City since 1975. Between 1995 and 2001, he was appointed to the farmer advisory committee for The Land Institute's Sunshine Farm Research Program, which explored the possibility of replacing fossil fuels, synthetic fertilizers, and pesticides with renewable energy technologies and other sustainable practices for raising crops and livestock. Mr. Burmeister had previously participated in multiple conferences related to sustainable agriculture in the cities of Great Bend and Salina in Kansas and in Rapid City, South Dakota, during the early 1990s.

Between 2008 and 2014, Mr. Burmeister was recruited as a board member of the Kansas-Oklahoma Conference Foundation of the United

Church of Christ. He had initially served on the Kansas-Oklahoma Conference Council between 1999 and 2003. Between 2005 and 2010, Mr. Burmeister found further success as a member of the board of trustees of the Clara Barton Hospital Foundation.

Throughout his career, Mr. Burmeister has contributed articles to several professional journals and publications in relation to agriculture and environmental conservation. He has also represented the local farming community as a participant in numerous community forums and political committees. Between 1976 and 1980, Mr. Burmeister served as a lobbyist and as a campaign organizer for the Union of Concerned Scientists, which is a nonprofit organization that strives to address several issues in relation to the environment such as climate change and energy shortages. In order to stay up to date with the latest developments in his field, Mr. Burmeister continues to maintain active affiliations with a host of professional organizations, including the Kansas Farmers Union and the American Solar Energy Society.

In 1952, Mr. Burmeister began doing fieldwork with tractors and implements for his father, Ferdinand Frederick Adam Burmeister. He had previously developed a fascination with the independence of his father's daily routine during his childhood. Mr. Burmeister also enjoyed riding his father's tractor while carefully observing the direct relationship between his father's duties and recurring meteorological events.

In 1960, Mr. Burmeister earned a Bachelor of Arts in chemistry and agriculture from Fort Hays State University. He subsequently pursued a volunteer position with the Peace Corps. Between 1961 and 1963, Mr. Burmeister broadened his agricultural engineering expertise while working in the Ludhiana District in Punjab State, India, on behalf of the aforementioned agency. Following his return to the United States, he served in the Kansas Army National Guard between 1963 and 1969.

In addition to his Christian faith, Mr. Burmeister attributes a great deal of his success to the guidance of his mentors, particularly his former teachers and pastors. He also credits the continuous prosperity of Paul Burmeister Farm to the perpetual expansion of his agricultural knowledge. Mr. Burmeister is extremely proud to have maintained the Burmeister family's ownership of the aforementioned farm for more than 90 years. Due to the unpredictable nature of his profession, he advises aspiring farmers to remember that new problems require new solutions as well as research into new sources of information. He has been honored with inclusion in the 76th edition of Who's Who in America.

John Frederick Derr, RPh, FASCP

Senior Strategy Consultant
The Loran Group, LLC

LIVINGSTON, MT UNITED STATES

S ince 2016, John Frederick Derr, RPh, FASCP, has thrived as a senior strategy consultant and founding partner with The Loran Group, LLC. With more than 60 years of experience in the health care industry to his credit, he specializes in helping health care organizations develop and implement innovative strategies to improve efficiency, profitability and patient care. Mr. Derr also focuses on guiding health care organizations through critical initiatives such as the launch of a new product or the introduction of advanced information technology into daily operations.

Alongside his responsibilities as a senior strategy consultant, Mr. Derr has excelled as the founder of the LTPAC Health IT Collaborative since 2005. Likewise, he has contributed to JD and Associates Enterprises, Inc. as the president and the chief executive officer for more than 25 years. Between 2021 and 2022, Mr. Derr was simultaneously appointed as the chief clinical technology adviser for eCare21 Inc.

Prior to the formation of The Loran Group, Mr. Derr held numerous leadership positions with Golden Living such as the strategic clinical technology adviser, senior vice president, chief information officer and chief technology officer between 2007 and 2013. He had previously found success as the executive vice president of the American Health Care Association and the National Center for Assisted Living for more than five years after serving as the vice president of marketing and as the vice president of mergers and acquisitions with the Sun Healthcare Group, Inc. between 1998 and 2001. During the early 1990s, Mr. Derr prospered as the president and chief executive officer of Innovative Health Concepts, Inc., which has since closed.

Between 1989 and 1991, Mr. Derr was appointed as the general manager of Kinamed Incorporated, a subsidiary of Japan's Kyocera Corporation. He had previously established his technological expertise as the president and chief executive officer of Westlake Group, Inc., which has since closed, throughout the late 1980s while simultaneously serving as a consultant for Siemens Medical Solutions USA, Inc. Between 1982 and 1985, Mr. Derr contributed to IRIS International, Inc., as the chief operating officer after finding success as the senior vice president of international marketing and as the president of the international equipment division of the Tenet Healthcare Corporation between 1980 and 1982.

In 1980, Mr. Derr excelled as the vice president and as the manager of the nuclear and ultrasound division of Siemens Medical Solutions USA, Inc. Throughout the late 1970s, he advanced to several leadership positions with G.D. Searle, LLC, which is now a subsidiary of Pfizer, Inc., such as the vice president of marketing. Mr. Derr had previously worked as the director of strategic planning and development at E. R. Squibb and Sons Inter-American Corporation between 1966 and 1974.

During his tenure at Golden Living, Mr. Derr was recruited to the U.S. Department of Health and Human Service's federal advisory committee for standards in software. Between 2008 and 2013, he simultaneously thrived as the chairperson of the American Society for Clinical Pathology Foundation. Mr. Derr had previously been appointed to the board of trustees of the Certification Commission for Health Information Technology in 2008.

Born in Chicago, Illinois, Mr. Derr obtained a Bachelor of Science in pharmacy from Purdue University in 1958 before serving in the U.S. Navy for more than five years, during which period he advanced to the rank of captain. He was subsequently promoted to the position of commanding officer with the U.S. Navy Reserve. Mr. Derr eventually issued his retirement from the military in 1989, at which point he was honored with a Meritorious Service Medal on behalf of the U.S. Navy. The former director of the Purdue Alumni Association's western region, he was also distinguished as an Outstanding Alumnus on behalf of Purdue University in 2006. 🌿

Raj Doppalapudi

Country Head
Privi Specialty Chemicals Limited

SOMERSET, NJ UNITED STATES

For more than 10 years, Raj Doppalapudi has thrived as the country manager of Privi Specialty Chemicals Limited, which provides a wide array of aroma and fragrance chemicals. With more than 25 years of experience as a corporate executive to his credit, he specializes in expanding Privi Specialty Chemicals' presence in Europe and North and South America. Mr. Doppalapudi also focuses on consistently improving Privi Specialty Chemicals' financial health and the efficiency of the aforementioned organization's daily operations, particularly in relation to manufacturing.

Prior to his appointment as the country head, Mr. Doppalapudi contributed to Privi Specialty Chemicals as the senior manager of global accounts between 2010 and 2013. During this period, he played an instrumental role in the formation of Privi Specialty Chemicals' manufacturing facilities in the United States as well as the recruitment of the facilities' team members. Mr. Doppalapudi had previously excelled as the manager of Privi Specialty Chemicals' exportation efforts between 1989 and 1998, at which point the aforementioned organization began exporting products to various European nations, particularly Germany.

In order to stay up to date with the latest developments in his field, Mr. Doppalapudi additionally maintains active affiliations with numerous professional organizations, including Women in Flavor and Fragrance Commerce, Inc., which offers professional development and networking services for male and female professionals in the international flavor and fragrance industry.

Born in Mumbai, India, Mr. Doppalapudi's decision to pursue a career as a corporate executive was chiefly inspired by his father, who helped establish Privi Specialty Chemicals during the early 1980s. Following his graduation from Bharat English School, he earned a Bachelor of Commerce at DAV University in Punjab, India, in 1998. Mr. Doppalapudi subsequently completed a postgraduate diploma in sales and marketing at India's National Institute of Sales and Marketing. He eventually concluded his education at St. Xavier's College in Mumbai, where he obtained a second postgraduate diploma in business management in 2004.

In 2013, Mr. Doppalapudi relocated to the United States to directly oversee the development of Privi Specialty Chemicals' new operations in the United States as well as the exportation of Privi Specialty Chemicals' signature products to multiple South American nations. Under his leadership, Privi Specialty Chemicals earned more than $1 million in annual revenue from their North and South American sales in less than one year. Thanks to his financial expertise, Mr. Doppalapudi gradually increased Privi Specialty Chemicals' annual revenue from North and South American sales to more than $30 million in less than 10 years.

In addition to his resilience and perseverance, Mr. Doppalapudi attributes a great deal of his success to the influence of his father as well as Mahesh Babani, who serves as Privi Specialty Chemicals' chairperson and managing director. In the coming years, he intends to increase Privi Specialty Chemicals' annual revenue to more than $50 million.

Arthur L. Fuller Sr.

Owner

ArtFul Enterprises International

HOUSTON, TX UNITED STATES

For more than 20 years, Arthur L. Fuller Sr. has thrived as the president and chief executive officer of ArtFul Enterprises International. With more than five decades of business consulting experience to his credit, he specializes in teaching aspiring entrepreneurs how to start e-commerce businesses and offer their products and services to customers based in different countries. Mr. Fuller also focuses on helping his clients expand their operations by honing their knowledge of various business practices, including digital marketing and franchising.

Alongside his responsibilities at ArtFul Enterprises International, Mr. Fuller excelled as the president of the Jean Richardson Fuller Foundation for Early Childhood Education between 1991 and 2010. He has also served as the co-founder and board member of the National Computer Graphics Foundation. Mr. Fuller has previously contributed to the Majestic Eagles, which supports African American-owned businesses, as the co-founder and the chairman of the board of directors. Likewise, he was also appointed as the executive secretary of the Houston Business and Professional Men's Club.

In 2020, Mr. Fuller garnered widespread recognition as the author of "Yes You Can: Against And Despite All Odds," published through Cobbin and Associates LLC. He had previously channeled his expertise in software engineering to release "Dynamics of Clipper: A Library for

Software Development" in 1988. Outside of his professional circles, Mr. Fuller has found further success as the chairman of the board of directors of the New Bethel Baptist Church Housing Corporation.

Between 1960 and 1990, Mr. Fuller was recruited as a supervisory naval architect with Naval Sea Systems Command, a branch of the U.S. Navy. Toward the beginning of this period, he helped establish the Advanced Research Projects Agency Network (ARPANET), which revolved around the technology that eventually evolved into the modern internet. Mr. Fuller was also appointed as the technical director of a project known as Computer Aided Ship Design and Construction (CASDAC), which was utilized to design several large naval vessels, including a nuclear aircraft carrier.

Born in Camden, Alabama, Mr. Fuller served in the U.S. Army and the U.S. Air Force before obtaining a Bachelor of Arts in mathematics and natural sciences at Miles College in 1958. Throughout the following three years, he completed postgraduate coursework in applied mathematics at New York University, where he simultaneously worked as a graduate assistant. During this period, Mr. Fuller worked in close proximity to one of the first installations of a commercial computer in the United States, which inspired his interest in technology. He was subsequently recruited as an instructor of mathematics at Miles College.

In addition to his faith, Mr. Fuller attributes a great deal of his success to the leadership skills he acquired while caring for his six younger siblings throughout his childhood. He also developed his intellect at a young age by reading nonfiction books, many of which helped him build a solid understanding of different industries and professions. Mr. Fuller is extremely proud to have played an instrumental role in the creation of ARPANET, which formed a new system of communication between different branches of the U.S. armed forces. Since his passion for reading directly contributed to his ascension from poverty, he advises aspiring entrepreneurs from impoverished communities to read books that feature realistic portrayals of different career paths.

Robert "Bob" Lee Hildebrand

Officer (Retired)
R.R. Donnelley & Sons Company

GLEN ELLYN, IL UNITED STATES

F or more than 20 years, Robert "Bob" Lee Hildebrand found success as an officer with R.R. Donnelley and Sons Company. Prior to his retirement, he specialized in the development and expansion of commercial printing facilities for R.R. Donnelley in several U.S. states as well as various nations in Europe and Asia. Mr. Hildebrand also focused on recruiting and overseeing employees of the aforementioned integrated communications company and ensuring appropriate compensation for their efforts.

During the 1950s and the 1960s, Mr. Hildebrand played an instrumental role in the development of numerous new facilities for the General Electric Company all over the world. In addition to identifying appropriate geographical locations for expansion, he developed sizable teams at new plants and actively maintained each plant's efficiency. Mr. Hildebrand additionally honed his expertise in employee relations and human resources while overseeing teams of employees at General Electric plants in Massachusetts, Indiana and Illinois.

Following his success with General Electric, Mr. Hildebrand accepted his initial position at R.R. Donnelley in 1968. Throughout the 1970s and 1980s, he gradually advanced to numerous leadership positions, such as the director of employee relations. After issuing his professional retirement in 1992, Mr. Hildebrand continued to contribute to R.R. Donnelley as a consultant in a part-time capacity for more than five years.

Born in Lincoln, Illinois, Mr. Hildebrand initially garnered widespread recognition as a talented basketball player. During the late 1940s, he was selected for an athletic scholarship to Illinois Wesleyan University, where he eventually obtained an associate degree in 1952. While attending the aforementioned institution, Mr. Hildebrand simultaneously thrived as a member of the Denver Central Bankers, which was part of the National Industrial Basketball League until the aforementioned league ceased operations in 1963.

Following these accomplishments, Mr. Hildebrand was recruited to participate in a management training program at General Electric. Between 1952 and 1955, he developed his leadership skills while accumulating a vast knowledge of many General Electric products, including light bulbs, electric generators, television sets, electric motors and aircraft engines. During this period, Mr. Hildebrand also learned the importance of employee satisfaction and engagement under the tutelage of business professors from Harvard University and several other prestigious academic institutions.

In recognition of his contributions to the Denver Central Bankers, Mr. Hildebrand was distinguished as an All-Star and an All-State basketball player in 1948, 1951 and 1952. In addition to his Christian faith, he attributes a great deal of his success to his humble approach to his work, which inspired him to continuously treat his employees with tremendous respect and to prioritize the needs of his employees above his own. Mr. Hildebrand is also extremely grateful to have participated in the aforementioned management training program with General Electric, which gave him the confidence to pursue increasingly challenging opportunities throughout his career. After completing the aforementioned program, he believed he had accumulated a similar degree of business expertise as a graduate of an esteemed Master of Business Administration program.

Since his retirement, Mr. Hildebrand has devoted significant attention to supporting a number of nonprofit organizations such as United Way Worldwide. In the coming years, he intends to spend more time with his five grandchildren, one of whom has since established his own prosperous career as an entrepreneur. In his spare time, Mr. Hildebrand relaxes by reading, renovating his home and maintaining his family's farm. ⚜

James Karas

Chief Executive Officer
Big Papa's TNT

SOMERSET, NJ UNITED STATES

With more than three and a half decades of experience to his credit, James Karas has distinguished himself with his multifaceted career journey. Bearing particular expertise in business consultation and spearheading new projects, he serves as the chief executive officer of Big Papa's TNT in Somerset, New Jersey. In addition, he has demonstrated proficiency in roles of high leadership in a variety of other roles, including as the chief executive officer of Savage Promotions since 1990 and the chancellor and chief executive officer of the International Center for Educational Advancement since 2015, having previously functioned as the organization's director of development for 25 years. Furthermore, Mr. Karas maintained involvement as the vice president of product development for XEL Advanced Technologies from 1994 until 1998, and has held a similar role on behalf of Specialty Products International since 1986.

Outside of his endeavors in entrepreneurship, Mr. Karas earned distinction for his commitment to physical fitness, and served as a promotor and sponsor for the International Federation of Body Building (IFBB) between 1986 and 1992. Concurrent with this role, he contributed in a similar fashion at the National Physique Committee (NPC) of New Jersey from 1986 to 1991, and with the Mr. Olympia, Ms. Olympia, Night of the Champions and Arnold Schwarzenegger Classic competitions, among others. Further showcasing his natural prowess, he wrote a sponsorship and promotional manual, whose third edition was released in 1987, and found success as a bail enforcement agent and bounty hunter in the New Jersey region from 1989 until 2010. During this time, he was notably inducted into the New Jersey Police Honor Legion for his role in saving the lives of two people from felons. Presently, he continues to function as a steward for the New Jersey Turnpike Authority.

Before venturing onto his vocational path, Mr. Karas sought an education at the New York Institute of Technology, where he studied between 1977 and 1978. Following this period, he attended Rutgers, the State University of New Jersey, from 1979 to 1980. Years later, Mr. Karas concluded his academic pursuits at Middlesex College from 1999 until 2000. Well qualified to work in his manifold fields, he was certified as a defensive driving instructor in the state of New Jersey in 2004, and received certification as a heavy equipment operator in 2010.

Long dedicated to civic advocacy, Mr. Karas is a member of the American Hellenic Educational Progressive Association, and has contributed extensively toward raising and helping to organize monetary fundraising events for U.S. soldiers. Professionally, he has also maintained his affiliation with the American Federation of Labor and Congress of Industrial Organizations and the International Federation of Professional and Technology Engineers.

In honor of the excellence he has consistently demonstrated throughout his career, Mr. Karas has received numerous accolades, including the Industry Innovation Award from the NPC / IFBB from John Kemper in 1987, as well as several "best in the show" trophies and plaques. He also earned a Rocket Racing Innovation and Achievement Award and an official recognition from the International Center for Educational Advancement. Reflecting on his career efforts, he credits much of his success to his propensity for hard work, ability to follow through on his plans, and learning from his mistakes. He also benefited richly from the tutelage of great mentors. Looking toward the future, Mr. Karas hopes to enter a well-earned retirement.

Margaret T. Ordoñez, PhD

Owner

Ordoñez Textile Conservation Services

SENOIA, GA UNITED STATES

S ince 2017, Margaret T. Ordoñez, PhD, has thrived as the owner of Ordoñez Textile Conservation Services. With more than 30 years of experience as a fashion professor to her credit, she specializes in the restoration and preservation of historic textiles from the early 20th century. Dr. Ordoñez also focuses on helping various museums and individual clients maintain the condition of textiles and other perishable fiber artifacts from different ancient civilizations.

Prior to the formation of Ordoñez Textile Conservation Services, Dr. Ordoñez excelled as a professor in the department of textiles, fashion merchandising, and design at the University of Rhode Island between 1979 and 2011. She has additionally found success as an educator at Kansas State University, where she developed her students' knowledge of multiple aspects of textile conservation such as textile cleaning, repair and stabilization. Dr. Ordoñez had previously worked as a chemistry teacher for high school students for more than five years, during which period she honed her expertise in identifying and analyzing natural fibers.

Throughout her career, Dr. Ordoñez has contributed articles to numerous professional journals and publications, including the International Journal of Costume and Fashion and Historical Archaeology, which is the official journal of the Society for Historical Archaeology. She has also been appointed as a copy editor of Dress, the Journal of the Costume Society of America. Likewise, Dr. Ordoñez has shared her expertise in textile conservation at conferences and workshops across the United States, such as the annual meeting of the American Institute for Conservation and the biennial North American Textile Conservation Conference. In order to stay up to date with the latest developments in her field, she continues to maintain active affiliations with the Conservation Society of America, the American Institute for Conservation, and the American Association of Textile Chemists and Colorists.

Born in Maryville, Tennessee, Dr. Ordoñez's interest in textiles was heavily inspired by her fascination with chemistry, which originally emerged during high school. She eventually pursued a formal education at the University of Tennessee, Knoxville, where she earned a Bachelor of Science in clothing and textiles as well as a Master of Science in clothing and textiles between 1961 and 1969. Dr. Ordoñez subsequently concluded her education in 1977, at which point she obtained a Doctor of Philosophy in textiles and clothing at Florida State University.

In 2022, Dr. Ordoñez found further success as a co-author of "Conservation Concerns in Fashion Collections: Caring for Problematic Twentieth-Century Textiles, Apparel and Accessories," which was released through the Kent State University Press. She had previously garnered widespread recognition as the author of 2001's "Your Vintage Keepsake: A CSA Guide to Costume Storage and Display." Following her retirement from the University of Rhode Island, Dr. Ordoñez was distinguished as a professor emerita in 2017.

A fellow of the Costume Society of America, Dr. Ordoñez attributes a great deal of her success to the support of her parents along with her patient and steadfast approach to her work. She is particularly proud to have influenced myriad students to pursue their own careers in relation to textile conservation while simultaneously preserving historic textiles at several museums, including the Tennessee State Museum and the Kentucky Museum. Since her inherent affinity for science played an instrumental role in her professional growth, Dr. Ordoñez advises aspiring textile conservation specialists to build a solid understanding of chemistry before attending college.

Peter J. Orzali

Investor
Orzali Holdings, LLC
HIGHLAND HEIGHTS, KY UNITED STATES

An experienced entrepreneur and investor, Peter J. Orzali has been innovating in the fields of business and pharmaceutical science for 50 years. As a young man, he got his start working at his father's pharmacy, but after his father's passing, he left the industry, not wanting to work for a chain drugstore. Mr. Orzali made his return to the pharmaceutical industry with Three Rivers Medical Center, where he served as the director of pharmacy from 1995 to 2004. He worked as the regional pharmacy director for Community Health Systems from 2000 to 2004 and the pharmacy director for Mercy Health Partners from 2004 to 2007. From 2007 to 2012, he served as the RS MS Clinical RPh with Humana.

In addition to his work in pharmaceutical science, Mr. Orzali has a history of successful business investments. From 1987 to 1999, he was an owner and partner at Patient-Aids, Inc. Since 1988, he has been a real estate business owner with the U.S. Post Office. He has made investments in the hospitality industry, including a partnership with Comfort Inn & Suites since 2005 and Inn & Suites in Wilder, Kentucky, since 2010. Though he retired from clinical pharmacy in 2012, Mr. Orzali has continued to invest in the medical industry, becoming a partner at Imbed Biosciences Inc. in 2018. He is also a partner at Braxton Brewing Company in Covington, Kentucky. At his son's encouragement, he became an investor with Owl's Brew, a beverage company selling tea cocktails, and they are set to construct an on-ground business in Cincinnati, Ohio, with an attached ice cream shop. The company has now branched out into a regional flavored alcohol brand, Garage Beer, with the slogan, "The garage is the mother of invention. And around here, we respect our mothers."

Mr. Orzali formed Orzali Holdings, LLC, to teach his three children the value of money. With Orzali Holdings, he has made a variety of real estate investments. Having received a bachelor of biological and chemical sciences from Thomas More University in Crestview Hills, Kentucky, Mr. Orzali appreciates the importance of secondary education, and he plans to contribute to the education of his nine grandchildren.

One of Mr. Orzali's greatest career honors was his appointment to the Kentucky State Board of Pharmacy by the governor of Kentucky, Ernie Fletcher, in 2009. After a year, he was elected president, and as president was a part of designing the Kentucky controlled substance program. He is a member of the Kentucky Pharmacy Association, the board of directors for the Kentucky Society of Health-System Pharmacists, the current vice president and past president of the Northern Kentucky Pharmacy Association, and a member of the Alpha Delta Gamma National Fraternity. Previously, Mr. Orzali received the Albert Nelson Marquis Lifetime Achievement Award and was named Innovative Pharmacist of the Year by Community Health Systems in 2001.

Mr. Orzali considers himself talented at identifying individuals with the potential to grow a business. Once he identifies a person with that capability, he spends time researching and meeting with them. An example of his success is the Braxton Brewing Company, which Forbes Magazine called the fastest-growing craft beer in the country in 2023. Before making any investment, he consults with both his personal attorney and certified public accountant. When approaching an investment in an industry he is not familiar with, he seeks out the expertise of professionals. Additionally, when buying or selling a company, he ensures all actions are conducted in a legal and tax-efficient manner.

John Joseph Raffaeli Jr.

President
C3 Investment Holdings LLC

COROLLA, NC UNITED STATES

A n independent human capital expert, education leader, entrepreneur and philanthropist, John Joseph Raffaeli Jr. spent 34 years of his career with major global corporations, including serving as senior vice president of human resources at Thomson Reuters, where from 1998 to 2011 he worked with senior management and the board of directors to develop human capital policies in support of the corporation's business strategies. Appointed to the corporation's disclosure committee as chair of global retirement, Mr. Raffaeli oversaw the administration and investment of nearly $5 billion of employee and company assets. With a Bachelor of Arts in social science from Waynesburg University in Waynesburg, Pennsylvania, and a Master of Science in industrial relations from West Virginia University in Morgantown, West Virginia, Mr. Raffaeli possesses a unique, multifaceted perspective on business.

Prior to his position at Thomson Reuters, Mr. Raffaeli worked as managing director of human resources at UBS, an investment banking and financial services company, from 1995 to 1998. He served as senior operating officer of human resources at Salomon Brothers from 1990 to 1995 and corporate general manager of industrial relations at Continental Can Company from 1976 to 1990. In addition to his extensive employment experience, Mr. Raffaeli has been cited in numerous national publications and appeared in a segment on CNBC featuring his successful implementation of the first large-scale, on-site managed health care network in the United States while at Salomon Brothers. During different points in his career, he was on the board of advisers of the Journal of Health Care Benefits, a contributing editor of Managing Employee Health Benefits magazine and a trustee of the Washington, D.C., think tank, the Employee Benefit Research Institute (EBRI).

A prolific writer, Mr. Raffaeli published several health-oriented articles, and between 2010 and 2020, he served as a visiting lecturer at two British universities, St. Mary's University and the University of Chester. Throughout the United States and Thailand, he taught strategic management, organizational behavior and leadership, global business, project management and managing change to hundreds of international post-graduate students. While living in New York state, he was a Master of Business Administration dissertation supervisor and a career school instructor in the state of New York, and he previously served on the board of directors for the University of Business and International Studies in Geneva, Switzerland.

Since 2011, Mr. Raffaeli has served as co-owner and president of C3 Investment Holdings LLC, presiding over vineyard, winemaking and real estate investments in Argentina, as well as a whisky distillery in Scotland. Through his subsidiary company, National Pastime Productions, LLC, he produced the stage play, "A Lucky Life," about baseball legend Lou Gehrig's life and battle with amyotrophic lateral sclerosis (ALS). Notably, Mr. Raffaeli was honored with the American Hero Award by the National Kidney Registry for his non-directed kidney donation in 2017.

Looking to the future, Mr. Raffaeli plans to write and publish books for his family, as well as continue growing C3 Investment Holdings, embracing his passion for winemaking. Upon retirement, he hired a life planner to create a roadmap for the next 30 years of his life that involves teaching, coaching and consulting, and having explored many of those avenues, he is preparing to embark on a new stage in his life.

Scott Alexander Rose, MBA, MNM, EdD, FP

Owner
Mainstreet Solutions LLC

BOCA RATON, FL UNITED STATES

I n 1993, Scott Alexander Rose, MBA, MNM, EdD, FP, created Mainstreet Solutions LLC, a specialty insurance agency where he serves as a certified international specialist. Prior to that, he worked as a performing arts teacher in Boca Raton, Florida, for 15 years. Dr. Rose began his career journey at Florida Atlantic University in Boca Raton, where he received a bachelor's degree in music education in 1981. A year later, he received a Bachelor of Fine Arts in theater arts from Florida Atlantic University and began teaching fine arts. In 1988, he was selected by the White House to serve as a Florida representative to the Office of Public Liaison during George H.W. Bush's presidency, which inspired him to transition into a career in insurance and set up Mainstreet Solutions, LLC. He returned to Florida Atlantic University for a master's degree in nonprofit management in 2012 and a Master of Business Administration in 2013. In 2015, he received a Doctor of Education from Lynn University in Boca Raton. Dr. Rose received the title of certified international specialist and a certificate in financial planning from Florida Atlantic University, both in 2013. He is also a certified fundraiser.

For his work in insurance, Dr. Rose has won multiple awards, including being named Top 2/12 by the South Florida Business Journal in 2020, Insurance Expert of the Year by International Lawyers Journal in 2021 and 2022, and Insurance Expert of the Year by Finance Monthly in 2021 and 2022. His doctoral thesis on learning theory received an award from the Carnegie Project on the Education Doctorate in 2016. Previously, Dr. Rose has been featured in Marquis Who's Who Top Business Owners and Entrepreneurs and is a past recipient of the Albert Nelson Marquis Lifetime Achievement Award. Since 2020, Dr. Rose has been a member of the Underwriters Association and the Palm Beach County Underwriters Association. He has also been a member of the Florida Association of British Business since 1996.

An avid volunteer worker, Dr. Rose served as president of Life Care Foundation on Disabilities, a nonprofit charity, from 2004 to 2015, and since 2015, he has worked with Limitless Horizons International. He is a past member of the Boca Raton Chamber of Commerce. In the future, Dr. Rose plans to continue his work with the community and with the insurance industry, as he is passionate about solving the health insurance issues that plague many Americans. He attributes his success to his commitment to caring for each client's particular needs regardless of profit, as he sees his work in the industry as primarily service-driven rather than profit-oriented. Though he is proud of the work he has done with Mainstreet Solutions LLC over the past three decades, Dr. Rose maintains the love he had for teaching and considers his most notable achievement to be the award he received from the Carnegie Project on the Education Doctorate. He has also been recognized with inclusion in the 76th edition of Who's Who in America. Dr. Rose is a vegetarian and has over 40 years' expertise in nutrition and yoga meditation.

Anil Saini

Chief Executive Officer
Pooja Trucking Inc.

Chief Executive Officer
SEI Transportation

HARRISBURG, PA UNITED STATES

E ntrepreneur Anil Saini has been the CEO of SEI Transportation since 2006 and the CEO of Pooja Trucking Inc. since 2010. Prior to his career in logistics and transportation, he was the owner of a bar and restaurant for 11 years. After receiving a bachelor's degree from the University of Delhi in Delhi, India, Mr. Saini immigrated to the United States and graduated with a Master of Business Administration from Temple University in 2006. He has also completed coursework from Temple University's Fox School of Business.

After being introduced to the logistics and transportation industry by his brother, an information technology professional and owner of a software company, Mr. Saini launched Madison Intermodal LLC, doing business as SEI Transportation, out of Harrisburg, Pennsylvania. The company, along with his other business endeavor, Pooja Trucking Inc., specializes in drayage, the transportation of freight from ports, typically by truck. Utilizing a combination of trucks and trains depending on the amount of goods, the company loads the vehicle and transports the goods out of Harrisburg to destinations across the country. By traveling for short distances of 200 miles, SEI Transportation saves fuel and manpower while also lessening environmental impact. The company's clients include household names such as Home Depot, Amazon and Walmart, with whom Mr. Saini has cultivated strong professional relationships due to his emphasis on customer service. Attributing his success to the support of his wife, Pooja Saini, and his own dedication, Mr. Saini is proud to have grown his company to 100 employees.

Because of his success in the industry, Mr. Saini has been featured in GQ, The Wall Street Journal, Forbes Magazine, Fortune Magazine and Millennium Magazine and won the 2021-2022 Best Intermodal Award from the Better Business Bureau. Previously, he has been featured in Marquis Who's Who Top Professionals and Who's Who of Top Executives and received the Albert Nelson Marquis Lifetime Achievement Award. Mr. Saini is a member of the Uniform Intermodal Interchange and Facilities Access Agreement, the Pennsylvania Motor Truck Association and the American Trucking Association. His hobbies include swimming, camping, golfing and skiing.

Dean Sivley

President
Berkshire Hathaway Travel Protection

MOUNT LAUREL, NJ UNITED STATES

S ince 2015, Dean Sivley has thrived as the president of Berkshire Hathaway Travel Protection, a division of Berkshire Hathaway Specialty Insurance. With more than 25 years of leadership experience in the travel industry to his credit, he focuses on increasing the popularity of AirCare travel insurance, which compensates air travelers for specific incidents such as flight delays, missed connections or misplaced baggage. Mr. Sivley also specializes in improving the technology behind various digital insurance services, providing mentorship to his younger colleagues and ensuring Berkshire Hathaway Travel Protection compliance with insurance filing regulations in all 50 U.S. states.

Prior to his appointment with Berkshire Hathaway Travel Protection, Mr. Sivley excelled as the chief executive officer of GroundLink Worldwide between 2013 and 2015. He had previously found success as the president of Travel Guard, which is owned by American International Group, Inc., between 2009 and 2013. During this period, Mr. Sivley simultaneously held a number of leadership positions with American International Group such as the president, the chief business officer and the chief operating officer of the aforementioned organization's accident and health insurance division.

Between 2004 and 2009, Mr. Sivley prospered as the senior vice president and as the chief operating officer of Orbitz for Business, the corporate travel brand of Orbitz Worldwide, Inc., which is a subsidiary of the Expedia Group. He had previously served as the chief strategy officer of Verticalnet, Inc., which was acquired by Bravo Solutions, between 1999 and 2000 after finding success as the president and the chief executive officer of the Atlas Travel and Technology Group during the late 1990s. Between 1995 and 1997, Mr. Sivley was appointed as the chief information officer and executive vice president of marketing at Rosenbluth International, which has since been acquired by American Express.

Alongside his responsibilities with Berkshire Hathaway Travel Protection, Mr. Sivley currently contributes to the United States Travel Insurance Association as a board member. He also supports several nonprofit organizations, including the United Way of Portage County in Stevens Point, Wisconsin. Mr. Sivley has also garnered recognition as a competitive tennis player and has earned first-place honors at numerous local tournaments for senior citizens.

Prior to his career in the travel industry, Mr. Sivley obtained a Bachelor of Science at the University of Wisconsin–Parkside in 1980. He subsequently worked as the chief information officer for Duracell Inc., owned by Berkshire Hathaway, for over 15 years. Toward the end of this period, Mr. Sivley concluded his education at the Columbia Business School, where he completed an Executive Master of Business Administration, with honors, in 1995.

In 2011, Mr. Sivley was selected for a Distinguished Alumni Award on behalf of the University of Wisconsin–Parkside. He is also particularly proud to have helped American International Group stabilize its financial health following the terrorist attacks of September 11, 2001, which dealt significant damage to the travel industry.

In the coming years, Mr. Sivley intends to further the growth of Berkshire Hathaway Travel Protection by improving the technology behind its primary services. He also aims to focus on maintaining a healthy lifestyle as well as his reputation as an active tennis player. Since his tendency to accept challenging projects directly contributed to the longevity of his career, Mr. Sivley advises aspiring corporate executives to continuously expand their skill sets by exploring new and unfamiliar areas of their industry.

Sandra Holbrook Childs

Volunteer & Contributor

Neighbors 4 Neighbors Food Bank

TOCCOA, GA UNITED STATES

S ince 2015, Sandra Holbrook Childs has served as a volunteer and as a contributor to Neighbors 4 Neighbors, which provides food for needy individuals and families based in Stephens County, Georgia. In these capacities, she specializes in coordinating the collection of donated groceries as well as their distribution at various locations such as the Open Arms Clinic and St. Matthias Episcopal Church. Ms. Childs also focuses on developing new programs to offer additional resources for impoverished households such as hygienic supplies and pre-paid vouchers for gasoline.

Prior to her recruitment with Neighbors 4 Neighbors, Ms. Childs excelled as a member of the Board of Education for the Stephens County School District between 2007 and 2015. She had previously thrived as a home economics teacher for high school and middle school students for more than 30 years. During the late 1980s and early 1990s, Ms. Childs found further success as a teacher for children with various learning disabilities.

Alongside her responsibilities with Neighbors 4 Neighbors, Ms. Childs has contributed to her local church as a Stephen minister for more than 10 years. In this capacity, she regularly helps fellow parishioners recover from a broad range of personal problems such as the loss of a family member or the dissolution of a marriage. Ms. Childs also frequently participates in charitable initiatives on behalf of the aforementioned church and solicits contributions from parishioners with the help of Neighbor 4 Neighbors' staff, all of whom serve the aforementioned organization in a volunteer capacity.

Moreover, Ms. Childs has served as a volunteer at numerous local soup kitchens. Following her retirement from her career as an educator, she played a central role in the development of a program that teaches reading to disabled adults. Throughout her involvement with Neighbors 4 Neighbors, Ms. Childs has consistently harnessed donations to her local church to amplify the aforementioned organization's charitable efforts, particularly those designed for the benefit of elderly individuals and single parents. In 2018, she helped Neighbors 4 Neighbors distribute more than 120,000 pounds of food to more than 7,500 impoverished households.

Born in Toccoa, Georgia, Ms. Childs' decision to pursue a career as a home economics teacher was chiefly inspired by her grandmother, who taught her how to sew at a young age. In 1965, she earned a Bachelor of Arts in vocational home economics from Georgia College and State University. While working as a home economics teacher, Ms. Childs obtained a Master of Arts from the aforementioned Milledgeville-based institution in 1975. She eventually concluded her education in 1987, at which point she completed a Master of Arts in special education at Georgia College and State University, which was formerly known as Georgia College.

In addition to her nurturing and compassionate personality, Ms. Childs attributes a great deal of her success to her parents, both of whom supported her decision to pursue a formal education and encouraged her to continuously further her professional expertise. She is extremely proud to have helped myriad students overcome learning disabilities as well as difficulties in relation to social skills and emotional stability. In her spare time, Ms. Childs relaxes by exercising her passion for decorative sewing to create clothing, draperies, quilts and various textile crafts. She advises aspiring educators to remember that they are solely responsible for their own actions, as opposed to the actions and behaviors of their students. For her achievements, she has been included in the 76th edition of Who's Who in America.

Connie Goodman-Milone

Humanitarian

Writer

Hospice Volunteer

MIAMI, FL UNITED STATES

For more than 30 years, Connie Goodman-Milone has found success as a poet and contributor of articles to myriad newspapers, book publications and literary journals. In these capacities, she specializes in composing written works involving themes of grief, loss and healing. She writes themes of nature in her haiku and free verse poetry. She is a leader in the writing community. As community relations director, she has a monthly column in the Author's Voice of the South Florida Writers Association. She is an editor and has contributed poetry, articles and photos for the Author's Voice as well. Ms. Goodman-Milone is a patient care volunteer with VITAS Healthcare. In her caring works, she highlights the value of philanthropy and humanitarianism in contemporary society.

Between 1995 and 2003, Ms. Goodman-Milone began developing a reputation as a prolific writer by contributing articles to numerous publications in relation to health care and poetry, including Medicinal Purposes Literary Review (poetry, photo), Today's Caregiver (poem), New Directions Social Work Advocate (article) and the Health and Social Services Networker (poem). She subsequently contributed several poems to Healthy Stories, the Grief Observer and VITAS Vital Signs (poetry and articles) between 2003 and 2008. Since 2002, Ms. Goodman-Milone has contributed letters to the editor to the Miami Herald. Since 2015, she has published several letters in the South Florida Sun Sentinel and in 2014, a letter in the San Antonio Express-News. She has contributed poems to literary journals such as Cadence: Florida State Poets Association Anthology (2008-2012) (2014-2023); Of Poets & Poetry (2014, 2022); Dark Wood (2018); 45 Magazine: Women's Literary Journal (2018-2020); the Florida State Poets Association Member Spotlight (2022); the National Endowment for the Arts Big Read Gratitude Notes (2023); Fractured by Cattails: Haiku Society of America Members' Anthology (2023); and Miami Poets Soiree (2023).

Between 2003 and 2005, Ms. Goodman-Milone was elected as the director of marketing for the South Florida Writers Association, which subsequently elected her to the position of director of community relations. Between 2006 and 2008,

she served as secretary of the association before being elected director at large for more than five years. Ms. Goodman-Milone eventually advanced to become the president of the South Florida Writers Association in 2015. She was elected to the position of secretary in 2016 and has served as community relations director since 2017.

During her tenure with the South Florida Writers Association, Ms. Goodman-Milone simultaneously prospered as the chairperson of the Creative Writing Committee of the nonprofit organization Junior Orange Bowl for more than 10 years. Since 2019, she found further success as the vice chairperson and director of the Creative Writing Committee. Ms. Goodman-Milone is a co-author of a forthcoming anthology known as the Bereavement Poetry Project. Alongside her career as a freelance writer, Ms. Goodman-Milone has served as a hospice volunteer for VITAS Healthcare for 23 years.

She also excels as a supporter of a host of nonprofit organizations, including the World Jewish Congress, USA for the United Nations High Commissioner for Refugees, the American Jewish World Service, United Service Organizations, the American Cancer Society, Sandy Hook Promise, the Children's Bereavement Center, Childrena's Cancer Research Fund, St. Jude Children's Research Hospital, The Nature Conservancy, Guiding Eyes for the Blind, the Humane Society of the United States and the American Society for the Prevention of Cruelty to Animals. As a testament to her passion for animal welfare, Ms. Goodman-Milone has thrived as a member of the National Wildlife Federation Leader's Club, a Wildlife Guardian for Defenders of Wildlife and as a Wildlife Rescue Team member for the World Wildlife Fund since 2014. She has additionally helped coordinate fundraising initiatives for the American Red Cross, the Susan G. Komen Foundation, the California Fire Foundation and the South Florida Writers Association. Ms. Goodman-Milone is a five-year survivor and captain for Susan G. Komen.

Since 2002, Ms. Goodman-Milone has contributed to the Southern Poverty Law Center as a member of the Leadership Council. From 2013 to 2015, she became an American Red Cross Champion and a Field Partner for Doctors Without Borders. She has been a dedicated supporter as a Sixth Ring member of the United States Olympic & Paralympic Foundation since 2019. She has served as a campaign volunteer for numerous Democratic political candidates in her home state of Florida. She is a member of the Democratic National Committee, the Academy of American Poets, the National Association of Social Workers, the National Writers Union and the National Association for Poetry Therapy. In 2018, Ms. Goodman-Milone was featured on a series of radio broadcasts with Close-Up Radio in relation to poetry, philanthropy and different ways of contributing to charitable organizations. She was honored with a profile interview as a Friend of the Miami Book Fair in 2023.

Born in Philadelphia, Pennsylvania, Ms. Goodman-Milone earned a Bachelor of Arts in Psychology at The George Washington University in 1985. She was subsequently recruited as an editorial assistant at Chelsea House Publishers, LLC. Toward the late 1990s, Ms. Goodman-Milone resumed her education at Barry University, where she earned a Master of Social Work. Through her studies, she had an internship in social work at the U.S. Department of Veterans Affairs Miami Medical Center. During 2000, she worked as a case manager in skilled nursing for HealthSouth Doctor's Hospital.

In 2019, Ms. Goodman-Milone won a Special Merit Award in the South Florida Writers Association Writing Contest. She had previously been honored with an Exemplary Medal by the Miami-Dade County School Board, District Nine in 2013. She was selected on behalf of the South Florida Writers Association for the Bill Katzker Member of the Year Award in 2003. In recognition of her contributions to VITAS Healthcare, Ms. Goodman-Milone has additionally been distinguished with accolades regarding length of service. In 2001, the VITAS Dade Program selected her as the Bereavement Volunteer of the Year. In 2021, she was honored by VITAS Healthcare with a VITAS Best Award. 🌿

E. Maynard Moore, PhD

Principal & Partner
CommunityNexus Consulting LLC

BETHESDA, MD UNITED STATES

Drawing on more than 45 years of experience in nonprofit organizing, E. Maynard Moore, PhD, has distinguished himself as the principal and partner at CommunityNexus Consulting LLC. Founded in 2005, the firm specializes in nonprofit management, with particular attention given to leadership development, integrity analysis, strategic planning, program evaluation, fundraising and promoting sustainability. Primarily located in and around the Mid-Atlantic states, many of Dr. Moore's clients work in the fields of social justice, higher education administration, charity and volunteerism.

Among his career accomplishments, Dr. Moore is most proud to have served as an account executive for the Habitat for Humanity International Capital Campaign from 1998 until 2001. The organization had initially engaged in a $20 million capital campaign to coincide with the 20th university of its founding. Instead, Dr. Moore organized a more ambitious $200 million fundraising campaign, which resulted in the most significant and large-scale project for which he has been responsible. Additionally, he was engaged by the Minority Health Professions Foundation to serve as its founding executive, a role he accepted on a temporary basis until someone from a minority community could be identified to assume the mantle of leadership. During this time, Dr. Moore is gratified to have led the organization in generating approximately $25 million in capital, a feat no one had anticipated.

Outside of his primary endeavors, Dr. Moore worked as the executive co-director of the Stewardship Center of the Baltimore-Washington Conference for the United Methodist Church from 2003 to 2005. In this role, he helped manage the charitable foundation of the annual conference and lent his aid in developing a support strategy for over 600 churches across the span of Maryland, the District of Columbia and West Virginia. In addition, he sat on the committee on gun violence for the National United Methodist Church and as a member of the Montgomery County Interfaith Organization.

To remain aware of developments in his field, he has long sustained his membership with WesleyNexus Inc., over which he has presided since 2011. Additionally, Dr. Moore served as the vice president of administration at the Institute on Religion in an Age of Science, a society of natural scientists, philosophy, and theologians who seek to provide a forum for informed and respectful inquiry within the intersection between science, religion and philosophy. In honor of his accomplishments in this role, he was bestowed with the President's Award for Exceptional Service. Furthermore, he has been a member of the Association of Fundraising Professionals for 50 years, the Methodist Federation of Social Action, and, on a personal level, the Potomac River Jazz Club.

Before embarking upon his professional journey, Dr. Moore studied history and sociology at Randolph-Macon College, from which he earned a Bachelor of Arts in 1959. Following this accomplishment, he went on to study at the Perkins School of Theology at Southern Methodist University, where he attained a Bachelor of Divinity and a Master of Sacred Theology.

He later received a Master of Arts in social ethics from the University of Chicago Divinity School in 1968 and a Doctor of Philosophy in adult education from Union Institute & University in 1974. Well-qualified in his field, he has also been certified as a fundraising professional and association executive via the Greater Washington Society of Association Executives.

Well-regarded for his achievements, Dr. Moore largely attributes his success to his deep and abiding religious faith, as well as his personal mission, which he has defined in five words: "promoting intellectual and spiritual coherence." Looking toward the future, he aspires to remain in good health and enjoy relationships with his wife, grandchildren, friends and family. 🌿🌿

Harry Shapiro

Former District Governor
Kiwanis International

Radio Disc Jockey & News Journalist (Retired)

GLENDALE, AZ UNITED STATES

For more than 30 years, spent between five years in New Jersey and 25 years in Arizona, Harry Shapiro found success as a disc jockey and news journalist for numerous radio stations and broadcasting companies. In this capacity, he specialized in conducting interviews with prominent entertainers in film and television. Mr. Shapiro also focused on reporting current events and breaking news stories to listeners based in the Phoenix Metropolitan Area.

In 1965, Mr. Shapiro graduated high school and worked at Seton Hall University's college radio station, eventually becoming sports director of that station by 1969. Throughout the following two decades, he served as a reporter and as a disc jockey for a host of local commercial radio stations such as KTAR-AM/FM/TV, which was an NBC affiliate in Phoenix that was owned by Combined Communications at the time, and KOOL-AM/FM/TV, which was a CBS affiliate that was owned by Chauncey and Associates.

Toward the end of his tenure as a disc jockey and journalist, Mr. Shapiro was appointed director of investor relations for the Glendale Chamber of Commerce in 1991, where he served until his retirement in January 2024.

Mr. Shapiro joined Kiwanis International in 1992. Between 2001 and 2002, he thrived as lieutenant governor of the Southwest district of the organization. In total, Mr. Shapiro held the role of lieutenant governor for three more terms: between 2009 and 2010, 2010 and 2011, and 2016 and 2017. Mr. Shapiro remains active as the chairperson of Kiwanis International's Southwest District Convention in 2024, having also held this role in 2003 and 2013. Mr. Shapiro eventually advanced to become the governor of Kiwanis International's Southwest District, the highest elected position in the district, for a one-year term in 2019. He is currently chairman of the Past Governor's Association for the Southwest District.

Since 1993, Mr. Shapiro has found further success as a member of the Glendale Ambassadors. Additionally, he serves on the Deer Valley Education Foundation as a board member. Moreover, Mr. Shapiro has previously harnessed his leadership skills to serve as the director of a district of the Arizona Jaycees and as the co-chairperson of the Seton Hall University Alumni Association in his home state of Arizona.

Born in Jersey City, New Jersey, Mr. Shapiro attended high school in North Arlington, New Jersey, during the early 1960s. His subsequent decision to pursue a career in broadcasting was heavily inspired by his growing reputation as a captivating public speaker. Mr. Shapiro completed a Bachelor of Arts in communication at Seton Hall University in South Orange, New Jersey, in 1970.

Throughout his career, Mr. Shapiro recorded more than 100 hours of interviews on an array of radio stations. He also excelled as an announcer for televised broadcasts of sporting events for multiple high school and professional football, basketball and baseball programs for more than 15 years. Likewise, Mr. Shapiro has contributed articles to several publications related to sports journalism.

In 2014, Kiwanis International selected Mr. Shapiro for the Walter Zeller Fellowship in recognition of his contributions to Kiwanis International's "Eliminate" project, which was a global campaign to diminish the prevalence of maternal and neonatal tetanus in underdeveloped nations. He had previously been distinguished with Kiwanis International's George F. Hixon Fellowship, which honors significant contributions to Kiwanis International's Children's Fund. In addition to his commitment to excellence, Mr. Shapiro attributes a great deal of his success to his ability to overcome adversity as well as his tendency to pursue increasingly challenging endeavors. In the coming years, he intends to further his involvement in various community organizations.

Keith D. Amparado

Emeritus President
Federation Board of Governors
SUNY Empire State University

NEW YORK, NY UNITED STATES

Drawing on more than 20 years of higher education leadership experience, Keith D. Amparado has thrived as the president emeritus of the Federation Board of Governors of Empire State University, which is part of the State University of New York (SUNY) system since 2022. In this capacity, he specializes in providing academic guidance and mentorship to incoming students of the aforementioned Manhattan-based institution. Mr. Amparado also focuses on promoting SUNY Empire State University's undergraduate and graduate programs to potential students from underserved communities as well as working professionals.

Prior to his appointment as the president emeritus, Mr. Amparado excelled as the president of the board of governors for SUNY Empire State University's Alumni/Student Federation between 2017 and 2019. He had previously found success as an assistant director at New York University for more than 15 years after initially working as a consultant for New York University's financial systems management unit. During the early 1990s, Mr. Amparado was appointed in this capacity for the New York City Department of Education on behalf of KDA Communications, which he helped establish in 1985. He currently serves as the president of the aforementioned marketing communications company.

Alongside his primary professional responsibilities, Mr. Amparado has simultaneously found further success as a board director of the

Shirley A. Chisholm Center for Equity Studies. Likewise, he has additionally prospered as the founder and group facilitator for a support group for caregivers for individuals with Alzheimer's disease at New York University since 2011. Mr. Amparado had previously shared his expertise with the aforementioned degenerative disease at speaking engagements and training seminars on behalf of CaringKind, the Heart of Alzheimer's Caregiving and the Alzheimer's Association for a number of years. In order to stay up to date with the latest developments in the marketing communications industry, he continues to maintain active affiliations with the Society for Technical Communication, the American Marketing Association, the Marketing Research Association, the Qualitative Research Consultants Association and the International Association of Business Communicators.

Born in Brooklyn, New York, Mr. Amparado initially developed his technical prowess while working as a systems analyst for Morgan Guaranty Trust Co., which is part of J.P. Morgan and Co., during the early 1980s. In 1988, he completed a Bachelor of Science at SUNY Empire State University. Mr. Amparado's eventual decision to establish a caregivers support group in relation to Alzheimer's disease was inspired by his mother, who succumbed to Alzheimer's disease in 2011.

In addition to his collaborative approach to his work, Mr. Amparado attributes a great deal of his success to his genuine passion for promoting diversity, equity and inclusion amongst the student population at SUNY Empire State University, where he has been designated as a lifetime board member of the Alumni/Student Federation. He has also been selected for inclusion in the 76th edition of Who's Who of America. During his tenure as the president emeritus of the Federation Board of Governors, he notably played an instrumental role in the development and implementation of a promotional initiative that significantly increased SUNY Empire State University's African American and Latino populations. Mr. Amparado is also deeply grateful for the support of his parents, both of whom taught him the importance of helping others at a young age. Due to the demanding nature of his profession, he advises aspiring academic administrators to pursue opportunities in areas of the higher education industry that align with their personal interests and goals.

Beverly L. Brechner, PhD

Professor Emerita
University of Florida

GAINESVILLE, FL UNITED STATES

For more than 35 years, Beverly L. Brechner, PhD, found success as an educator in the department of mathematics at the University of Florida College of Liberal Arts and Sciences. Prior to her retirement, she specialized in honing her students' knowledge of various branches of topology, including geometric topology and continuum theory. Dr. Brechner also regularly harnessed her expertise with prime ends and dynamical systems to help her students understand the role of mathematics in the fields of neuroscience and cognitive development.

In 1962, Dr. Brechner began her academic career as an instructor at Louisiana State University. She served in this capacity until 1964, at which point she was promoted to the position of assistant professor at the aforementioned Baton Rouge-based institution. Dr. Brechner was eventually recruited as an assistant professor at the University of Florida in 1968.

Between 1971 and 1983, Dr. Brechner excelled as an associate professor at the University of Florida, where she subsequently thrived as a professor throughout the following two decades. During the late 1970s and the early 1980s, she simultaneously found further success as a visiting associate professor at the University of Michigan and The University of Texas at Austin. Following her retirement in 1983, Dr. Brechner was distinguished as a professor emerita on behalf of the University of Florida.

Alongside her primary responsibilities as an educator, Dr. Brechner was appointed governor of the Florida section of the Mathematics Association of America between 1980 and 1983. Throughout her career, she has also contributed more than 25 articles to several professional journals and publications, including Topology and Its Applications, Fundamenta Mathematicae and the Annals of the New York Academy of Sciences. In order to stay up to date with the latest developments in her field, Dr. Brechner continues to maintain active affiliations with the Mathematics Association of America, the American Mathematical Society, and the Society for Industrial and Applied Mathematics.

After obtaining a Bachelor of Science in mathematics at the University of Miami in 1957, Dr. Brechner earned a Master of Science in mathematics from the aforementioned Coral Gables-based institution. In 1961, she attended a topology conference organized by the National Science Foundation, which solidified her decision to pursue a career as a mathematics educator. Dr. Brechner subsequently concluded her education at Louisiana State University, where she completed a Doctor of Philosophy in mathematics in 1964.

In 1989, the Mathematical Association of America selected Dr. Brechner for the George Pólya Award, which honors expository excellence in articles published in the College Mathematics Journal. In addition to her postgraduate education, she attributes much of her success to her parents, who consistently encouraged her and her siblings to pursue a formal education. Dr. Brechner also drew tremendous inspiration from the work of R.H. Bing and Deane Montgomery, both of whom are widely recognized as pioneers in the field of topology.

In the coming years, Dr. Brechner intends to focus on deepening her understanding of mathematics' influence on advanced technology such as artificial intelligence. Since her imagination and creativity continuously contributed to her professional growth, she advises aspiring mathematics educators to pursue their own passions and interests with the utmost determination. Dr. Brechner also frequently encouraged her graduate students to develop an exceptional work ethic and to approach increasingly daunting areas of mathematics without apprehension.

Michael A. Cervantes

Elementary School Educator (Retired)
El Rancho Unified School District

SAN GABRIEL, CA UNITED STATES

For more than 35 years, Michael A. Cervantes found success as an educator for elementary school students within the El Rancho Unified School District in Pico Rivera, California. Prior to his retirement, he specialized in helping students of Latin American descent improve their abilities to read and write in the English language. Mr. Cervantes also focused on developing new methodologies for evaluating a student's proficiency with the English language and maintaining close relationships with his students' parents.

In 1972, Mr. Cervantes began his academic career as a fifth grade teacher at the Valle Lindo School District, where he additionally worked as a bilingual teacher between 1975 and 1976. Toward the late 1970s, he excelled as a third grade teacher with the aforementioned district before serving in this capacity at the El Rancho Unified School District for more than five years. During this period, Mr. Cervantes simultaneously contributed to the El Rancho Unified School District as a kindergarten teacher.

Between 1984 and 1989, Mr. Cervantes worked as a second grade teacher at the El Rancho Unified School District, which subsequently appointed him as a fourth grade teacher and first grade teacher throughout the early 1990s. Toward the beginning of this period, he was simultaneously recruited as a teacher of Spanish as a second language for the El Rancho Unified School District's Gifted and Talented education program. Between 1995 and 1997, Mr. Cervantes thrived as a fifth grade teacher at the El Rancho Unified School District before finding further success as a fourth grade teacher at the aforementioned district for more than five years.

Throughout the 2000s, Mr. Cervantes contributed to the El Rancho Unified School District as a fifth grade teacher as well as a second grade teacher and as a third grade teacher. In 2010, he issued his professional retirement. Mr. Cervantes currently excels as a mentor for college students enrolled in education programs at various universities throughout his home state of California on behalf of the Alumni Association of California State University, Los Angeles.

Alongside his responsibilities as an educator, Mr. Cervantes has served as the vice president of the El Rancho Federation of Teachers since 1991. He has also been appointed to numerous committees within the El Rancho Unified School District in relation to language arts curricula, criteria for student report cards and the selection of books for literacy education. Between 1990 and 1994, Mr. Cervantes was recruited as the publisher of the official newsletter of the El Rancho Federation of Teachers. He had previously accepted a position as the chairperson of the El Rancho Unified School District parent participation committee in 1988.

Since 2019, Mr. Cervantes has additionally found success as a student sponsor for San Gabriel Mission High School's "Adopt a Student" program. He has also served as a co-coordinator of multiple programs and subcommittees for the San Gabriel Mission Church in relation to charitable initiatives for displaced children from Latin America, religious education and helping Latin American immigrants secure U.S. citizenship. Between 1998 and 2004, Mr. Cervantes was recruited as a co-editor of the San Gabriel Mission Church's souvenir program. He currently contributes to the San Gabriel Mission Catholic Community as an extraordinary minister of Holy Communion.

Born in Altadena, California, Mr. Cervantes earned a Bachelor of Arts in English at California State University, Los Angeles in 1971. He subsequently completed a Master of Arts in education at the aforementioned Los Angeles-based institution. Mr. Cervantes eventually concluded his education in 1985, at which point he obtained a Master of Arts in Chicano studies at California State University, Los Angeles.

In 2019, Mr. Cervantes was selected for an Alumni Recognition Award on behalf of San Gabriel Mission High School. He has also garnered recognition for his direct contributions to the establishment of several academic scholarships for at California State University, Los Angeles, such as the New World Scholarship, the Leader Scholarship, the Maria Dolores Cervantes Scholarship and the New World Essay Scholarship. Mr. Cervantes is particularly proud to have played an instrumental role in the development of the El Rancho Unified School District's bilingual education program. Since his holistic approach to his work continuously contributed to his success, he advises aspiring educators to determine the underlying causes of their students' struggles by speaking with their parents as well as their previous teachers. He has been included in the 76th edition of Who's Who in America.

Diane Davis-Deckard

Visual Arts Teacher (Retired)
Bloomington High School North

FORT COLLINS, CO UNITED STATES

For more than 35 years, Diane Davis-Deckard found success as an art teacher for elementary, middle school and high school students. Prior to her retirement, she specialized in honing her students' proficiency with various forms of visual art such as drawing, painting and sculpting. Ms. Davis-Deckard also focused on promoting her older students' work in exhibitions and competitions in order to maximize their eligibility for artistic scholarships as well as their acceptance into prestigious collegiate art programs across the United States.

After beginning her teaching career at Lakeview Elementary School, Ms. Davis-Deckard was recruited as an art teacher at Spencer Elementary School and Gosport Elementary School, both of which are part of Spencer – Owen Community Schools, between 1981 and 1983. She subsequently served in this capacity at multiple elementary schools within the Martinsville Schools Metropolitan School District, including Poston Road Elementary School, Centerton Elementary School and North Elementary School. Between 1984 and 1985, she excelled as an art teacher at Clear Creek Elementary School. Toward the beginning of this period, she simultaneously found further success as an art teacher at Batchelor Middle School, where she worked for more than five years.

In 1984, Ms. Davis-Deckard was additionally appointed as an art teacher at Broadview Elementary School, which has since closed. She subsequently thrived in this capacity throughout the 1980s and the 1990s. In 1991, Ms. Davis-Deckard also contributed to Grandview Elementary School as an art teacher. Between 1992 and 2018, she prospered as an art teacher at Bloomington High School North before issuing her professional retirement.

Alongside her primary responsibilities as an educator, Ms. Davis-Deckard was recruited as the coordinator of Bloomington High School North's annual "Evening of the Arts" event between 1995 and 2018. Likewise, she was appointed as the fundraising coordinator for the aforementioned high school's visual arts department in 1998. Between 2004 and 2018, Ms. Davis-Deckard simultaneously served in this capacity and as an exhibit coordinator for the Monroe County Art Teachers. She had previously contributed to the aforementioned organization as a meeting coordinator during the 1990s.

Throughout her career, Ms. Davis-Deckard and her students have provided paintings and murals to numerous local organizations such as the Greater Bloomington Chamber of Commerce, Bloomington Hospital, which is a part of the Indiana University Health system, and The Herald-Times, which is owned by Schurz Communications. Since 2011, she has continued to contribute original decorative art to Bloomington High School North. Ms. Davis-Deckard has also maintained an active affiliation with the Indiana Retired Teachers Association since 2018.

Born in Denver, Colorado, Ms. Davis-Deckard's decision to pursue a career as an art educator was chiefly inspired by her father, who enjoyed his own prosperous career as a trumpet instructor. In 1973, she obtained a Bachelor of Arts in fine arts at Indiana University Bloomington. During the early 1980s, she returned to the aforementioned institution to complete a Master of Science in art education.

In 2015, Ms. Davis-Deckard was selected for a Star of Excellence Award for Outstanding Service and Dedication on behalf of the Monroe County Community School Corporation. She had previously been celebrated with an Indiana Heritage Arts Teacher of the Year Award on behalf of the Historic Brown County Art Gallery. In addition to her ambitious and energetic personality, Ms. Davis-Deckard attributes a great deal of her success to her exceptional work ethic. In the coming years, she intends to devote more attention to creating and promoting her own original paintings.

Lawrence K. Duffy, PhD, MS

Professor
University of Alaska Fairbanks

FAIRBANKS, AK UNITED STATES

R ecognized for more than five decades of notable contributions as an educator, Lawrence K. Duffy, PhD, MS, has enjoyed a fulfilling career as a professor at the University of Alaska Fairbanks. Rising to his current role in 1992, he specializes in the subjects of chemistry and biochemistry, and has held numerous roles of high leadership at the institution. Among them, he served as the director of the Resilience and Adaptation Program from 2013 until 2020, as the interim dean of the university's graduate school between 2007 and 2012, and as the president of the faculty senate in 2000. He previously availed himself as the associate dean for graduate studies and outreach at the College of Natural Science and Mathematics from 2000 to 2006 and as the head of his department from 1994 until 1999. Dr. Duffy initially joined the faculty staff at the university in 1969 as a teaching assistant in the chemistry department and later worked as a research assistant at the school's Institute for Arctic Biology in 1974.

Hailing from a wide-ranging career in the field of academia, Dr. Duffy has lent his expertise to numerous other institutions of higher learning, including the University of the Arctic, Roxbury Community College, Harvard Medical School, and the University of Texas Medical Branch. Outside of his primary endeavors, he continues to serve as the vice chairman of the advisory board of the National Science Board's

Air Pollution Control Commission. Previously, Dr. Duffy was a member of the curriculum advisory board of both Ilisaġvik College and the Fairbanks North Star Borough School District, and directed the Alaska Basic Neuroscience Program.

Dr. Duffy has been a member of several important organizations relevant to his field, including the American Association for the Advancement of Science, the American Chemical Society and the New York Academy of Sciences. Moreover, he served as a past president of the American Society of Circumpolar Health, the American Institute of Chemists and his local chapter of Sigma Xi. Furthermore, he has contributed as a member of the editorial boards of Advances in Clinical Toxicology and Science of the Total Environment, which are prominent journals in their respective fields.

Likewise known for his contributions as a civic-minded citizen, Dr. Duffy served on the board of directors of the Alzheimer's Disease Association of Alaska from 2014 to 2021, with his previous stint ranging from 1994 to 1995. Notably, he also presided over the organization in 1999. Additional roles to his credit include his work on the science advisory board of the American Federation for Aging Research and as a member of the institutional review board of the Fairbanks Memorial Hospital. Dr. Duffy also served to the rank of a lieutenant in the U.S. Navy Reserve between 1971 and 1973.

Before embarking upon his professional journey, Dr. Duffy studied at Fordham University, where he earned a Bachelor of Science in 1969. Following this accomplishment, he went on to study at the University of Alaska Fairbanks, from which he received a Master of Science in 1972 and graduated with a Doctor of Philosophy in 1977. He subsequently undertook postdoctoral fellowships at Boston University and the Roche Institute of Molecular Biology and coursework at the University of Texas Medical Branch and Harvard Medical School.

For his extensive accomplishments, Dr. Duffy has been bestowed with numerous accolades. He was recognized with inclusion in the 76th edition of Who's Who in America. To wit, he earned the Bullock Award from the University of Alaska in 2021, a Camille & Henry Dreyfus Foundation Award from the American Chemical Society in 2020, an Excellence in Interdisciplinary Science Award from the Western Alabama Interdisciplinary Science Conference in 2012, and the Sven Ebbesson Neuroscience Service Award in 2007, as well as many merits from the University of Alaska Fairbanks and innumerable other institutions. In accounting for his standout success, Dr. Duffy largely credits the influence of several mentors, under whose tutelage and guidance he greatly benefited. Among his most dearly held achievements, he is most proud to have done the same for many students in his own right and hopes to continue doing so for years to come.

Charlene Ellen Fried

Teacher
Sierra Vista High School

Lecturer
California State University, Los Angeles

Adjunct Faculty Member
Loyola Marymount University

SEAL BEACH, CA UNITED STATES

For more than 50 years, Charlene Ellen Fried has thrived as a bilingual teacher at Sierra Vista High School in Baldwin Park, California. She is an expert in teaching social-emotional learning, English and English as a second language. Throughout her career, she has focused on preparing her students for prosperous careers where they can reach out to generously serve their communities. Having served a diverse population of students throughout her distinguished tenure, she became recognized as the school's first bilingual teacher on campus.

In 2023, Ms. Fried was selected as a recipient of the Water Education Grant Program on behalf of the Upper San Gabriel Municipal Water District. In accordance with the aforementioned grant, she facilitated a collaborative project in which students discussed, developed and implemented different strategies for minimizing water waste within their households and communities. She started the unit by discussing bucket fillers (people who communicate using kind words) to bucket dippers (people who communicate using unkind words). The goal was to first discuss the differences between a bucket filler and a bucket dipper, then discuss water waste and water conservation, and finally, show the relationship between bucket fillers and dippers and water waste and water conservation. As a final project, the students drew their perceptions of the problem of water waste and water conservation and presented their projects to the class. They created a water conservation event and invited their classmates to the event to help conserve water in their own communities. This project will be published in the spring edition of the CABE Multilingual Educator, and at their 2024 conferences. Ms. Fried will conduct workshops to share this project with other educators.

Apart from teaching at the high school level, Ms. Fried also teaches at the university level. She was invited to teach at California State University, Los Angeles, and Loyola Marymount University. She serves as a Lecturer B at CSULA, in the Charter College of Education. She teaches ELD methodology classes, classroom management and a variety of other classes in the credential program. She also supervises student teachers. She is a part-time lecturer at Loyola Marymount University and teaches ELD and Spanish methodology classes, literary classes, assessment classes, and classes focusing on ways to successfully work with the diverse student populations that the credential candidates will work with at the local schools.

As an extension of her work, Ms. Fried has been active as a workshop presenter for the California Association for Bilingual Education (CABE), the National Association for Bilingual Education (NABE) and other organizations. During her career, she has been invited to study and tour schools in Spain and Mexico. Her international travels have been instrumental in her insights regarding various school systems' structures and priorities abroad. Ms. Fried continues to study the Mayan language, and she and her son, Jose Luis Perez, have worked as volunteers in Quintana Roo, Mexico, to advance Spanish and English literacy among the Mayan-speaking children to help them expand academic and employment opportunities.

In an attempt to understand her diverse student population, she spent one year driving from Los Angeles to Rio de Janeiro and two summers traveling all over Asia. Looking toward the future, Ms. Fried is considering volunteering with both CABE and NABE in retirement, as well as volunteering in Quintana Roo. She wants to continue traveling. She believes that people's stories define who they are and empower them to accomplish their dreams and share them with others. She also wants to continue writing, which has been critical to her success as an effective writing teacher. Her students have won the CABE and NABE essay writing contests for the past three years.

Drawing inspiration from her late husband, who passed away from COVID-19, she wants to continue his legacy of teaching. He was a dedicated elementary school teacher and Vietnam War veteran.

Highly educated, Ms. Fried received a Bachelor of Arts in English and public speaking from San Francisco State University in 1968 and a Master of Science in bilingual cross-cultural education from Pepperdine University in 1984. Additional educational pursuits to her credit include certification in Spanish from the University of Salamanca and the University of Valencia in Spain. She also holds credentials as a bilingual cross-cultural specialist in bilingual education in Spanish from Pepperdine University.

In light of her success, Ms. Fried was recognized by both CABE and NABE as the Bilingual Teacher of the Year. She also received the Corazon Award from CABE and, among other accolades, in 2023, was named Woman Educator of the Year by California Senator Susan Rubio. Aside from these many honors, Ms. Fried has appeared in various news outlets and on podcasts, including EdSource Magazine in 2021 and 2022, regarding her unique classroom approach. The Baldwin Park Unified School District also recognized Ms. Fried in May 2022 by naming the Sierra Vista High School Library the Charlene Fried Library in her honor.

Willie Johnson Jr., PhD

Milwaukee County Supervisor
Milwaukee County Board of Supervisors

MILWAUKEE, WI UNITED STATES

W ith several decades of public service to his credit, Willie Johnson Jr., PhD, has distinguished himself as the 2nd District Supervisor of the Milwaukee County Board of Supervisors since 2022. Currently serving his eighth term in office, he was first elected as the county supervisor of the 13th District in 2000. As a duly elected representative, Dr. Johnson is primarily responsible for addressing issues related to community and economic development. He serves on numerous projects, initiatives, task forces and committees to best serve the needs of his 52,000 constituents. Among them, he sat on the steering committee of the Wisconsin Department of Transportation's (WISDOT) Marquette Interchange Project Disadvantaged Business Enterprise (DBE), chaired the labor development committee of the WISDOT Southeast Freeways Milwaukee County Urban DBE Advisory Committee, and was appointed by Governor Jim Doyle to the State of Wisconsin's Minority Business Development Board in 2004.

Prior to his election, beginning in 1987, Dr. Johnson worked as a financial assistance worker and a social worker on behalf of the Financial Assistance and Child Welfare divisions of the Milwaukee County Department of Human Services for several years. Previously, he had volunteered on behalf of the Milwaukee Minority Chamber of Commerce in 1986, through which he assisted minority-owned businesses in becoming certified for the city's Minority Business Enterprise Program.

Dedicated to civic advocacy in various forms, Dr. Johnson serves as a board member of Economics Wisconsin, Milwaukee Innercity Congregations Allied for Hope, the Milwaukee County Historical Society and the Wisconsin Counties Association, of which he is a past president. Additionally, he is the president of the Wisconsin County Mutual Insurance Corporation and a Scoutreach program commissioner for the Three Harbors Council of the Boy Scouts of America. In addition, he served as a member of the Urban Economic Development Association of Wisconsin and Rebuilding Together of Greater Milwaukee. To name only a few of his other previous community affiliations, Dr. Johnson also maintained involvement with the Harambee Ombudsman Project, the Riverwest Neighborhood Association, the Great Harambee Neighborhood Initiative, the University of Wisconsin-Milwaukee (UWM) Center for Economic Education and the Local Initiatives Support Corporation of Milwaukee, among many others.

To commemorate his numerous accomplishments, Dr. Johnson has been bestowed with a wealth of accolades throughout the course of his career. To wit, he was named a Minority Small Business Champion by the U.S. Small Business Administration in 2015, received a special recognition from the Wisconsin Women's Business Initiative Corporation in 2012 and earned a Golden Shovel Award from WISDOT in 2010. He was further bestowed with an outstanding service recognition from the Wisconsin Minority Business Opportunities Committee in 2008, a "To Do What Is Just" Award from the Milwaukee Innercity Congregations Allied for Hope in 2005, and a Merit Award from the Milwaukee County Disadvantaged Business Enterprise Program in 2001, in addition to the many other merits he has accrued over the years.

Before venturing onto his vocational path, Dr. Johnson studied political science at Northwestern University, where he earned a Bachelor of Arts in 1981. Following this accomplishment, he undertook coursework toward a Master of Public Administration at UWM. Dr. Johnson later attended the Wisconsin University of Theology, from which he received a Master of Arts and a Doctor of Philosophy in humanities.

As a commitment to his field, Dr. Johnson has been active with several worthy organizations. Among them, he is a member of the National Association for the Advancement of Colored People, the Milwaukee Urban League, 100 Black Men of Greater Milwaukee, the National

Forum for Black Public Administrators, the National Association of Black County Officials, the National Association of Social Workers and the National Museum of African American History and Culture.

In accounting for his success, Dr. Johnson largely credits his deep and abiding Christian faith and his steadfastly positive demeanor. Among his most dearly held accomplishments, he is particularly proud to have always distinguished himself as an advocate for minority business development and a champion of women entrepreneurship. Looking toward the future, he aspires to continue achieving reelection and serve as a humble servant of the people to whom he has dedicated his life and soul.

Lynn R. Kahle, PhD

Professor Emeritus
University of Oregon

EUGENE, OR UNITED STATES

F or 43 years, Lynn R. Kahle, PhD, has thrived as an educator. Though now retired, he is a professor emeritus of marketing at the University of Oregon's Lundquist College of Business. He began his career as a visiting assistant professor at the University of Nebraska in Lincoln, Nebraska, from 1977 to 1978, and after completing a doctorate, he was a postdoctoral fellow at the University of Michigan in Ann Arbor, Michigan, from 1978 to 1980. After completing his postdoctoral study, he went on to work as an assistant professor at The University of North Carolina at Chapel Hill from 1980 to 1983. In 1983, he joined the department of marketing at the University of Oregon in Eugene, Oregon, where he remained until 2017, when he was named professor emeritus by the university. From 2018 to 2020, Dr. Kahle taught at Pace University before officially retiring in 2020.

Like most professors, Dr. Kahle's first step into the field of education was getting an education himself. He began by attending Concordia College in Portland, Oregon, earning an associate degree in 1971 before going on to attain a bachelor's degree at Concordia College in Fort Wayne, Indiana, where he graduated with distinction in 1973. Soon after, in 1974, Dr. Kahl graduated from Pacific Lutheran University with a master's degree. He pursued a doctorate at the University of Nebraska and graduated in 1977, then did his postdoctoral study at the University of Michigan from 1978 to 1980.

Dr. Kahle has authored several books on marketing, particularly on values and lifestyle marketing, including "Communicating Sustainability for the Green Economy," published in 2014 and co-authored by Eda Gurel-Atay, "Belief Systems, Religion, and Behavioral Economics: Marketing in Multicultural Environments," published in 2013 and co-authored by Elizabeth Minton and "Marketplace Lifestyles in an Age of Social Media: Theory and Method," published in 2012 and co-authored by Pierre Valette-Florence. In 2019, he served as the editor of "Consumer Social Values," a book on behavioral science and economics, and in 2022 he was the editor-in-chief of the American Psychology Association (APA) Handbook of Consumer Psychology.

Along with his published works, he has received numerous awards, including the Stotlar Award for Education from the Sports Marketing Association in 2014, the Lundquist College of Business Thomas C. Stewart Distinguished Professor Award in 2014, the Lifetime Achievement Award from the Consumer Behavior Special Interest Group of the American Marketing Association in 2013 and the National Research Service Award from the University of Michigan from 1978 to 1980. Previously, Dr. Kahle has been recognized by Marquis Who's Who through the Albert Nelson Marquis Lifetime Achievement Award, along with being selected for inclusion in Who's Who in America and Who's Who in the World and named a Marquis Who's Who Top Professional. He has also been featured in Marquis Who's Who Millennium Magazine.

Dr. Kahle served his community as a member of the board of directors for the Organization for Economic Initiatives in Eugene, Oregon, from 1988 to 1996. Prior to his position on the board, he was president of the Commission on Rights of Aging in Eugene from 1987 to 1989 and a member of Eugene's Human Rights President's Council from 1988 to 1991. He is an active member of the American Psychological Association, which he served as chair of the membership board in 2019 and as a council representative from 2013 to 2019. Formerly, he was president of the Society for Consumer Psychology from 1997 to 1998.

In the future, Dr. Kahle would like to continue enjoying his retirement and traveling the world. Now that he is no longer teaching, he can devote more time to his hobbies, which include hiking, tennis and reading.

Paul L. Maier, PhD

Writer

Professor Emeritus
Western Michigan University

KALAMAZOO, MI UNITED STATES

An accomplished author, professor and minister, Paul L. Maier, PhD, has enjoyed a long and vibrant career. In 1958, Dr. Maier began working at Western Michigan University in Kalamazoo, Michigan, as the campus chaplain, which led him to a concurrent career as a professor of ancient history. Though Dr. Maier left the chaplain position in 1999, he remained as a professor at the university until 2011, when he ultimately retired and was granted the title of professor emeritus.

Dr. Maier is a graduate of Harvard University, where he obtained a Master of Arts in 1954. After completing his master's degree, he went on to study at Concordia Seminary, a Lutheran seminary in St. Louis, Missouri, earning a Master of Divinity in 1955. Soon after, Dr. Maier's education took him to Switzerland on a Fulbright scholarship, where he received a Doctor of Philosophy from the University of Basel, graduating summa cum laude in 1957. Dr. Maier holds two honorary Doctor of Letters, one from Concordia Seminary, received in 1995, and another from Concordia University Irvine, received in 2007. He also holds an honorary Legum Doctor from Concordia University Ann Arbor received in 2000.

As well as his career in education and ministry, Dr. Maier is a prolific author of historical fiction and nonfiction. His published nonfiction works include "The Genuine Jesus: Fresh Evidence from History and Archeology," "In the Fullness of Time: A Historian looks at Christmas, Easter, and the Early Church" and "The Da Vinci Code - Fact or Fiction?" Examples of his religious fiction include "A Skeleton in God's Closet," "More Than a Skeleton," "Pontius Pilate" and "The Flames of Rome." Dr. Maier has also written books for children, including "Martin Luther: A Man Who Changed the World" and "The Very First Christmas." He is the editor and translator of "Josephus - The Essential Writings" and "Josephus - The Jewish War" and a contributor of over 300 articles and reviews to professional journals. Having appeared in documentaries and television series, Dr. Maier's voice is respected in his field and outside of it. For the entirety of 2004, he was a featured guest on the Canadian Christian talk show "100 Huntley Street."

Dr. Maier is a member of The Phi Beta Kappa Society and an honorary member of Beta Sigma Psi. For his outstanding achievements over his lengthy career, Dr. Maier has won many awards, including the Gold Medallion Book Award from the Evangelical Christian Publishers Association (ECPA) in 1989 and the Alumni Award for Teaching Excellence in 1974. Previously, he won the Albert Nelson Marquis Lifetime Achievement Award and was featured as a Marquis Who's Who Top Professional. In his spare time, Dr. Maier enjoys photography, and he is passionate about nature preservation.

Margie L. McInerney, PhD

Professor of Management
Marshall University

HUNTINGTON, WV UNITED STATES

For more than 30 years, Margie L. McInerney, PhD, has thrived as a professor of management at Marshall University in Huntington, West Virginia. In this capacity, she specializes in building her students' knowledge of human resource management, collective bargaining and organizational behavior. Dr. McInerney also focuses on helping her students understand the roles of diversity, equity and inclusion, and ethical management tactics in the growth of a successful business.

After working as an adjunct instructor at Wesleyan College between 1979 and 1980, Dr. McInerney was recruited as a teaching assistant and a research assistant at The Ohio State University between 1980 and 1983. Throughout the following three years, she excelled as an assistant professor at the University of North Carolina Wilmington. In 1986, Dr. McInerney was appointed as an assistant professor at Marshall University, where she gradually advanced to become an associate professor in 1986 before her promotion to the position of professor in 1990.

Alongside her primary responsibilities as an educator, Dr. McInerney found further success as the director of Marshall University's Doctor of Nurse Anesthesia Practice and Management program in 1991. Between 1983 and 1985, she served as a board member of the Community Boys and Girls Club of Wilmington. Dr. McInerney has also contributed to the Labor and Employment Relations Association as a member of the automobile industry council.

Throughout her career with Marshall University, Dr. McInerney has additionally contributed to multiple academic institutions as an adjunct faculty member, including Ohio University and Central Michigan University. In 2019, she garnered widespread recognition as the author of a chapter titled "Integrating Artificial Intelligence into Traditional University Business Management Programs," which was included in the academic book "Artificial Intelligence and its Impact on Business." Moreover, Dr. McInerney has served as an administrative adviser to the international college sorority of Delta Zeta since 2011.

Born in Frankfurt, Germany, Dr. McInerney's decision to pursue a career as an educator was heavily inspired by her aunt, who enjoyed her own prosperous career as a teacher for middle school students. In 1975, she obtained a Bachelor of Science, Bachelor of Arts at the University of Akron. Dr. McInerney subsequently earned a Master of Business Administration at Marshall University before working as a bank examiner and comptroller with the U.S. Department of the Treasury between 1977 and 1979. In 1983, she concluded her education at The Ohio State University's Max M. Fisher College of Business, where she completed a Doctor of Philosophy in human resource management.

In recognition of her contributions to Marshall University, Dr. McInerney has been celebrated with a Distinguished Service Award and a Charles E. Hedrick Outstanding Faculty Award. She has also been inducted into the Marshall University chapter of the Society of Human Resource Management's Hall of Distinction. In 2017, Dr. McInerney was selected for a "Meet the Scholars Award" on behalf of the advisory board of the Pensole Lewis College of Business and Design in Detroit, Michigan.

In addition to her genuine passion for her work, Dr. McInerney attributes a great deal of her success to her interest in myriad areas of business management. She also draws inspiration from her goal of eventually sharing her research with her colleagues and students. In the coming years, Dr. McInerney intends to continue helping aspiring entrepreneurs learn how to treat their future employees with kindness and respect.

Lawrence J. McKenzie Jr.

Author

Professor
West Virginia University at Parksburg

DAVISVILLE, WV UNITED STATES

For more than 20 years, Lawrence J. McKenzie Jr. has thrived as a professor of English, philosophy and ethics at West Virginia University at Parkersburg. In this capacity, he specializes in honing his students' abilities to effectively express their ideas through the written word. Mr. McKenzie also focuses on helping his students harness various rhetorical tools and techniques to support alternative perspectives with compelling arguments.

Prior to his recruitment at West Virginia University at Parkersburg, Mr. McKenzie worked as an instructor of humanities at the University of Charleston between 1998 and 2000. He had previously begun his academic career as an adjunct instructor of British literature at Marietta College. In addition to the aforementioned academic subjects, Mr. McKenzie served as a professor of composition and rhetoric at West Virginia University at Parkersburg between 1998 and 2012. Toward the middle of this period, he additionally contributed to West Virginia University at Parkersburg as a professor of the philosophy of religion.

Alongside his primary responsibilities as an educator, Mr. McKenzie found further success as a member of West Virginia University at Parkersburg's library committee between 2010 and 2011. He had previously been appointed as a member of the aforementioned university's internationalization committee in 2007. Since 2004, Mr. McKenzie has simultaneously excelled as a board member of the West Virginia Consortium for Faculty and Course Development in International Studies.

Between 2000 and 2005, Mr. McKenzie was recruited as the secretary of the executive board as well as the acquisitions editor for the Mountain State Press. During the middle of this period, he also found success as the acquisitions editor of the West Virginia Writers Association, Inc. In 2006, Mr. McKenzie garnered further recognition as the editor of a collection of short stories titled "Mountain Voices: Illuminating the Character of West Virginia."

Outside of his professional circles, Mr. McKenzie served as the president of the Community Acres Homeowners Association, Inc., in Davisville, West Virginia, between 2003 and 2005. Toward the late 1990s, he was appointed as a pastor at Hyatt Memorial United Methodist Church. Mr. McKenzie had previously contributed to the Ostrander United Methodist Church as an associate pastor and director of community youth programs.

Born in Cumberland, Maryland, Mr. McKenzie earned a Bachelor of Arts in philosophy and religion at the University of Charleston in 1994. During this period, he simultaneously worked as an associate pastor and theological intern at St. Andrew United Methodist Church. Throughout the following four years, Mr. McKenzie obtained a Master of Arts in theological studies at the Methodist Theological School in Delaware, Ohio.

In 2013, Mr. McKenzie was honored as a Faculty Member of the Year on behalf of West Virginia University at Parkersburg. He had previously been selected for the aforementioned institution's "Unsung Hero" award in 2003. Moreover, Mr. McKenzie has additionally been distinguished as a fellow of the West Virginia Humanities Council.

Mr. McKenzie attributes a great deal of his success to his students, who regularly inspire him to channel his own creativity and experiences into his lessons. He is also extremely grateful to have honed his expertise under the mentorship of Reverend Robert G. Newman, PhD, who served as a professor of religion at the University of Charleston for more than 30 years. In order to stay up to date with the latest developments in his specialty areas, Mr. McKenzie continues to maintain active affiliations with the West Virginia Education Association, the National Council Teachers of English and the American Philosophical Association.

Gayle Granatir Michael, BA, MA

Political Consultant
Educational Consultant

BALA CYNWYD, PA UNITED STATES

For more than 30 years, Gayle Granatir Michael, MA, BA, has thrived as a private political and educational consultant. Widely renowned for her leadership roles in multiple political organizations, she focuses on helping the Montgomery County Office of Children and Youth investigate and address reports of abuse, neglect and dependency of children under the age of 18 in Montgomery County, Pennsylvania. In the latter capacity, Ms. Michael simultaneously provides private tutoring services in a broad range of subject areas in relation to language arts and communication.

Ms. Michael began her teaching career at the Rose Tree Media School District in Pennsylvania, where she also served as a coach between 1960 and 1963. She subsequently found further success in both capacities at Woodrow Wilson High School, which is part of New Jersey's Camden City School District, for a number of years before returning to Pennsylvania to work as a teacher and as a coach for the Norristown Area School District during the late 1960s. Between 1972 and 1973, Ms. Michael excelled as an instructor at Rutgers University – Camden.

Following her success as an educator, Ms. Michael shifted her focus to politics in 1989, at which point she was recruited as a board member for the Republican Women of the Main Line. Likewise, she accepted a position as a committeewoman for the Montgomery County Republican Party in 1992. Since 1995, Ms. Michael has also prospered as a co-founder and as a board member for the Montgomery County Republican Women's Leadership, which eventually promoted her to the position of chairperson between 2010 and 2014.

In 2020, Ms. Michael served as the campaign manager for Judge Paula Patrick's candidacy as a member of the Pennsylvania Supreme Court. In the aforementioned Pennsylvania township of Bala Cynwyd, she currently contributes to the Belmont Hills Library as a member of the board of trustees, and she has spearheaded several fundraising initiatives to maintain the library's financial health. Thanks to her widespread reputation, Ms. Michael regularly shares her expertise on the role of women in politics as a guest speaker at academic institutions across the United States. She has also held numerous leadership positions with the Montgomery County Office of Children and Youth such as the vice chairperson and the chairperson of the board of directors.

Ms. Michael's decision to pursue a career in politics was heavily inspired by her admiration for Jacqueline Kennedy Onassis. In 1960, she obtained a Bachelor of Arts from Temple University. While working as a teacher and a coach for Woodrow Wilson High School, Ms. Michael concluded her education at St. Joseph's University, earning a Master of Arts in 1967. Since 1992, she has continued to contribute to St. Joseph's University as a member of the National Alumni Board. To honor her for her achievements, she was included in the 76th edition of Who's Who in America.

An active affiliate of the National Federation of Republican Women, Ms. Michael attributes a great deal of her success to her ability to listen carefully during conversations with her colleagues. She is incredibly proud to have formed genuine relationships with many of her former students. Following her tenure as a teacher with the Norristown Area School District, Ms. Michael was deeply honored when her students presented her with a personalized charm bracelet. In the coming years, she intends to revisit her passion for international travel and explore several foreign European nations, particularly Croatia.

Donald B. Peck

Director (Retired)
Center for Elementary Science
Fairleigh Dickinson University

GENEVA, IL UNITED STATES

Donald B. Peck's philosophy is that science is the active pursuit of new knowledge about our physical world. It is about asking questions, getting our hands dirty and seeking answers. Science is something we do, and it can be taught that way. To this end, he promoted research programs in high school and "research" activities in elementary schools.

Mr. Peck led a long and distinguished career in education that spanned more than 40 years while specializing in chemistry, geology and mineralogy. Prior to retiring, he served as the director of the Center for Elementary Science at Fairleigh Dickinson University in New Jersey between 1987 and 1996. During his tenure on campus, Mr. Peck specialized in geology and focused heavily on curriculum and instruction for elementary school children. He and his team were invited to teach their approach to elementary school science education in Puerto Rico by Merck Pharmaceutical Company and in South Korea by the Korean National University for Education.

During an earlier stage of his career, Mr. Peck taught and held administrative roles in the public school system. He initially taught chemistry and physics at Litchfield High School in Litchfield, Connecticut, during the early 1950s and subsequently spent more than 20 years in New Jersey as the director of science curriculum and instruction at Scotch Plains-Fanwood Public Schools and as the supervisor of science curriculum and instruction at Woodbridge Township School District. Mr. Peck also had the opportunity to teach chemistry and geology on the Torrington and Waterbury campuses at the University of Connecticut during the 1960s.

Mr. Peck's research was supported through a fellowship from the National Science Foundation. He also earned the opportunity to visit the laboratories of General Electric while continuing his studies.

Apart from his extensive career in education and research, Mr. Peck has become a well-written writer, co-authoring numerous science textbooks for Holt Rinehart and Winston, Silver Burdett Ginn, and Houghton Mifflin publishers during the course of 20 years. In 2007, he also authored "Mineral Identification: A Practical Guide for the Amateur Mineralogist" via the Mineralogical Record. The book's second edition was released in 2016.

In retirement, Mr. Peck enjoys involvement with various local non-profit and civic initiatives. Among his efforts, he has volunteered his time to his local Habitat for Humanity.

A graduate of Bates College, Mr. Peck earned a Bachelor of Science in chemistry in 1953. He subsequently attended Union College, earning a Master of Science in science teaching in 1960. Additionally, he studied in the Doctor of Philosophy program at the University of Maryland in 1971, sponsored by the National Science Foundation. Mr. Peck is recognized as a life member of the National Science Teachers Association.

Anita H. Prince, PhD

Assistant Superintendent of School Operations
Virginia Department of Corrections

CHESTERFIELD, VA UNITED STATES

For more than 15 years, Anita H. Prince, PhD, found success as an educator and academic administrator with the Virginia Department of Corrections and the Virginia Department of Education. Prior to her retirement, she specialized in providing primary and lower secondary education to inmates of various correctional facilities for adults and children within the aforementioned U.S. state. Dr. Prince also focused on building her students' knowledge of relevant skills for the current workforce in order to prepare them for prosperous careers following the completion of their sentences.

Between 1999 and 2000, Dr. Prince was recruited as a professional development coordinator for the Virginia Adult Learning Resource Center of Virginia Commonwealth University. During the early 2000s, she excelled as a program improvement specialist for the Virginia Department of Education's office of adult education and literacy. Dr. Prince subsequently thrived as the assistant superintendent for academic programs with the Virginia Department of Correctional Education, which has since merged with the Virginia Department of Corrections, between 2004 and 2012.

Throughout the following three years, Dr. Prince found further success as the director of academic programs for the Virginia Department of Corrections. During this period, she oversaw the administration of educational services for more than 5,000 adult inmates on an annual basis. Between 2015 and 2018, Dr. Prince prospered as the assistant superintendent for school operations at the aforementioned government agency before issuing her professional retirement.

Alongside her primary professional responsibilities, Dr. Prince has previously served as the president of the Virginia Association for Adult and Continuing Education. Likewise, she has additionally contributed to the Correctional Education Association as an auditor. In order to stay up to date with the latest developments in her field, Dr. Prince continues to maintain an active affiliation with the Coalition on Adult Basic Education.

After obtaining a Bachelor of Science in psychology and biology at Radford University, Dr. Prince worked in numerous local and statewide social service agencies for more than 20 years. In 1984, she resumed her education at Virginia Commonwealth University, where she eventually earned a Doctor of Philosophy in adult education, social policy and social planning. Dr. Prince subsequently completed a second Doctor of Philosophy in education, social work and social policy at Virginia Commonwealth University in 1989.

In honor of her contributions to the field of child welfare, Dr. Prince has previously been recognized by the children's division of the American Humane Association. In addition to her genuine passion for education, she attributes a great deal of her success to the influence of her mother, who taught her the importance of building a viable professional skill set at a young age. Dr. Prince also credits her exceptional work ethic to her mother's prosperous career as a registered nurse and an officer of the U.S. Navy.

In the coming years, Dr. Prince intends to further her involvement in multiple community organizations, particularly in relation to child welfare and adult education. She currently works as a rehabilitation assistant and as a Tai Chi instructor in a part-time capacity. Due to the many similarities between education and mentorship, Dr. Prince advises aspiring educators to prepare themselves for their careers by pursuing opportunities to serve as mentors to their peers. During her childhood, she frequently shared her knowledge of different academic disciplines with her younger friends and family members.

Lawrence H. Rubly, MBA

Chief Operating Officer
Austin University

LAKE FOREST, IL UNITED STATES

Hailing from over 50 years of experience in his chosen field, Lawrence H. Rubly, MBA, has distinguished himself through his work as the chief operating officer and vice president of Austin University since 2018. In this capacity, he oversees all university operations, including overseas work, through which he leverages his vast experience in international education. Bearing additional expertise in career teaching and global training development, Mr. Rubly previously found success in a similar capacity at American Tech and Management University, where he also served as the dean of the business school from 2013 to 2018. Additional leadership roles in education to his credit include his work as the director of the School of Allied Health at Coyne College, the president of the International Academy of Design and Technology, the director of distance learning and online business development at DeVry University and the associate academic dean at the Keller Graduate School of Management.

Outside of his roles in academic leadership, Mr. Rubly served as an adjunct professor at Oakton Community College from 1983 until 2020. Throughout this period, he initiated the Global Business Studies Program and created the Certificate in Global Business, which allowed international students to earn a U.S. learning credential entirely online within a year. He has also availed himself on behalf of students as the executive vice president and senior fellow for distance learning at the World Engagement Institute since 2012. Prior to his work in the field of education, he built a prolific career in the private sector as a managing partner at Tech Management Consulting Ltd from 1983 to 1990 and as a contracts manager for Telemedia Inc. between 1973 and 1981. During this time, he cultivated his international expertise by developing a long-distance learning method using portable cassette tapes to teach foreign languages to U.S. executives.

Known for his contributions as a civic-minded citizen, Mr. Rubly has served on the board of directors for The Cradle Adoption, a nonprofit organization that has helped match more than 16,000 children with loving families since 1923. Adjacent to this role, he chairs the board committee for Adoption Learning Partners, which provides online and in-person training for applicants regarding all aspects of adoption. Mr. Rubly also sat on the board of trustees for Kuwait Technical College from 2002 until 2020.

Before embarking upon his professional journey, Mr. Rubly studied linguistics at the University of Notre Dame, from which he earned a Bachelor of Arts in 1969. Following this accomplishment, he served in the U.S. Army Security Agency until 1972, whereupon he returned to Notre Dame and received a Master of Arts in 1974. Mr. Rubly continued his studies in linguistics at the Illinois Institute of Technology, graduating with a Master of Science in the same year. A decade later, he completed his academic efforts at Southern Illinois University, receiving a Master of Business Administration in marketing and finance in 1984.

In accounting for his success, Mr. Rubly largely credits his ability to remain focused, as well as his desire to innovate and tread new ground in the field. Furthermore, he has always benefited from a nurturing support network and collaboration with talented colleagues. Among his most notable achievements, he is particularly proud to have helped teach English to members of the Royal Saudi Naval Forces and helped build programs for international business at the college level. Looking toward the future, Mr. Rubly would like to continue sustaining his language education efforts in Egypt.

James J. Secosky

Teacher (Retired)
Bloomfield Central School District

LOVELAND, CO UNITED STATES

Hailing from more than 25 years of experience in the field of science education, James J. Secosky has now distinguished himself through his work in astronomy. Bearing a wealth of knowledge surrounding the planet Mars, he has devoted a great deal of time and attention to conducting research through programs set up by the National Aeronautics and Space Administration, which allow amateur astronomers to conduct their own investigations into the red planet. At his suggestion, thousands of pictures, many of which bear unique scientific value, have been taken by the Mars Global Surveyor and Mars Reconnaissance Orbiter satellites, and are regularly posted to his online social media accounts. An exhaustive cataloger of the facts surrounding the solar system's fourth planet, Mr. Secosky also routinely updates the Marspedia online encyclopedia and hopes to serve as an intermediary between the science and general public regarding Martian studies.

Prior to his turn toward amateur astronomy, Mr. Secosky worked as a science teacher on behalf of the Bloomfield Central School District in New York from 1971 until 1998, during which time he taught grades seven to 12, coached wrestling teams, conducted geology field trips, and administrated a support group for students who struggled with substance abuse problems. Following this period, he focused more intently on service as a college educator and served as an adjunct instructor at Portland State University and Finger Lakes Community

College, the latter for which he also worked as a microbiology labora-tory technician for several years.

Outside of his primary endeavors in education, Mr. Secosky has spoken before over 100 audiences regarding discoveries made by the Hubble Space Telescope from 1991 until 2008. Likewise, he has deliv-ered speeches at conventions of the Mars Society, the Science Teach-er's Association of New York State, the Rochester Academy of Science and the National Science Teachers Association on multiple occasions. Well-regarded as a vast font of knowledge in his area of expertise, he has also been interviewed by National Public Radio, contributed as a writer for the Holt Science & Technology Earth Science textbook, and taught classes at the Rochester Museum and Science Center, among other accomplishments to his credit.

Mr. Secosky first sought an education at Pennsylvania Western Uni-versity in California, Pennsylvania, from which he earned a Bachelor of Science in secondary education, with a particular focus in biology, in 1971. Graduating cum laude, he is proud to have both made the wres-tling team and been a member of the Theta Xi fraternity. Following this accomplishment, he went on to attend the State University of New York at Genesco and graduated with a Master of Arts in biology in 1977. After concluding his academic efforts, Mr. Secosky went on to be certified as a teacher of general science, biology, chemistry and Earth science in the state of New York.

To commemorate his numerous accomplishments, Mr. Secosky has received several accolades throughout the course of his career. Among them, he was included in the 76th edition of Who's Who in America. He received the Marian S. Hallock Award from the Bloomfield Central School District, which honors employees who touch the lives of stu-dents in special ways, in 1989. Additionally, he earned a Professional Excellence Award from Pennsylvania Western University in 1994 and the John Q Award from the Council on Alcoholism in the Finger Lakes during the same year. Among his most cherished achievements, how-ever, Mr. Secosky is most proud to have been one of the first amateur applicants to be given access to the Hubble Space Telescope and to have served as an executive officer for the Mars Society's habitation simulation mission in Utah in 2013. Looking toward the future, he aspires to continue serving as an inspiration to others.

Spending his early years doing a number of physically intensive jobs, including farm work, yard work and paper routes, Mr. Secosky has remained physically active through the decades. In addition to wrestling in college, he credits his years of practicing judo for helping him to grow significantly regarding discipline and focus. He is also thankful for his wife of more than 50 years, who supported him as he strove to change the world. Furthermore, Mr. Secosky is the proud father of one son, who is a geophysicist and church elder, and grandfather to two grandsons, both of whom have achieved the rank of Eagle Scout.

Lucy Mae Svang Selander, BA

Librarian

Minneapolis Public Library

MINNEAPOLIS, MN UNITED STATES

For more than 50 years, Lucy Mae Svang Selander, BA, has served her community as a youth services librarian working with children and teens. She began her career as a part-time library aide in 1965 before receiving a Bachelor of Arts in sociology and library science from the University of Minnesota Twin Cities in Minneapolis, Minnesota, in 1969. After graduating, she became a library aide with the history department of the Minneapolis Public Library in Minneapolis, Minnesota, until 1970, when she was promoted to librarian assistant at the East Lake branch of the Minneapolis Public Library, overseeing their adult section. From 1973 to 1982, she worked as the librarian assistant for the children's section of the Roosevelt branch of the Minneapolis Public Library. At the Minneapolis Public Library's Nokomis branch, she worked as a librarian assistant from 1982 to 2009, when she moved to the Hennepin County Library's East Lake and Roosevelt branch, where she remained for a year. From 2010 to 2017, Ms. Selander worked as a librarian in the youth services at the Oxboro branch of the Hennepin County Library, which had, at that point, merged with the greater Minneapolis Public Library. Ms. Selander retired in 2017 but remains passionate about reading and children's literacy.

As a child, Ms. Selander had a love of reading instilled in her by her mother, Marion. Her mother, a former schoolteacher, began reading to her and her twin sister, Marie, in preschool and continued for years. During the summer, her mother would read to her and the neighborhood children, breathing life into classic books like "Red Badge of Courage," "Treasure Island" and "Little House in the Big Woods." Since then, Ms. Selander has had an interest in working with libraries, hoping to share her love of reading. Another mentor of hers was her uncle, George N. Aagaard, the former dean of the University of Washington School of Medicine, who was featured in Who's Who in America when she was young. It has been her dream to be featured in Who's Who in America and see her name listed with her uncle's.

Seeing children return to the library again and again, including bringing their own children later in life, is one of the highlights of Ms. Selander's career. Now that she is on Facebook, she can see where the children she read to have gone with their lives, including becoming teachers, professors and working professionals. Throughout her long career, Ms. Selander has had the unique experience of watching library science change and technology advance, with libraries first transitioning from paper records to automation and from card catalogs and microfiche to computers. By the time she retired, the library had digitized its records and began using computers for tasks that were once completely manual. Ms. Selander considers her greatest achievements to be the encouragement of children to read, doing story times and visiting schools, and participating in different book clubs and programs for children.

A member of the American Library Association, the Minnesota Library Association and the American Association of University Women (AAUW), Ms. Selander continues to be an advocate for libraries and encouraging children to read.

Lieda A. Shadwick, MAT

Career and Technical Education Educator
Riverview Gardens High School

COLLINSVILLE, IL UNITED STATES

F or more than 20 years, Lieda A. Shadwick, MAT, has thrived as a career and technical education educator at multiple high schools across the United States. In this capacity, she specializes in helping her students learn how to design websites and develop the knowledge and skills necessary to manipulate different forms of computer applications. Ms. Shadwick also focuses on building her students' understanding of the various components of a successful small business, particularly in relation to marketing and advertising.

In 1999, Ms. Shadwick began her teaching career at Venice High School in Illinois, where she worked as a career and technical education educator. Between 2001 and 2002, she served as a career and technical education educator at Livingston High School before finding further success in this capacity at Northwestern Junior/Senior High School in Palmyra, Illinois, between 2004 and 2005. Throughout the following five years, Ms. Shadwick was appointed as a career and technical education educator at Riverview Gardens High School in St. Louis, Missouri.

Between 2011 and 2012, Ms. Shadwick excelled as a career and technical education educator and as an adviser to the yearbook club at Confluence Preparatory Academy. She subsequently prospered as a business educator at R.G. Central Middle School for more than five years, where she also prospered as an assistant girls' basketball coach. Since 2019, Ms. Shadwick has worked as a career and technical education educator at the aforementioned St. Louis-based high school, where she also served as a yearbook adviser for four years.

Alongside her primary responsibilities as a career and technical education educator, Ms. Shadwick has simultaneously served as a teacher of English as a second language through VIPKid, now known as VIP Teach, in an independent contractor capacity since 2018. During the early 2000s, she was additionally appointed as a substitute teacher with Collinsville Community Unit School District 10 and Cahokia Unit School District 187. Between 2009 and 2011, Ms. Shadwick was recruited as the vice president of the Collinsville High School Band Parents Association. From 2011 until 2012, she served as the CHS Band Parents Association president. In order to stay up to date with the latest developments in her field, she continues to maintain active affiliations with the National Education Association, the Missouri chapter of the aforementioned labor union and DECA, Inc.

Prior to her success as an educator, Ms. Shadwick served in the U.S. Army/Army Reserves for more than five years. During this period, she participated in the Gulf War and gradually advanced to the rank of sergeant. Following her exit from the military, Ms. Shadwick obtained a Bachelor of Science in business administration and a Bachelor of Music in music performance at Southern Illinois University Edwardsville. During the early 2000s, she concluded her education at Webster University, where she earned a Master of Arts in Teaching in education technology.

In 2010, Ms. Shadwick was honored as the "Teacher of the Year" on behalf of Riverview Gardens High School. In addition to her compassionate and empathetic personality, she attributes a great deal of her success to her ability to foster productive communication with students from various cultural or economic backgrounds. Ms. Shadwick also draws tremendous inspiration from her mother, who emigrated to the United States from her native country of Lithuania before enjoying her own prosperous career as an educator. In the coming years, she intends to pursue a graduate degree in relation to teaching English as a second language while devoting more time to her passion for photography.

Anita Skop

Superintendent (Retired)
District 15
New York City Department of Education

WEST NYACK, NY UNITED STATES

For more than 35 years, Anita Skop found success as an educator, staff developer and academic administrator with the New York City Department of Education. Prior to her retirement, she focused on overseeing the implementation of curricula and providing faculty members with the necessary resources to maximize student achievement. Ms. Skop also specialized in increasing educational equity within numerous school districts and creating a welcoming and accommodating environment for students of various ethnic backgrounds.

Between 1985 and 1991, Ms. Skop began her academic career as a first grade teacher at Public School 199 Frederick Wachtel in Brooklyn, New York, which is part of New York City District 21. She subsequently worked as a second grade teacher at the aforementioned public school before her appointment as a teacher for the Global Learning and Observation to Benefit the Environment (GLOBE) program between 1994 and 1996. Throughout the following five years, Ms. Skop excelled as a staff developer for New York City District 21.

Between 2001 and 2003, Ms. Skop was recruited as the director of literacy and social studies for Brooklyn School District 19, which is part of the New York City Department of Education. She subsequently thrived as a regional instructional specialist for the New York City Department of Education's District 5, which promoted her to the position of local instructional superintendent between 2004 and 2007. After finding further success as a lead senior achievement facilitator with the New York City Department of Education, Ms. Skop prospered as the community superintendent for the aforementioned school system's District 15 for more than 10 years. Between 2022 and 2023, she contributed to the New York City Department of Education as a senior adviser to the deputy chancellor before issuing her professional retirement.

Alongside her responsibilities with the New York City Department of Education, Ms. Skop has served as an educational adviser and adjunct professor at Touro University for more than 20 years. Between 1998 and 2001, she was additionally appointed as a presenter for a language parts program known as "Project Read." During her tenure as an educator at Public School 199, Ms. Skop simultaneously worked as an instructor for the Midwood Development Corporation between 1987 and 1994.

Throughout her career, Ms. Skop has participated in multiple committees and initiatives through the New York City Department of Education in relation to English, language arts and literacy. In 1995, she was recruited to the selection committee for the New York State Teacher of the Year. During this period, Ms. Skop additionally served as the president of the New York chapter of the National Network of State Teachers of the Year.

Born in Brooklyn, New York, Ms. Skop's decision to pursue a career as an educator was chiefly inspired by her genuine passion for the field of education. In 1985, she obtained a Bachelor of Arts in English with a minor in education at Brooklyn College, which is part of the City University of New York system. Ms. Skop subsequently earned a Master of Science in special education at Adelphi University. Toward the late 1990s, she completed an advanced certificate in administration at the aforementioned Brooklyn-based institution.

In 2022, Ms. Skop was celebrated with a Leadership Award on behalf of Educators for Student Success. She had previously been honored with the Shirley Chisholm Women of Excellence Award on behalf of the New York State Senate. In 1994, the New York State Education Department selected Ms. Skop as the New York State Teacher of the Year. Moreover, she has also been recognized as an "Outstanding Educator" on behalf of the United Federation of Teachers.

In addition to her compassionate personality, Ms. Skop attributes a great deal of her success to her ability to speak to children with exceptional kindness and respect. She is particularly proud to have accompanied one of the chancellors of the New York City Department of Education to Washington, D.C., to speak with multiple lawmakers about the future of the education sector. In the coming years, Ms. Skop intends to share her expertise in literacy in a consultant capacity while maintaining her responsibilities as an adjunct professor at Touro University.

Marilynn J. Smiley, PhD

Distinctive Teaching Professor Emerita
State University of New York at Oswego

OSWEGO, NY UNITED STATES

For more than 50 years, Marilynn J. Smiley, PhD, found success as an educator and academic administrator at the State University of New York (SUNY) at Oswego. Prior to her retirement, she specialized in honing her students' knowledge of music that originated in ancient Greece, the Middle Ages and the Renaissance. Dr. Smiley also focused on helping her students understand the evolution of music throughout history as well as the influence of iconic classical composers, particularly Ludwig Van Beethoven.

Between 1953 and 1961, Dr. Smiley began her academic career as a music teacher at a public school in Logansport, Indiana. She was subsequently recruited as a faculty member of the music department of the aforementioned New York-based institution, which promoted her to the position of distinguished teaching professor in 1974. Dr. Smiley thrived in this capacity until 2014, at which point she was designated as a distinctive teaching professor emerita on behalf of SUNY Oswego. Between 1976 and 1981, she simultaneously served as the chairperson of SUNY Oswego's music department.

Alongside her primary responsibilities at SUNY Oswego, Dr. Smiley has found further success as the president of the board of directors of the Oswego Opera Theatre for more than 10 years. Likewise, she currently excels as the president of the Oswego branch of the American Association of University Women. Dr. Smiley had initially served in this capacity between 1984 and 1986.

Moreover, Dr. Smiley additionally contributed to the American Association of University Women of New York State as a historian between 2004 and 2013 and as the director of diversity between 1993 and 1996. During the latter period, she was simultaneously appointed as a board member of the New York State-St. Lawrence Chapter, American Musicological Society. Dr. Smiley had previously prospered as the chairperson of the New York chapter of the American Musicological Society between 1975 and 1977.

In 2013, Dr. Smiley garnered further recognition as a co-editor of "Remarkable Women in New York State History," which was released through the History Press. She has also contributed articles to numerous professional journals and publications. In order to stay up to date with the latest developments in her field, Dr. Smiley maintains active affiliations with the Renaissance Society of America, the College Music Society, the Music Library Association and the Medieval Academy of America.

Born in Columbia City, Indiana, Dr. Smiley's decision to pursue a career as a music educator was chiefly inspired by her proficiency with multiple musical instruments, particularly the piano and the flute. After obtaining a Bachelor of Science at Ball State University, she earned a Master of Music in musicology at Northwestern University in 1958. Dr. Smiley eventually concluded her education at the University of Illinois, where she completed a Doctor of Philosophy in musicology in 1970.

In honor of her contributions to SUNY Oswego, Dr. Smiley was selected for the Chancellor's Award for Excellence on behalf of the directors of the SUNY system in 1973. She has also been honored with inclusion in the 76th edition of Who's Who in America. In addition to her genuine passion for music, she attributes a great deal of her success to the guidance and support of her own music teachers. In the coming years, Dr. Smiley intends to play an instrumental role in the development and production of an operetta titled "The Golden Cage." She had previously been celebrated for her research efforts for "The Golden Cage" in an extensive feature in the Syracuse Post-Standard in 2022.

Marilee Ann Snider

Educator & Learning Specialist (Retired)
Fairfield-Suisun Unified School District

FAIRFIELD, CA UNITED STATES

For more than 50 years, Marilee Ann Snider found success as a teacher and learning specialist. Prior to her retirement, she focused on helping elementary and middle school students improve their proficiencies in various academic subjects, including reading, writing, social studies and mathematics. Ms. Snider also specialized in creating new strategies for adapting instruction to meet the needs of children with severe behavioral disorders or intellectual disabilities.

Between 1962 and 1965, Ms. Snider began her academic career as a teacher in San Diego, California. Throughout the following 20 years, she served in this capacity at a school in Riverside, California. Toward the middle of this period, Ms. Snider was simultaneously recruited as an educator and as a learning specialist with the Fairfield-Suisun Unified School District, where she subsequently worked for more than 35 years.

During the beginning of her tenure with the Fairfield-Suisun Unified School District, Ms. Snider found further success as the manager of a resource room program for children with special needs between 1977 and 1985. She also contributed to the aforementioned school district as the instructor of an experimental emergency medical response course for educators and other staff members. Ms. Snider was additionally recruited as a teacher at a diagnostic center in Solano County,

California, which has since closed, for more than five years. In 2015, she issued her professional retirement.

Following her retirement, Ms. Snider excelled as an educator for children with special needs at Cordelia Hills Elementary School in a volunteer capacity between 2016 and 2018. She subsequently served in this capacity between 2022 and 2023. In order to stay up to date with the latest developments in her field, Ms. Snider continues to maintain an active affiliation with the California Retired Teachers Association. She also regularly contributes to multiple nonprofit organizations and medical research organizations, including St. Jude Children's Research Hospital, Habitat for Humanity for International and multiple organizations in relation to animal rights.

Born in Denver, Colorado, Ms. Snider's decision to pursue a career as an educator was chiefly inspired by her natural comfort in a class-room setting. In 1962, she earned a Bachelor of Arts in elementary education at San Diego State University. While working as a teacher, Ms. Snider simultaneously completed a Master of Arts in education at the University of California, Riverside. She eventually concluded her education at the University of San Francisco, where she obtained a Master of Arts in administration and supervision in 1985.

In recognition of her contributions to the Fairfield-Suisun Unified School District, Ms. Snider was distinguished as the Teacher of the Year. In 1992, she was appointed president of the Beta Psi chapter of Delta Kappa Gamma. Along with her genuine passion for her work, Ms. Snider attributes a great deal of her success to the support of her family members as well as her colleagues.

During her tenure as the president of the Beta Psi chapter of Delta Kappa Gamma, Ms. Snider was deeply honored to coordinate numer-ous fundraising initiatives for fellow educators. Under her leadership, the aforementioned chapter also supported scholarships for multiple education students. Since her confidence in her professional skill set played an instrumental role in the longevity of her career, Ms. Snider encourages aspiring educators to focus on developing their own strengths in order to eventually cultivate the skills of their students.

Eugene Thompson

Head Men's Tennis Coach
Virginia State University

Assistant Women's Basketball Coach
Virginia State University

HOPEWELL, VA UNITED STATES

F or more than 15 years, Eugene Thompson found success as the assistant coach of the women's basketball team and as the head coach of the men's tennis team at Virginia State University. With more than five decades of experience as an athletic coach and as an educator to his credit, he notably guided the former team to five championship victories within the National Collegiate Athletics Association's Division II. In addition to basketball and tennis, Mr. Thompson has garnered further recognition as a track and field coach for college and high school students across the United States.

Prior to his recruitment at Virginia State University, Mr. Thompson worked as a teacher and head basketball coach at Conrad Schools of Science and Alexis I. du Pont High School between 2000 and 2004. During this period, he was simultaneously appointed as the head of the men's and women's tennis teams at Lincoln University, which had initially recruited him as the head of the men's tennis team in 1994. Mr. Thompson had previously thrived as a teacher as well as a coach of the football, basketball, and track and field teams at Wilmington High School for more than 20 years.

Alongside his responsibilities as a head coach and assistant coach, Mr. Thompson contributed to Virginia State University as an adjunct professor and coordinator of the aforementioned institution's fitness center. In order to stay up to date with the latest developments in the tennis community, he continues to maintain active affiliations with the United States Tennis Association and the American Tennis Association. Moreover, Mr. Thompson currently excels as a mentor for 100 Black Men of America, Inc.

Born in Newport News, Virginia, Mr. Thompson completed undergraduate coursework at Compton College before serving in the U.S. Army between 1959 and 1962. He subsequently earned a Bachelor of Science in health, physical education and recreation at Elizabeth City State University in 1966, at which point he was recruited as the head football and basketball coach at Southwestern High School. After further success in both capacities at Douglas High School, Mr. Thompson concluded his education at Virginia State University, where he obtained a Master of Education in 1971.

Throughout his career, Mr. Thompson worked as a coach at the Five-Star Basketball Camp in New York City for more than 30 years, during which period he collaborated with several renowned basketball coaches, including Hubei Brown, Rick Pitino and John Calipari. He also shared his coaching expertise with a number of iconic professional basketball players, including Christian Laettner, Grant Hill and Vince Carter. Moreover, Mr. Thompson is extremely proud to have guided the basketball team at Wilmington High School to state championship victories in 1978, 1983 and 1988.

In recognition of his contributions as a basketball, tennis, and track and field coach, Mr. Thompson was inducted into the Delaware Sports Hall of Fame in 2022. He had previously been inducted into the Delaware Afro-American Sports Hall of Fame, Inc. in 2009. Furthermore, Mr. Thompson has additionally been honored with the Eve Kraft USTA Community Service Award on behalf of the United States Tennis Association and an Achievement Award on behalf of the National Association of Basketball Coaches. The former organization had previously distinguished him as the "Coach of the Year" for the Middle States division.

Jeremy B. Utt, EdS, NBCT

Teacher

Stafford County Public Schools

GARRISONVILLE, VA UNITED STATES

Passionate about teaching from an early age, Jeremy B. Utt, EdS, NBCT, has served the state of Virginia as a public school educator for nearly 20 years. Graduating in 2003 with a Bachelor of Arts in government and public policy from William & Mary, a university in Williamsburg, Virginia, Mr. Utt decided to follow his childhood dream of becoming a teacher, pursuing a Master of Arts in Education in curriculum and instruction from William & Mary. While a student at William & Mary, Mr. Utt assisted with the re-establishment of the Virginia Alpha Chapter of Pi Gamma Mu, an international honor society in the social sciences. After receiving his degree in 2006, he began teaching at the Isle of Wight County Schools in Windsor, Virginia, where he remained until 2010. He spent another five years as a teacher at the Hampton County Schools in Hampton, Virginia. Since 2015 he has served as an educator for the Stafford County Public Schools in Stafford, Virginia. In addition to serving as a teacher, he served a year as the mathematics specialist for a middle school. At his current school, in addition to his teaching duties, he serves as the sponsor of the Junior Beta Club he founded in 2021 and as the chapter adviser of the National Junior Honor Society Chapter.

Throughout the course of his career, Mr. Utt learned that teaching a wide variety of subjects has improved the quality of his instruction, as he has taught most mathematics courses from sixth grade up to AP

Calculus BC. In terms of conveying information, he gained a depth of understanding of mathematics that he did not possess at the start of his career. As a veteran teacher, he understands and relates to students more than he did in his first few years of teaching, and he has cultivated a wide range of experience dealing with children from various backgrounds, ethnicities, abilities and circumstances.

For demonstrating excellence as a teacher, he has won numerous awards, including Master Teacher of Honor from Kappa Delta Pi in 2021, Phi Delta Kappa Distinguished Educator from Phi Delta Kappa International in 2019 and Teacher of Honor from Kappa Delta Pi in 2010. In 2006, when he had only just begun teaching, he received the Meritorious New Teacher Candidate Designation. Previously, he received the Albert Nelson Marquis Lifetime Achievement Award and was featured in both the 76th edition of Who's Who in America and among Marquis Who's Who Top Educators. Mr. Utt considers his most notable professional achievement to be his becoming a National Board Certified Teacher, the highest and most respected certification a teacher may obtain.

Looking to the future, Mr. Utt plans to continue as a teacher. Though he is not actively seeking an administrative role, if he felt called to do so in the future, he would take a role as a central office coordinator or director. Having earned an education specialist degree in educational leadership from Old Dominion University in 2018, he is contemplating returning to school to receive a Doctor of Education in gifted administration.

Michael J. Walzer

Teacher & Coach (Retired)
Akron Public Schools

AKRON, OH UNITED STATES

For more than 30 years, Michael J. Walzer thrived as an educator for elementary, middle and high school students at Akron Public Schools. Prior to his retirement, he specialized in honing his students' knowledge of math, science and history. Mr. Walzer also served as a coach for numerous middle school sports programs, including soccer and track.

Between 2008 and 2019, Mr. Walzer found further success as a substitute teacher for various school districts in Summit County, Ohio, where he taught physical education, special education and art in a part-time capacity. He has additionally excelled as a poll worker for the Summit County Board of Elections since 2016. Moreover, Mr. Walzer has contributed to the Mustill Store Museum and House in Akron, Ohio, in multiple volunteer capacities for more than 10 years.

Following his retirement from his career with Akron Public Schools in 2006, Mr. Walzer garnered recognition as a frequent contributor to the Akron Beacon Journal. Three of his poems have been published by Eber and Wein Publishing: 2014's "Staking a Claim," 2017's "The Many Colors of Vinny Vango" and 2022's "Hula Hoopla." Mr. Walzer also harbors a deep passion for hiking and has maintained an active affiliation with the Akron Metro Parks Hiking Club since 2012.

Mr. Walzer's initial interest in pursuing a career as an educator emerged during his senior year of high school, at which point he worked as a math tutor for third grade students. He also displayed a natural talent for math at a young age. While attending elementary school, Mr. Walzer regularly achieved perfect scores on math examinations despite devoting minimal effort.

Mr. Walzer developed his athletic prowess during high school as well. He earned first-place honors in numerous track competitions and developed a local reputation for his ability to run one mile in just over four and a half minutes. During the early 1970s, Mr. Walzer notably placed 13th in a statewide middle-distance running competition.

In 1976, Mr. Walzer obtained a Bachelor of Science in elementary education at Kent State University. He was subsequently recruited as an educator with Akron Public Schools, where he worked until he issued his professional retirement in 2006. Mr. Walzer continues to contribute to the Kent State Alumni Association's High School Scholarship Fund in order to support the tuitions of future students of the aforementioned Ohio-based institution.

Mr. Walzer is deeply honored to have helped multiple sports teams attain undefeated records. He is particularly proud of the accomplishments of his soccer players, most of whom were based in urban areas. Mr. Walzer was also recruited as a soccer coach at Litchfield Middle School for 17 years, winning at least nine out of 10 games every season.

Mr. Walzer attributes a great deal of his success to his Roman Catholic upbringing on behalf of his late parents, Robert and Alice. He also credits his younger brother, the late Stephen Walzer, for exemplifying the importance of enjoying the act of playing a sport, rather than focusing entirely on the outcome of the game. Due to the inevitability of losses and disappointing performances in sports, Mr. Walzer strongly advises aspiring coaches to learn from their mistakes and acknowledge flaws in their coaching strategies without shame or embarrassment. In the coming years, he intends to pursue a position as a substitute teacher while composing more poems and spending more time with his two grandnieces and three grandnephews. He has been honored for his achievements in the 76th edition of Who's Who in America.

Glenn A. Burdick

Dean Emeritus
University of Southern Florida

DADE CITY, FL UNITED STATES

Drawing on over five decades of experience in the field of physics, Glenn A. Burdick distinguished himself as the dean of the College of Engineering at the University of Southern Florida prior to his retirement in 1986, whereupon he was granted emeritus status. Having joined the faculty staff at the university in 1965 as a professor of electrical engineering, he went on to secure his position as a dean in 1979. Previously, Dr. Burdick worked as an instructor at the Georgia Institute of Technology from 1956 until 1959, having first served as a special tool designer for the university in 1954.

Outside of his work in the realm of education, Dr. Burdick was active as the president of Burdick Engineering and Science Inc. from 1983 until the company's dissolution in 2013. Prior to this role, he had worked decades earlier in the private sector as a senior member of the research staff at Sperry Microwave in Oldsmar, Florida, from 1961 to 1964. He initially garnered expertise in his field as an office manager with Statewide Contractors in Las Vegas, Nevada, in 1955. Additionally, before embarking upon his professional journey, Dr. Burdick served his country as a member of the U.S. Air Force between 1950 and 1954.

Though his career has been filled with many memorable moments, Dr. Burdick is most proud to have endowed the Glenn A. and Joyce M. Burdick Scholarship fund at the Georgia Institute of Technology, which is bestowed to students who demonstrate scholastic excellence and leadership at the university's School of Physics within the College of Sciences. Among other achievements to his credit, he is also gratified to have spearheaded the invention of an underground pipeline leak detector and a method for effective sailboat mast insulation.

As a commitment to his field, Dr. Burdick has been active with several industry-related organizations throughout his career. To wit, he served as the vice chairman of the Southeastern Region of the National Society of Professional Engineers from 1986 until 1988 and as a member of various other societies, including the New York Academy of Sciences, the National Academy of Forensic Engineering, the American Association of Forensic Sciences and the Florida Engineering Society, among several others. Likewise dedicated to civic endeavors, he was an appointed member of the State of Florida's Energy Task Force between 1980 and 1985, as well as a member of the Pinellas County High-Speed Rail Task Force and the Tampa Bay Foreign Affairs Committee throughout the 1980s.

Well-regarded for his myriad accomplishments, Dr. Burdick has garnered several accolades throughout his career. Among them, he was named the Engineering Faculty Member of the Year by the State of Florida in 1986 and the Engineer of the Year by the Florida Engineering Society in 1981. Furthermore, the University of Southern Florida named its largest building within the College of Engineering the Glenn A. Burdick Hall in his honor. Dr. Burdick has also been elected to National Science Foundation and Woodrow Wilson fellowships and as a Texas Gulf Scholar throughout the late 1950s and early 1960s.

Having long believed in the value of a quality education, particularly in physics and the sciences as a whole, Dr. Burdick first studied at the Georgia Institute of Technology, where he earned a Bachelor of Science and a Master of Science in 1958 and 1959, respectively. After graduating, he went on to attend the Massachusetts Institute of Technology, from which he received a Doctor of Philosophy in 1961.

Robert A. Childs

Senior Vacuum Engineer & Technical Supervisor (Retired)
Plasma Science and Fusion Center
Massachusetts Institute of Technology

Vacuum Engineer & Instructor
RAC Consulting

HULL, MA UNITED STATES

G raduating from Bourne High School in Massachusetts in 1965, Robert A. Childs subsequently spent time in the U.S. Air Force, where he became certified as a level five telecommunication specialist in 1968. In 1969, he joined the Massachusetts Institute of Technology and worked with the instrumentation labs at the Draper Laboratory until 1970, when he became an electronic technician in the institute's Center for Space Research. During this time, he assisted in the development of the RF interferometry experiment that was used on the Apollo 17 mission to the moon. As part of this, they tested prototypes on glaciers, and he received special hazardous conditions training for this work. Their last test was on the Taku glacier of the Juneau ice field in Alaska.

Mr. Childs remained with MIT in the Plasma Science and Fusion Center for the next three decades as a vacuum engineer and technical supervisor until his retirement in 2007. Starting out as an electronics technician in 1973, he notably designed and constructed the Alcator A and Alcator C tokamaks. His success in these endeavors, including numerous additional diagnostic experiments for the Alcator series, led to his promotion to the role of vacuum lab technical supervisor in 1981.

This saw his responsibilities grow to encompass supervising all activities in the vacuum lab and instructing technicians, graduate students and physicists in the proper cleaning, assembly and testing of various equipment and other apparatus in the lab. Throughout this period, Mr. Childs furthered his skills by taking continuing education courses through MIT's Lowell Institute and the American Vacuum Society.

Furthermore, Mr. Childs consulted internally across a number of Plasma Science and Fusion Center projects as well as in other departments. One such consulting job became a full-time assignment as the field manager and engineer responsible for heat treating the central solenoid model coil for the U.S. module of the International Thermonuclear Experimental Reactor design program. He worked from 1996 to 1998 at a heat-treating company in Dayton, Ohio, to heat treat 10 large superconducting coils in the world's largest commercially available vacuum furnace. Mr. Childs' success on this project led to him being recruited by Mitsubishi Electric to help them with their insert coils being made for the same ITER program from 1998 to 1999.

By the time Mr. Childs retired in 2007, he was in charge of the design, operation and maintenance of the vacuum systems for the Alcator CMOD Tokamak fusion reactor experiment, which saw funding from the Office of Fusion Energy within the U.S. Department of Energy. This experiment was the third in a series of large fusion experiments at MIT and, as such, required the highest level of ultra-high vacuum standards. In addition to design and construction, Mr. Childs was responsible for reviewing and providing technical advice on the designs of numerous diagnostic experiments and upgrades that were being added to the system.

Following his retirement, Mr. Childs became a consultant with RAC Consulting, where he remains to this day, offering his expertise and skill in vacuum system design, analysis and troubleshooting; cryogenic design; material processing; and plating and metal surface processing. He has also remained active with the American Vacuum Society, which he first joined in 1978. Currently, he is the chair of the exhibitor and manufacturers committee, a member of the long-range planning group, and an instructor for vacuum technology short courses, and he previously served as president in 2004. A well-regarded author in his field, Mr. Childs has presented his work at industry conferences and had numerous articles published in professional journals.

For his years of excellence, Mr. Childs has been the recipient of a number of honors and accolades. In 1991, he was presented with a letter of recognition from MIT for designing and creating an interactive plasma display demo for the Plasma Science and Fusion Center's high school outreach program. He went on to receive a certificate of merit from the Department of Energy for his work on the U.S. module of the ITER central solenoid model coil in 1997. The American Vacuum Society has awarded Mr. Childs twice for his service, first in 1999 with the George T. Hanyo Award and again with the society's Honorary Membership Award in 2011. He has additionally been honored with inclusion in the 76th edition of Who's Who in America.

Chi Che "Franklin" Hsu

Professor (Retired)
Bates Technical College

FEDERAL WAY, WA UNITED STATES

L ooking back on a successful career, Chi Che "Franklin" Hsu celebrates 20 years as an educator and 45 years in the field of engineering. Originally from Taiwan, Mr. Hsu immigrated to the United States in 1971, going on to receive a Bachelor of Science in electrical engineering from Southern Illinois University in Carbondale, Illinois, in 1980 and a Master of Science in electrical engineering from the university in 1982.

Mr. Hsu began his engineering career at The Boeing Company in 1984, serving as a design engineer at the company's office in Seattle, Washington. In 1988, he left Boeing for a position as a senior project engineer at Honeywell, Inc., in Albuquerque, New Mexico, but he later returned to Seattle in 1993 to work as an electronics engineer at BioSonics, Inc. Remaining in Washington state, Mr. Hsu served as an embedded software engineer at Heart Interface Corporation in Kent for two years, spending another two years as an electrical engineer at Applied Precision, Inc., in Issaquah. Mr. Hsu began working as a hardware test engineer for the Microsoft Corporation in 1998 before transitioning to senior software engineer at Avocent in 1999.

While working at Avocent, Mr. Hsu was asked by a local university to conduct a lecture, and after speaking to students and relaying his knowledge, he realized that he, like his father, an engineering professor, had a passion for teaching. Shortly after, he became an instructor at DeVry University, teaching full-time while growing his martial arts studio, the Institute of Chinese Martial Arts, where he taught kung fu and tai chi. Leaving DeVry in 2007, Mr. Hsu became an adjunct instructor at ITT Technical Institute, where he worked for seven years before joining the faculty at Bates Technical College, where he served as a tenured instructor until his retirement in 2022. To commemorate his professional accomplishments, he has been included in the 76th edition of Who's Who in America.

Attributing his success to his faith, Mr. Hsu hopes to continue educating others even in his retirement. Throughout his career, Mr. Hsu's proudest moments occurred during times when he had the opportunity to positively impact the lives of students. Seeing his students go on to become successful professionals and achieve their goals filled him with an immense sense of satisfaction and purpose, driving him to further himself as a teacher.

In the future, Mr. Hsu hopes to travel and support his two children as they pursue their careers. A devout Christian, Mr. Hsu is interested in writing a book to share the importance of faith with others as well as sponsoring a child in Tanzania, Africa, so they can have a proper Christian education.

Harry W. Jarnagan

Program Executive
Hill International Inc.

FEDERAL WAY, WA UNITED STATES

F or more than 40 years, Harry W. Jarnagan has thrived as an executive and project manager in the civil engineering and development industry. In this capacity, he specializes in overseeing the design, construction, and rehabilitation of public facilities and structures such as bridges, tunnels and civil centers. Mr. Jarnagan also focuses on determining accurate budgets for different projects and minimizing each project's impact on the surrounding natural environment.

Between 1980 and 1985, Mr. Jarnagan honed his leadership skills as a project manager for Dunbar and Dickinson, Inc. in Clute, Texas. He subsequently found further success as a cost engineer for Bechtel Energy, owned by the Bechtel Corporation, before his appointment as a project controls engineer with the Tennessee Valley Authority between 1987 and 1988. Throughout the following two years, Mr. Jarnagan worked as a project controls engineer for Fluor Daniel, which is part of the Fluor Corporation.

During the early 1990s, Mr. Jarnagan prospered as a project controls engineer and as a supervisor for Morrison-Knudsen, which is now owned by AECOM Technology Corporation. Between 1995 and 1997, he was recruited as a program controls manager for the United States Enrichment Corporation. Mr. Jarnagan subsequently excelled as a controls manager for the International Technology Group's western region.

In 1998, Mr. Jarnagan accepted a position as a vice president with the Mott MacDonald Group, where he worked for more than 20 years. During this period, he notably served as a program manager for the Washington State Department of Transportation's replacement of a major elevated freeway known as the Alaska Way Viaduct, which had previously been damaged by an earthquake. Between 2018 and 2022, Mr. Jarnagan was additionally appointed as a project manager for the Central Puget Sound Regional Transit Authority's design and construction of a light railway extension known as the Federal Way Link Extension.

In 2022, Mr. Jarnagan was recruited as a vice president and senior program manager for Hill International Inc. in Seattle, Washington. Since 2023, he has contributed to the aforementioned construction organization as a program executive. In this capacity, Mr. Jarnagan currently focuses on overseeing an initiative to convert the Washington State Ferries' fleet of vessels to a hybrid-electric power system.

Alongside his primary professional responsibilities, Mr. Jarnagan has previously served as the president of the Association for the Advancement of Cost Engineering. Between 2003 and 2007, he excelled as the chairperson of the construction of the Beach Boys Historic Landmark, which commemorates the site of the childhood home of Brian, Dennis and Carl Wilson of the Beach Boys. Outside of his professional circles, Mr. Jarnagan has additionally contributed to the Great Lakes Shipwreck Historical Society in various volunteer capacities.

Born in Cedar Rapids, Iowa, Mr. Jarnagan served in the U.S. Army between 1975 and 1980, during which period he advanced to the ranks of first lieutenant, second lieutenant and captain. Toward the beginning of this period, he simultaneously earned a Bachelor of Science at the U.S. Military Academy. Mr. Jarnagan eventually concluded his education at Texas A&M University, where he obtained a Master of Science in civil engineering in 1984.

In recognition of his contributions to the Mott MacDonald Group, Mr. Jarnagan has been honored with multiple accolades, including a Customer Care Award and a Program Management Award. He has also been celebrated with a Lifetime Achievement Award on behalf of the Association for the Advancement of Cost Engineering, which has also distinguished him as a fellow and an honorary lifetime member. In the coming years, Mr. Jarnagan aims to devote more time toward his passion for visiting historic lighthouses across the United States.

Richard E. Kolsch

Senior Geotechnical Engineer (Retired)
Amtrak

POTTSTOWN, PA UNITED STATES

For more than 30 years, Richard E. Kolsch found success as a senior geotechnical engineer in the railroad industry. Prior to his retirement, he specialized in the stabilization and repair of rock slopes, bridges, tunnels and embankment dams. Mr. Kolsch also focused on designing switching yards, obtaining permits for major projects, interpreting seismographic readings and protecting trains from landslides.

After working as a geologist for a highway construction company known as Glasgow, Inc. for more than five years, Mr. Kolsch began his career in the railroad industry in 1979, at which point he was recruited as a senior geotechnical engineer for the Consolidated Rail Corporation. He subsequently thrived in this capacity throughout the following two decades. Toward the end of this period, Mr. Kolsch notably participated in the reconstruction of the West Point Tunnel, which is located beneath the U.S. Military Academy at West Point, New York.

Between 2001 and 2011, Mr. Kolsch was appointed a senior geotechnical engineer with the National Railroad Passenger Corporation, also known as Amtrak. During this period, he played an instrumental role in the stabilization of the Thames River Bridge, which spans from New London, Connecticut, to Groton, Connecticut. Mr. Kolsch additionally helped stabilize Amtrak's Northeast Corridor, an electrified railroad line spanning from Boston, Massachusetts, to Washington, D.C.

Born in Pottstown, Pennsylvania, Mr. Kolsch's decision to pursue a career as a geologist was heavily inspired by his fascination with local rocks and minerals, which initially emerged during his childhood in Queens, New York. He eventually developed a fascination with Earth science, which influenced him to study geology at Villanova University. In 1967, Mr. Kolsch earned a Bachelor of Science in geology from the aforementioned Pennsylvania-based institution.

After completing his undergraduate degree, Mr. Kolsch served in the U.S. Army for more than five years. During this period, he furthered his geological expertise while participating in the construction of numerous major roadways. Mr. Kolsch gradually advanced to the rank of captain before exiting the military in 1971, at which point he was recruited by the aforementioned highway construction company to monitor the drilling and blasting of rock quarries for the extraction of minerals. He also assisted in the construction of multiple interstate highways in several U.S. states, including West Virginia and Kentucky.

Along with his extensive experience in construction, Mr. Kolsch attributes a great deal of his success to the guidance of his former professors and superiors. Specifically, his first construction superintendent taught him the value of time management and continuously encouraged him to pursue increasingly demanding projects. Throughout his career, Mr. Kolsch additionally drew tremendous inspiration from his wife, who helped him build an honorable reputation by prioritizing the needs of his colleagues and customers above his own.

In the coming years, Mr. Kolsch intends to continue enjoying his well-deserved retirement while spending more time with his four grandchildren. He also aims to further his involvement in his local church and other community organizations while continuing to exercise his passions for yardwork, housework and target shooting. Since his ethical approach to his work directly contributed to the longevity of his career, Mr. Kolsch advises aspiring geotechnical engineers to base their decisions on their own morals and values rather than the opinions of others or their desire to grow their personal wealth.

Andre "Andrzej" Z. Manitius, PhD

Professor
Department of Electrical and Computer Engineering
George Mason University

MCLEAN, VA UNITED STATES

F or more than 30 years, Andre "Andrzej" Z. Manitius, PhD, has found success as an educator and academic administrator with the department of electrical and computer engineering at George Mason University's Volgenau School of Engineering. With more than six decades of academic experience to his credit, he specializes in building his students' knowledge of the mathematical aspects of control theory, particularly in relation to dynamical systems. Dr. Manitius also focuses on helping his students understand the role of control engineering in the development of sustainable technology and the manufacturing of sustainable goods.

Between 1974 and 1983, Dr. Manitius worked as a researcher and as a professor of mathematics at the University of Montreal in Quebec, Canada. He subsequently thrived in the latter capacity at the Rensselaer Polytechnic Institute in Troy, New York, throughout the following five years. In 1988, Dr. Manitius accepted his current position as a professor of electrical and computer engineering at George Mason University. Between 1998 and 2014, he simultaneously found further success as the chairperson of George Mason University's department of electrical and computer engineering.

Toward the middle of his tenure at the Rensselaer Polytechnic Institute, Dr. Manitius was additionally recruited as the director of an applied mathematics program at the National Science Foundation. Between 1987 and 1988, he contributed to the aforementioned independent government agency as the deputy director of the division of mathematical sciences. Dr. Manitius had previously been appointed as a member of the selection committee for grant programs in relation to pure and applied mathematics with the Natural Sciences and Engineering Research Council of Canada during the early 1980s.

Throughout his career, Dr. Manitius has contributed articles to a host of professional journals and publications, including the Journal of Differential Equations, Systems and Control Letters and the Society for Industrial and Applied Mechanics' Journal on Control Optimization. Between 1979 and 1989, he served as an associate editor of the Institute for Electrical and Electronics Engineers' Transactions on Automatic Control. In order to stay up to date with the latest developments in his field, Dr. Manitius maintains active affiliations with the Society for Industrial and Applied Mathematics, the Institute for Electrical and Electronics Engineers, the American Mathematics Society and the International Neural Network Society.

Born in Poland, Dr. Manitius earned a Master of Science in electrical engineering at the AGH University of Science and Technology in 1960. Throughout the following 10 years, he worked as a research assistant and as an adjunct professor at the Warsaw University of Technology, where he also obtained a Doctor of Philosophy in automatic control and electrical engineering in 1968. Following his relocation to the United States in 1972, Dr. Manitius honed his academic expertise as a visiting associate professor at the University of Minnesota.

In 2022, Dr. Manitius was presented with the David J. King Teaching Award at George Mason University's Celebration for Teaching Excellence. He had previously been recognized with the Institute of Mathematics of the Polish Academy of Sciences' Prize for outstanding scientific achievements in mathematics in 1972. Dr. Manitius is particularly proud to have helped establish multiple undergraduate and graduate programs at George Mason University such as the Master of Science in computer engineering program and the Master of Science in computer forensics program. Due to the collaborative nature of his profession, he advises aspiring engineering professors to draw influence from the research of their peers and educators.

Farzad Shahbodaghlou, PhD

Professor of Engineering
California State University, East Bay

FREMONT, CA UNITED STATES

R ecognized for over two and a half decades of contributions to the field of engineering, Farzad Shahbodaghlou, PhD, has earned distinction through his accomplishments as an academic and consultant to the construction industry. In addition to his service as a professor on behalf of students, he has found success as a graduate adviser and, most prominently, as the founding director of the construction management program at California State University, East Bay, also known as CSUEB, since 2009. Throughout this time, Dr. Shahbodaghlou is proud to have cultivated the program's expansion from six students at its inception to over 200 students in 2015.

Prior to his work at CSUEB, Dr. Shahbodaghlou served as a tenured associate professor at Bradley University, where he specialized in civil engineering and construction from 1987 until 1998, during which time he worked as a faculty adviser to the university chapter of Associated General Contractors. Following this period, he entered the private sector and distinguished himself as the director of corporate training and customer satisfaction for DPR Construction Inc. in Redwood City, California, between 1997 and 2002, after which he consulted on behalf of various clients as the owner of Process Improvement Consulting Inc. from 2002 to 2008. During this time, Dr. Shahbodaghlou held a part-time role as an adjunct professor at San Jose State University, after which he returned to teaching on a full-time basis.

Adjacent to his main responsibilities in the field, Dr. Shahbodaghlou has contributed extensively to the Bradley University student chapter of the American Society of Civil Engineers as a supervisor for the construction of playgrounds between 1989 and 1997, and as a faculty adviser on several occasions. Likewise, he served as a reviewer for the Journal of Professional Issues in Engineering Education and Practice from 1993 until 1996. To remain aware of developments in his field, Dr. Shahbodaghlou has also maintained his affiliation with the Construction Management Association of America, of which he has been a board member of the Northern California chapter, the Mechanical Contractors Association of America, of which he is a student chapter adviser, and the honorable societies of Phi Kappa Phi, Tau Bate Pi and Phi Eta Sigma.

Dr. Shahbodaghlou was first inspired to specialize in his field due to the influence of his cousin, who immigrated to the United States during the 1950s and became an engineer with the support of Ohio Northern University. Following his example, Dr. Shahbodaghlou attended the same university and graduated with a Bachelor of Science in civil engineering, with highest distinction, in 1982. He subsequently transferred to Purdue University, from which he earned a Master of Science in civil engineering and a Doctor of Philosophy in 1987.

Though his professional journey has been filled with highlights, Dr. Shahbodaghlou is most proud to have interacted with a variety of talented students whose enthusiasm for their future careers has provided a limitless source of motivation. He is gratified to have seized the opportunity to positively impact so many lives who will, in turn, pass on his teachings to future generations of students in their own right. Looking toward the future, Dr. Shahbodaghlou aspires to continue presiding over the civil engineering program at CSUEB and laying the foundation for future careers.

In Memoriam

Richard V. Shanklin III, PhD

Mechanical Engineer

MCLEAN, VA UNITED STATES

For more than 40 years, Richard V. Shanklin III, PhD, found success as a mechanical engineer, program manager and director for the public and private sectors. In these capacities, he specialized in the design and evaluation of various technologies involving the generation of magnetohydrodynamic (MHD) power for a broad range of commercial applications. Dr. Shanklin also focused on overseeing the production of combustion technology for the aerospace industry as well as the production of synthetic fuels from coal, shale and heavy crude oil.

Between 1959 and 1960, Dr. Shanklin began his career as an engineering assistant with Phillips Petroleum Company, which is now known as the Phillips 66 Company. He subsequently worked as an associate engineer for the Boeing Company before his appointment as a design engineer for the Arnold Research Organization (ARO), which operated the U.S. Air Force's Arnold Engineering Development Complex in Tennessee before ARO's closure in 1980. During the late 1960s, Dr. Shanklin prospered as the chief engineer for J.B. Dicks and Associates, Inc., which has since closed.

Between 1971 and 1972, Dr. Shanklin excelled as an associate professor of mechanical engineering at Nashville State Technical, which is part of Nashville State Community College. He subsequently served as an assistant professor at the University of Tennessee before finding further success as a senior scientist with Systems Research Laboratories, Inc. in Dayton, Ohio, for a number of years. Between 1975 and 1977, Dr. Shanklin thrived as an assistant director of the MHD division of the U.S. Energy Research and Development Administration, which has since been dissolved.

Toward the late 1970s, Dr. Shanklin was recruited as a senior staff engineer for the energy systems division of TRW Inc., which has since closed. Between 1978 and 1979, he contributed to the aforementioned government organization as the director of the MHD division. Dr. Shanklin subsequently held numerous leadership positions with TRW Inc.'s energy systems division, including the manager of combustion programs and the assistant operations manager of process development.

Between 1982 and 1986, Dr. Shanklin served as a project officer with the Synthetic Fuels Corporation, which has since closed. Throughout the following five years, he worked as a director for BDM Federal, Inc. in McLean, Virginia. Dr. Shanklin continued to share his expertise in mechanical engineering with multiple organizations in a consultant capacity until 2018, when he passed away at the age of 80.

Born in Brooklyn, New York, Dr. Shanklin's interest in engineering was heavily inspired by his grandfather, who enjoyed a prosperous career as a mining engineer. In 1959, he obtained a Bachelor of Science in mechanical engineering at Duke University. While working as a design engineer with ARO, Dr. Shanklin simultaneously earned a Master of Science at the University of Tennessee. He eventually concluded his education in 1971, completing a Doctor of Philosophy at the aforementioned Knoxville-based institution.

During his tenure with the U.S. Energy Research and Development Administration, Dr. Shanklin was celebrated with multiple accolades in relation to special achievements. He was particularly proud of his contributions to the aforementioned government organization, during which period he frequently traveled to Russia to discuss the latest advancements in MHD with engineers from numerous European nations. In 1976, Dr. Shanklin was honored with a George Westinghouse Silver Medal on behalf of the American Society of Mechanical Engineers. He has also been commemorated with inclusion in the 76th edition of Who's Who in America.

Robert "Moss" Cartwright

Senior Managing Director of Institutional Sales and Trading
Mesirow Financial

WHITE PIGEON, MI UNITED STATES

L everaging well over five decades of experience in his chosen field, Robert "Moss" Cartwright has earned distinction as the senior managing director of institutional sales and trading at Mesirow Financial, a financial advisory firm that provides its services in wealth management, capital markets and investment banking services. Having held this role since 2010, Mr. Cartwright is largely responsible for liaising with 10 large accounts, as well as conducting financial research and sharing his findings with customers. In this respect, he has learned well the value of forging long-lasting relationships with clients and promoting individual collaboration across firms, and he is proud to have cultivated a reputation as someone who can be trusted to look out for the best interests of his investors and portfolio managers.

Prior to his work at Mesirow Financial, Mr. Cartwright served as the head of taxable fixed income at William Blair LLC from 1983 until 2010, having worked as the vice president and head of corporate bonds for First MidAmerica Inc. between 1981 and 1983. He previously built a prolific career in institutional research and sales at various other financial firms, including Dean Witter Reynolds, PaineWebber & Co., Bear Stearns and Eastman Dillon Union Securities. Working in Chicago, Illinois, throughout much of his career, Mr. Cartwright began in the research and trust department of the First National Bank in 1969. He had become involved in the financial sector by a stroke of good fortune, having started his career as a bellhop at a hotel in Chicago.

Mr. Cartwright first sought an education at what is now North Park University, where he participated in numerous sports, served as the president of his local Viking Club, and earned a Bachelor of Arts in 1968. Following his entry into the realm of finance, he pursued certification in various securities licenses, including Series 63, 79T, 57TO, 7TO, 55 and 24, among several others. Mr. Cartwright is proud to have distinguished himself through his tireless research in the trading of bonds. Recognizing his accomplishments, he was notably invited to speak before the Institutional Investors Bond Conference in 1980.

As a commitment to his field, Mr. Cartwright has been active with several industry-related organizations, including the Chicago Bond Club. Likewise committed to civic service, he has sat on the board of directors for the Hinsdale Community House Basketball Program, volunteered at the Hinsdale Youth Center, and served as president of the Clarendon Hills Little League.

Mr. Cartwright attributes his success to the fact that he works long hours and puts in an exhaustive amount of research into the art of bond trading. Likewise, he benefited richly from the tutelage of various mentors, including his parents, George and Edna, and his wife, Shelley. Among his most cherished achievements, he is most gratified to have maintained his platform at Mesirow. He has been selected for inclusion in the 76th edition of Who's Who in America. Looking toward the future, he aspires to continue enjoying the perks of his career and working to secure the best deal possible for his clients. He is exploring private financing for credit tenant leases and ground leases. He looks forward to his free time, enjoying spending time with family and friends, boating, golfing, and skiing.

Laurie Cooperman Rosen

Chief Financial Officer
Rent-A-CFO

LAS VEGAS, NV UNITED STATES

For more than 40 years, Laurie Cooperman Rosen found success as a day trader, financial auditor and chief financial officer in a consultant capacity. Prior to her retirement, she specialized in helping small businesses improve their financial health, establish competitive compensation packages and explore the potential risks and rewards of significant capital expenditures. Ms. Cooperman Rosen also focused on providing general bookkeeping and tax preparation services while ensuring accurate financial reporting and maintaining her clients' compliance with various financial regulations.

Toward the late 1970s, Ms. Cooperman Rosen began her financial career with Citibank, N.A., which is a subsidiary of Citigroup Inc. During her tenure with the aforementioned financial services organization, she served as an auditor at Citigroup Centre in London, England. Ms. Cooperman Rosen was subsequently appointed as an auditor for a financial services company called Crocker Bank which specialized in foreign exchange trading. She eventually found further success as a foreign exchange trader for the Bank of America Corporation.

In 1998, Ms. Cooperman Rosen established Rent-A-CFO. During her tenure with Rent-A-CFO, Ms. Cooperman Rosen was notably recruited as the financial manager for the Oakland School for the Arts in Oakland, California. She additionally provided an array of financial planning services and coordinated fundraising initiatives for the West Contra Costa

Youth Service Bureau for several years. In 2022, Ms. Cooperman Rosen issued her professional retirement. Alongside her primary professional responsibilities, she has previously contributed to the Oakland Business Improvement District as a board member and treasurer.

Born in Philadelphia, Pennsylvania, and raised in New Jersey, Ms. Cooperman Rosen's decision to pursue a career in the financial services industry was heavily inspired by her exceptional typing skills, which initially emerged while attending Fair Lawn High School. She eventually obtained a bachelor's degree in economics and music at Tufts University. Between 1974 and 1976, Ms. Cooperman Rosen completed a Master of Business Administration in finance and operations management at the Wharton School of the University of Pennsylvania.

Ms. Cooperman Rosen's most significant achievement was purchasing and developing a property in downtown Oakland at former Mayor Jerry Brown's suggestion. He also selected her to be the chief financial officer for the aforementioned Oakland School for the Arts. The Oakland property had more than 30 tenants in the 27,000-square-foot building, which Ms. Cooperman Rosen and her husband owned from 2004 until 2015. They ultimately sold the property at the peak of the market.

In late 2016, Ms. Cooperman Rosen moved to Nevada but continued to keep a residence in California. She remained serving as a consultant with the California Capital and Commercial Group, which was helping develop the Port of Oakland and the aforementioned West Contra Costa Youth Service Bureau, among other clients. She served on the board of her homeowner's association located on the Chabot Golf Course in Oakland through which she owned a home from 1997 until 2017.

In addition to her exceptional work ethic and meticulous personality, Ms. Cooperman Rosen attributes her success to her talent as a pianist, which enabled her to type numbers with tremendous speed and accuracy. During her sophomore year at Fair Lawn High School, she was selected for the aforementioned school's Best Typist Award. In the coming years, Ms. Cooperman Rosen intends to continue staying up to date with the latest developments in the stock market while maintaining a healthy lifestyle. Likewise, she also aims to devote more time to building her knowledge of naturopathic medicine and holistic health remedies.

Emma S. Shinn, MBA, CPA

Vice President & Chief Financial Officer
Shinn Consulting

LITTLETON, CO UNITED STATES

Over a career of 53 years, Emma S. Shinn, MBA, CPA, has garnered extensive expertise in management accounting. In 1968, Ms. Shinn received a Master of Business of Administration in accounting from the College of Business Administration at American University in Washington, D.C., making her the only woman in her master's graduating class, and she became a certified public accountant in 1984. As the vice president and chief financial officer of Shinn Consulting, Ms. Shin specializes in setting up accounting systems for corporate clients, designing and implementing them as a management tool in addition to a financial reporting mechanism. This allows the company to utilize its resources and make them available to managers. She acts as an interpreter of financial information, developing charting mechanisms by selecting specific areas and metrics to measure, which can be extracted from the accounting system. This allows companies to manage themselves with true information, including historical data that helps them plan for company growth.

When Ms. Shinn entered the accounting industry over five decades ago, management processes were solely manual. However, she has always been a champion of technology and innovation and is currently working toward incorporating more automation to accelerate both the accounting and management processes. Although her primary focus is accounting, she takes a holistic approach to business that incorporates different departments into a cohesive whole.

Ms. Shinn considers her most significant achievement to be developing an accounting system specialized for home builder companies. Her system not only maximizes profitability but ensures excellence in all processes and procedures, including quality and customer satisfaction. Shinn Consulting provides both consulting services and extensive training in accounting processes and procedures to builder staff, as well as teaching staff to read and understand complex financial information. By following the system's targets, builders can easily track their progress and profitability. Ms. Shinn's work in streamlining the accounting process for home builder companies has earned her recognition in the industry.

Ms. Shinn is a pioneering influence in the home building industry, with expertise that revolves around utilizing accounting information to assist managers in becoming better at managing their businesses. She prides herself on having never been a public accountant, dealing with financials for taxes or external investors. Instead of financial gain, she focuses on helping management use their accounting database to its full potential. Ms. Shinn wrote her first book on accounting for home builders, "Accounting & Financial Management for Residential Construction," in 1972 and has since updated it eight times, with the latest update in 2020.

Ms. Shinn attributes her success to her focus and the values impressed upon her by her family. Within her family, she has had many role models, including an aunt who became the first female doctor in Panama and another aunt who earned a doctorate in nutrition from Harvard and worked in the Panamanian government as a nutritionist. Her father encouraged her to strive for success, saying she could achieve anything with hard work. Even when Ms. Shinn reaches her goals, she always seeks to improve and simplify her work to make it more accessible, as she hopes to help others achieve their goals by providing them with tools and guidance to succeed.

As Ms. Shinn looks to the future, she is focusing on stepping away from her active role in Shinn Consulting to spend more time with her family. She aims to cement her legacy in the industry and make Shin Consulting an heirloom she can pass on to her children.

Paul Bardack, JD

Executive Director (Retired)
Maryland Small Business Development Center

SILVER SPRING, MD UNITED STATES

P aul Bardack, JD, has had an extraordinary career. Even better, he helped create an extraordinary family and surrounded himself with extraordinary friends.

Mr. Bardack co-conceived America's Enterprise Zone program, one of our nation's most widely used economic development tools, as staff to a South Bronx U.S. congressman. He managed small business efforts for the City of Cleveland Department of Economic Development, and he was senior economic development policy adviser to a New Jersey governor. He was tasked by President George H.W. Bush to calm Los Angeles after the deadly Rodney King riots; his success in that role, while serving as Deputy HUD Assistant Secretary, was honored by the Los Angeles mayor. He practiced tax law for a large New York firm and also ran his own economic development consulting company. Further, Mr. Bardack led federal, state and local entrepreneurial development and advocacy efforts for the National Mentoring Partnership (now MENTOR).

Changing careers, Mr. Bardack helped build successful eLearning lines of business, first for Booz Allen Hamilton and, subsequently, for SAIC. He shaped MyJewishLearning.com as the influential website's first chief executive officer. He also headed America's leading eLearning trade group, the United States Distance Learning Association. He was a leader of one of the federal government's primary online learning programs, the Department of Defense's Advanced Distributed Learning

Initiative. In a singular honor, he was selected several times to represent the United States globally before UNESCO in the organization's online learning public policy deliberations.

Mr. Bardack helped Maryland small businesses survive, as head of the state's Small Business Development Center, during the COVID-19 pandemic that cut short the dreams of far too many entrepreneurs.

Mr. Bardack guided several D.C. area and nationally prominent Jewish organizations through his service on their boards of directors, and he also became active in Maryland Democratic politics. He contributed to Barack Obama's first presidential campaign as an online education policy adviser, and he helped bring Major League Baseball to Washington, D.C.

Mr. Bardack's career was built on a solid foundation: a New York City public school education; a Bachelor of Arts in political science from Yale University; a Juris Doctorate from American University's Washington College of Law (he is a member of the D.C. Bar); a solid Jewish education; the support of his parents and the joy in learning and reading with which he was raised; the nonstop love of his wife; the encouragement of his three children, their spouses and his grandchildren; and the inspiration of his extended family and friends.

If Mr. Bardack could offer advice to other professionals, it would be this: "Work hard, be the best prepared in the room, and remember that you can get so much more done if you don't care who gets the credit."

Richard B. Callahan

Director of Recreation and Parks (Retired)
City of Annapolis, Maryland

ANNAPOLIS, MD UNITED STATES

For more than 30 years, Richard B. Callahan found success as the director of the City of Annapolis Recreation and Parks. Prior to his retirement, he specialized in overseeing the expansion and ongoing maintenance of various recreational sites, public facilities and community centers. Mr. Callahan also focused on establishing recreational athletic programs and recruiting participants from numerous underserved communities.

Under Mr. Callahan's leadership, the City of Annapolis Recreation and Parks developed the first summer recreational basketball league in the aforementioned city's history. During the 1970s, 1980s and 1990s, the aforementioned league was attended by myriad renowned coaches of collegiate basketball programs, including Charles "Lefty" Dreisell, who served as the head coach of the University of Maryland's men's basketball team for more than 15 years, and John Robert Thompson Jr., who served as the head coach of Georgetown University's men's basketball team for more than 20 years. Toward the late 1990s, the basketball court at Annapolis's Truxtun Park was named in Mr. Callahan's honor by Dean Johnson, who was appointed as the mayor of Annapolis between 1997 and 2000.

Following his tenure with the City of Annapolis Recreation and Parks, Mr. Callahan thrived as a member of the board of commissioners of the Housing Authority of the City of Annapolis for more than 10 years. During this period, he played an instrumental role in the refurbishment of myriad athletic facilities for more than five public housing projects such as swimming pools and basketball courts. In 2006, Mr. Callahan notably spearheaded the construction of a new baseball field for residents of public housing that was eventually named in his honor.

A native of Maryland's Eastern Shore, Mr. Callahan attended Annapolis High School, where he garnered widespread recognition for his talent for basketball. Thanks to his athletic prowess, he was selected for an athletic scholarship to Washington College in Chestertown, Maryland. While attending the aforementioned institution, Mr. Callahan found further success as a lacrosse player, which resulted in his designation as an All-American. He eventually obtained a Bachelor of Science in psychology and education in 1960.

Following these accomplishments, Mr. Callahan accepted a position as an assistant with the City of Annapolis Recreation and Parks. He was subsequently recruited as the aforementioned department's director following the exit of the former director. In 1966, Mr. Callahan facilitated the construction of the city of Annapolis's first public swimming pool. During the late 1960s, he also helped ensure the safety of the city of Annapolis amid nationwide protests in response to the assassination of Dr. Martin Luther King Jr.

In 2019, Mr. Callahan was honored with a Peacemaker Award on behalf of the Dr. Martin Luther King Jr. Committee of Anne Arundel County. He has also been recognized with multiple accolades in relation to athletics on behalf of Washington College such as the Thomas Reeder Spedden Award. Likewise, Mr. Callahan has additionally been inducted into Washington College's Athletic Hall of Fame.

Along with his exceptional work ethic, Mr. Callahan attributes a great deal of his success to his ability to gain the trust of his local community. He also credits his stellar reputation amongst minority communities to his close relationship with Roger Moyer, who was appointed as the mayor of Annapolis, Maryland, between 1965 and 1973. In his spare time, Mr. Callahan continues to stay up to date with multiple collegiate sports programs, specifically the men's basketball team of the U.S. Naval Academy.

In Memoriam

Wendell J. Dillinger

President & Treasurer

Middletown & Hummelstown Railroad

MIDDLETOWN, PA UNITED STATES

L ong driven by the adage "where there's a will, there's a way," Wendell J. Dillinger found success as the president and treasurer of the Middletown and Hummelstown Railroad (M & H Railroad), a shortline railroad service that operates freight and passenger trained between Middletown and Hummelstown, Pennsylvania. Established in 1888 and assuming independent operation in 1976, M & H Railroad primarily uses a vintage 1955 diesel locomotive for its tourist services, as well as a number of entertaining and educational events. In his role with the company, which he held from 1980 until his passing in December 2023, Mr. Dillinger was largely responsible for maintaining oversight of business operations and compiling quarterly reports for the Federal Railroad Administration. In total, he leveraged well over 75 years of experience in his chosen field.

Mr. Dillinger worked with numerous transportation services, including as an accountant at the Chicago and Northwestern Transportation Company, the president of the Iowa Terminal Railroad, and in various roles at Prairie Bus Lines, Blue Bird Coach Lines and the Chicago Burlington and Quincy Railroad. His first position in the field was at the Chicago Aurora and Elgin Railroad, following the writing of his thesis paper on the Philadelphia Suburban Transportation Company, which focused on how the company survived and thrived during the travails of the Great Depression.

Having always been fascinated with history and restoration work, Mr. Dillinger spent his time writing the history of the M & H Railroad.

He was also an avid genealogist. A prolific author, he wrote on the subject of his work at the Chicago Aurora and Elgin Railroad in the article "My Job Developed a Plan to Restore Passenger Service on the CA&E." He was featured in First and Fastest, a quarterly publication of the Shore Line Interurban Historical Society, long held to be a premier example of railroad journalism.

Mr. Dillinger first sought an education at Otterbein University, from which he earned a Bachelor of Arts. Following this accomplishment, he studied at the Wharton School of the University of Pennsylvania, graduating with a Master of Business Administration. To remain aware of developments in his field, he previously maintained his affiliation as a member of the Tourist Railway Association Inc. Additionally, he was a past member of Rotary International and the U.S. Army.

Ronald J. Dolecki

Intelligence Analyst (Retired)
The Central Intelligence Agency

HUNTINGTOWN, MD UNITED STATES

F or more than 30 years, Ronald J. Dolecki found success as an intelligence officer with the Central Intelligence Agency (CIA). Prior to his retirement, he specialized in interpreting photographic images provided by strategic reconnaissance satellites on behalf of the CIA's Directorate of Science and Technology. Mr. Dolecki also composed more than 50 comprehensive intelligence reports about various U.S. adversaries throughout his career and authored a training manual.

Born in Oil City, Pennsylvania, Mr. Dolecki served in the U.S. Army during the mid-1960s. During this period, he underwent extensive training in topographic engineering at the U.S. Army installation of Fort Belvoir in Fairfax County, Virginia. Mr. Dolecki subsequently harnessed his newfound expertise to provide geospatial information and services such as terrain analyses and visualization to operators of military helicopters and tactical vehicles. He would later hone his skills at the CIA for interpreting satellite images of several countries then hostile to the United States.

Following his exit from the military, Mr. Dolecki earned a bachelor's degree in 1970 from Pennsylvania Western University, which was formerly known as Clarion University of Pennsylvania. After working for the Pennsylvania Department of Transportation for a brief period, he was invited by the CIA to participate in their recruitment process in

Washington, D.C. The CIA then sent Mr. Dolecki to Omaha, Nebraska, to undergo their required training as a satellite photo interpreter before officially beginning a career in which he thrived from 1971 until 2004. During this period, he regularly shared his photographic interpretation skills with the National Geospatial-Intelligence Agency, a combat support agency within the U.S. Department of Defense.

Between 2004 and 2006, Mr. Dolecki also excelled as an intelligence analyst with Booz Allen Hamilton Inc. Throughout the next two years, he found further success as a geospatial specialist with Courage Services, Inc., which is a subsidiary of CENTRA Technology. Mr. Dolecki provided his services to that employer before issuing his permanent professional retirement in 2008.

In recognition of his contributions to the CIA, Mr. Dolecki has been honored with many accolades, including two "Report of the Year" Awards and nine "Exceptional Performance" Awards. Likewise, he has been celebrated with a Distinguished Civilian Service Medal on behalf of the National Geospatial-Intelligence Agency and a "Team Appreciation Award" on behalf of Booz Allen Hamilton. Moreover, Mr. Dolecki has also been selected for numerous accolades on behalf of the U.S. armed forces, including a Meritorious Unit Commendation, a Good Conduct Medal, an Operation Desert Storm Service Award, a National Defense Medal, and an Operation Enduring Freedom Award. In 2022, he was recognized with a Prisoner of War Medal commemorating his captivity by guerilla insurgents in Africa way back in 1965. During that remarkable ordeal, he escaped captivity after being given up for dead.

Due to his widespread reputation as an intelligence officer, Mr. Dolecki has been featured in several major publications throughout his career, such as the Baltimore Sun. He is also the featured subject of three YouTube videos and was included in the 76th edition of Who's Who in America. Along with his faith, he attributes a great deal of his success to the perseverance and adaptability he developed during his military service, which helped him prepare for his career with the CIA. Mr. Dolecki is particularly proud to have directly contributed to the advancement of Operation Desert Storm, which influenced his selection for the National Geospatial-Intelligence Agency's Distinguished Civilian Service Medal. Furthermore, he was deeply honored to have been presented with the aforementioned accolade by James Clapper, who served as the director of the National Geospatial-Intelligence Agency from 2001 to 2006 and as the U.S. director of national intelligence between 2010 and 2017. 🌿🌿

David John Flounders Sr.

Owner & President

SSSVP Inc.

LINEVILLE, AL UNITED STATES

A s the president, owner and co-founder of Samson's Strength Sustainable Veterans Project (SSSVP), Inc., David John Flounders Sr. has proven himself to be a capable and successful entrepreneur. SSSVP, Inc., founded in 2016 and located in Lineville, Alabama, is a certified 501-c3 charitable organization that assists veterans struggling with homelessness. Assisting veterans is a deeply personal endeavor for Mr. Flounders, who is a veteran himself. Mr. Flounders enlisted in the U.S. Navy in 1983, serving as a mechanist's mate first class in steelwork for a decade and serving an additional three years in the U.S. Navy Reserve. He dedicated 19 years to the Connecticut Army National Guard, working as a security officer, an environmental officer, a suicide prevention officer and an Applied Suicide Intervention Skills (ASIST) instructor, before medically retiring in 2014.

Always looking to broaden his horizons, Mr. Flounders earned a Bachelor of Science in liberal arts from Excelsior University, a private online university based out of Albany, New York, in 2011. Prior to receiving a bachelor's degree, he completed two years of pre-medicine coursework at the University of Pittsburgh Johnstown in Johnstown, Pennsylvania. Mr. Flounders continues to strive for further education, currently pursuing a Masterson Method certification. The Masterson Method, a form of equine bodywork training, will expand Mr. Flounders' knowledge base and reflect his commitment to advancing his expertise in equine therapy, a fundamental part of the therapeutic services offered by SSSVP. Mr. Flounders and his wife are immersed in further developing their equine therapy, building a program on their ten-acre property. His wife, Kathleen, has a background in equine experiential therapy dating back to her master's degree thesis in 1991, bringing a wealth of expertise to the project. The couple has adopted five mustangs and received an additional two from Mustang Leadership Partners, LLC., in Chattanooga, Tennessee.

Mr. Flounders became interested in building his own business in 2015 while participating in an entrepreneurship boot camp for veterans with disabilities organized by the Institute for Veterans and Military Families at Syracuse University in Syracuse, New York. The program aimed to assist veterans like himself in establishing their businesses. Although initially planning a full-time career in leatherwork, a cherished hobby of his, Mr. Flounders ultimately decided to launch a nonprofit venture and began developing SSSVP.

SSSVP has been awarded a $147,000 grant through the Alabama Department of Veterans Affairs, and Mr. Flounders plans to use the grant to finish the veteran housing they have begun developing as well as building an extra barn to expand their equine experiential learning therapy. For their equine therapy, SSSVP has partnered with Equine Empowered Therapy, an established therapy organization for veterans struggling with the transition from service member to civilian. Other organizations they collaborate with include the Veterans Fishing Organization Inc. and Central Alabama Veterans Collaborative, enhancing support for veterans in the organization.

Having worked in a variety of fields, Mr. Flounders is proud of both his military service and his work with SSSVP. While a military steelworker, he was a part of the recommissioning crew for the USS Missouri (BB-63), an Iowa-class battleship completed in 1944, serving on board from 1984 to 1988. For two years, he worked aboard the USS Fulton (AS-11), a submarine tender famous for its use in World War II, helping to decommission the 50-year-old ship.

Mr. Flounders credits his success to his strong work ethic and the tireless support of his wife. To those interested in pursuing a career in nonprofit work or entrepreneurship, he advises being open to all opportunities that may come.

In Memoriam

Herman Keizer Jr.

Army Chaplain (Retired)

U.S. Army

CALEDONIA, MI UNITED STATES

For more than 30 years, Herman Keizer Jr. found success as a chaplain for the U.S. Army. Prior to his retirement, he specialized in conducting religious worship services and providing spiritual guidance for members of the U.S. Army in the U.S. and abroad. Chaplain Keizer also focused on helping members of the U.S. Army overcome symptoms of post-traumatic stress disorder and adapt to new, peaceful lifestyles following the end of their military careers.

Throughout his tenure as a military chaplain, Chaplain Keizer accompanied the U.S. Army to numerous foreign conflicts such as the Vietnam War, where he was injured in a helicopter accident, falling 150 feet. He provided spiritual and mental health counseling to U.S. troops within multiple infantry divisions. He subsequently served in this capacity for the U.S. Army's 25th Infantry Division, which is based at Schofield Barracks in Wahiawa, Hawaii. Between 1994 and 1997, Chaplain Keizer was appointed as a chaplain for the U.S. Army Garrison Stuttgart in Southwest Germany. During this period, he coordinated annual conferences for fellow military chaplains based in participating nations of the North Atlantic Treaty Organization (NATO).

Between 2000 and 2002, Chaplain Keizer was assigned to the ambassador at large for international religious freedom in the U.S. Department of State. He subsequently issued his retirement from the U.S. Armed

Forces before finding further success as the director of chaplaincy ministries for the Christian Reformed Church in North America for more than five years. Between 2012 and 2014, Chaplain Keizer continued to thrive as the co-director of the Soul Repair Center of the Brite Divinity School in Fort Worth, Texas, which educates religious leaders and professional caregivers about counseling veterans of the U.S. Armed Forces who have been affected by moral injury.

During his tenure with the Christian Reformed Church in North America and the Brite Divinity School, Chaplain Keizer simultaneously contributed to the Calvin Institute of Christian Worship in Grand Rapids, Michigan, as a consultant for veterans of the U.S. Armed Forces who suffer from post-traumatic stress disorder and moral injury. In 2011, he was appointed president of the U.S. Army Chaplain Corps Regimental Association. Likewise, Chaplain Keizer also found success as a board member of the Grand Rapids Area Center for Christian Ecumenism as well as the Heartside Ministry. He additionally served as a national chaplain for the Military Order of the Purple Heart and as the president of the Army and Navy Club of Grand Rapids until 2017, at which point he passed away following a sudden intracerebral hemorrhage.

Born in Chicago, Illinois, Chaplain Keizer earned a Bachelor of Arts in philosophy and Greek at Calvin University in 1965. He subsequently obtained a Bachelor of Divinity in theology at Calvin Theological Seminary in 1968, at which point he also became an ordained minister with the Christian Reformed Church in North America. During the late 1970s, Chaplain Keizer resumed his education at Columbia Teachers College, where he completed a Master of Arts in education. In 1979, he earned a Master of Theology from the New York Theological Seminary.

In recognition of his military service, Chaplain Keizer has been honored with a host of accolades, including a Purple Heart, five Bronze Star Medals, including one with a "V" device for valor, four Legion of Merits, a Defense Superior Service Medal and a Soldier's Medal. He has additionally been celebrated with a Distinguished Alumni Award on behalf of Calvin Theological Seminary and one from Calvin University, and a Distinguished Service Award on behalf of the American Association of Professional Chaplains. In 2022, Chaplain Keizer was selected for induction into the Michigan Military and Veterans Hall of Honor.

Morgan Little, MS, MBA

Advisory Committee
Texas Veterans Commission

DRIPPING SPRINGS, TX UNITED STATES

Drawing on years of industrial and military experience, Morgan Little, MS, MBA, served on all three advisory committees for the Texas Veterans Commission. Previously, he served his country for over three decades in the U.S. Navy and the U.S. Navy Reserve, in addition to the pharmaceutical industry. His overseas service during his initial military experience was in Vietnam and Korea, followed by a reserve mobilization supporting U.S. and NATO forces in Bosnia for two years. Over the years, he served as a unit executive and repair officer in nine units and a commanding officer of four reserve units. Throughout his career, Mr. Little has given back to his community through various local veterans' organizations, such as the Austin Military Service Coalition, where he served as president for two years. The Austin coalition had approximately 100,000 members and was comprised of over 30 local military organizations to communicate the interests of Austin's veterans to county and state government officials. Later, he served as chairman of the Texas Coalition of Veterans Organizations for six years, which had over 600,000 members and included more than 30 state-wide veterans' organizations. For five years, he was president of the National Association of Destroyer Veterans, which has 14,000 members.

Proficient in his field, Mr. Little received a Bachelor of Science in agriculture from the University of Arizona in 1964. To enhance his professional acumen, he earned a Master of Science in animal science and biostatistics from his alma mater in 1966, and completed a Master of Business Administration in decision sciences from Rider University in Lawrenceville, New Jersey, in 1978. Educated in animal physiology, animal breeding, reproduction and milk secretion physiology, animal nutrition, animal diseases, animal parasitology and biostatistics, including study design and experimental and mathematical statistics, he was soon certified as a professional animal scientist (animal biometrics) by the American Society of Animal Science. Later, as a naval reservist, he was certified as a nuclear, biological and chemical (NBC) defense officer after working with the U.S. Navy's only forward-deployed chemical and biological decontamination facility at the U.S. Naval Hospital Sigonella in Sicily. He wears the U.S. Navy Command Ashore badge and was selected for and completed all three resident reserve officer courses at the U.S. Naval War College in Newport, Rhode Island.

In recognition of his professional expertise, Mr. Little received a Dedicated Service Award in 2009 from the Executive Committee of the Texas Committee for Employer Support of the Guard and Reserve. Previously, he was given a Seven Seals Award from the Texas Committee for Employer Support in 2006. He received the Reserve Organization of America's Sea Service Section Anchor Award in 2016. While his career has been filled with highlights, he takes pride in having completed his master's degree before beginning his career in the U.S. Navy. Commissioned in July 1968, he attended a three-week course in Long Beach, California, and subsequently spent 18 months aboard the U.S.S. Epperson (DD 719) homeported at Pearl Harbor in Hawaii. In June 1969, the ship deployed to the Western Pacific in the Gulf of Tonkin and Sea of Japan for six months. Before the ship arrived in the Western Pacific, the North Koreans shot down a U.S. Navy EC-121 Constellation surveillance aircraft over the Sea of Japan, in which 33 lives were lost. In December 1969, Mr. Little returned from overseas. He was released from active duty in July 1971 and acquired a position in the pharmaceutical industry, where he worked for 37 years before his involvement with the Austin Military Service Coalition and the Texas Coalition of Veterans Organizations. The cornerstone of his success lay with the U.S. Navy because it allowed him to mature as a human being. Mr. Little intends to expand his career growth in the coming years.

Beth A. Lockhart

Owner
Dragon's Lair Art and Gourds

Avionics Systems Specialist (Retired)
Tinker Air Force Base

HARRAH, OK UNITED STATES

F or more than 30 years, Beth A. Lockhart has found success as a visual artist and as the owner of Dragon's Lair Art and Gourds. In this capacity, she focuses on composing paintings of animals and fictional characters on unique surfaces, including gourds, eggs and human skulls. Ms. Lockhart also frequently harnesses her expertise with acrylic oil to create paintings of animals such as horses, deer and cats as well as various creatures of medieval folklore, particularly dragons, gnomes and unicorns.

Alongside her career as an artist, Ms. Lockhart simultaneously thrived as an aircraft mechanic and as an avionics systems specialist with the Oklahoma National Guard for more than 20 years. During this period, she regularly assessed the condition and functionality of numerous military aircraft at Tinker Air Force Base such as the Boeing KC-135 Stratotanker, which is widely recognized as the primary source of aerial refueling for the U.S. Air Force. Ms. Lockhart also specialized in evaluating the efficacy of multiple digital systems such as the airborne early warning and control system (AEWC), which enables pilots to detect aircraft, ships, vehicles, missiles and other incoming projectiles at long ranges.

Prior to her appointment with the Oklahoma National Guard, Ms. Lockhart honed her avionics skills as an aviation mechanic for the U.S.

Department of Defense toward the late 1980s. She had originally been appointed to a clerical position with the U.S. armed forces, but her creative personality inspired her to undergo additional training as an aircraft mechanic. In 2022, Ms. Lockhart issued her retirement from her military career.

Throughout her career with Dragon's Lair Art and Gourds, Ms. Lockhart has consistently showcased her artwork at myriad artistic festivals and crafts fairs, including the Medieval Fair of Norman, Oklahoma, the annual Rose Rock Music Festival in Noble, Oklahoma, and the Oklahoma State Fair in Oklahoma City, Oklahoma. In addition to providing guests with her vast selection of painted gourds, eggs, skulls and acrylic paintings, she conducts demonstrations and workshops in which she explains her innovative technique for utilizing the round shape of gourds to create the bodies of different animals such as horses, ducks, penguins and cows. Ms. Lockhart has also garnered recognition for combining gourds and pinecones to create rounded birdhouses.

Born in Jackson, Mississippi, Ms. Lockhart's artistic talents initially emerged toward the beginning of her military career. During this period, she frequently composed sketches in between aircraft inspections. Ms. Lockhart's decision to pursue her artistic endeavors while simultaneously working as an aircraft mechanic was also influenced by the support of her husband, who enjoyed his own prosperous career as an aircraft electrician with the U.S. Air Force before issuing his retirement.

Toward the beginning of her military career, Ms. Lockhart was recognized as the U.S. Air Force's "Mechanic of the Month." Along with her sizable customer base, she attributes a great deal of her success to her consistent expansion of her professional network of fellow artists and artistic patrons. Ms. Lockhart also credits her widespread reputation to her desire to cater to the specific interests of her customer base, rather than attempting to satisfy a broader range of artistic tastes and preferences.

In the coming years, Ms. Lockhart aims to participate in more art festivals across her home state of Oklahoma. She is extremely proud to have distributed a considerable portion of her earnings from the aforementioned festivals to several charitable organizations. Since her notably confident approach to her work has played a central role in her artistic career, Ms. Lockhart advises aspiring artists to pursue their creative endeavors with the utmost determination.

Donald Patrick Loren

Distinguished Professor of Practice
National Defense University

ALEXANDRIA, VA UNITED STATES

D rawing on more than 20 years of experience as a homeland security adviser, Donald Patrick Loren has thrived as a distinguished professor of practice at the National Defense University since 2021. In this capacity, he specializes in honing his students' abilities to develop comprehensive strategies for protecting the national security of the United States. Highly esteemed for his decades of military service, Mr. Loren also focuses on helping his students create realistic responses to contemporary threats to national security by harnessing the latest and most advanced military technologies and resources.

Prior to his tenure at the National Defense University, Mr. Loren was appointed deputy assistant secretary for plans and posture with the Office of the Secretary of Defense, which is part of the U.S. Department of Defense. Between 2017 and 2018, he excelled as the assistant secretary of operations, security and preparedness for the U.S. Department of Veterans Affairs. Mr. Loren had previously found success as the chief executive officer and president of Old Dominion Strategies LLC, which provided strategic advice to the U.S. Department of Defense's Defense Threat Reduction Agency and the U.S. Department of Homeland Security, for more than five years.

Between 2007 and 2009, Mr. Loren contributed to the U.S. Department of Defense as the deputy assistant secretary of defense and homeland security integration after working as the deputy director of operations support at the National Counterterrorism Center, which is part of the Office of the Director of National Intelligence. Likewise, he also served as the deputy director of politico-military affairs in relation to Europe, Russia, Africa and the North Atlantic Treaty Organization (NATO). Between 1999 and 2001, Mr. Loren prospered as the principal adviser to the operational commander of combat forces at NATO and as the commander in chief of NATO's Allied Forces Southern Europe command. He had previously been recruited as the deputy director of the strategy and policy division of the Office of the Chief of Naval Operations in the late 1990s.

Alongside his responsibilities as an educator, Mr. Loren has actively contributed to the Homeland Security Advisory Council in various capacities for more than 10 years. Between 2012 and 2015, he was appointed as the chairman of the board of directors of the National Association of Uniformed Services. Mr. Patrick has additionally served as a board member for the Northern Virginia Chamber of Commerce as well as myriad nonprofit organizations, including Hope for the Warriors and America's Adopt a Soldier. Thanks to his widespread reputation, Mr. Loren has been recruited as an adjunct lecturer at multiple prestigious academic institutions, including the Naval Postgraduate School, Syracuse University, The George Washington University and Old Dominion University. During the early 1980s, he garnered further recognition as the author of "The Shipboard Guide to Physical Fitness," which was released through the U.S. Naval Institute's Naval Institute Press.

Born in New York City, Mr. Loren earned a Bachelor of Science in operations analysis at the U.S. Naval Academy in 1974. He subsequently held numerous leadership positions with the U.S. Navy such as lieutenant, lieutenant commander and operations officer. Mr. Loren eventually resumed his education at Old Dominion University, where he obtained a Master of Science in education in 1983.

After serving as a commanding officer on the USS Elrod, Mr. Loren completed postgraduate coursework at Harvard University and the Massachusetts Institute of Technology. He subsequently thrived as a commander for a squadron of warships known as Destroyer Squadron 28 for the U.S. Navy between 1995 and 1997 before finding further success as the executive assistant to the commander in chief of the U.S. Naval Forces Europe and Africa. During the early 2000s, Mr. Loren advanced to become the deputy director of surface ships at the Office of the Chief of Naval Operations. Following his promotion to the rank of rear admiral, he issued his retirement from the U.S. Armed Forces.

In recognition of his military service, Mr. Loren has been honored with a host of accolades, including a Bronze Star, a Defense Superior Service Medal, a Legion of Merit, a Meritorious Service Medal, a Defense Meritorious Service Medal and a Joint Commendation Medal. He has also been celebrated with a Conspicuous Service Cross on behalf of the New York State Senate. In 2022, Mr. Loren was selected for induction into the National Defense University Joint Forces Staff College National Hall of Fame.

John J. McDaniel

Chief Executive Officer
Wounded Warriors in Action Foundation Inc.

APOLLO BEACH, FL UNITED STATES

Since becoming a soldier in 1983, John J. McDaniel has served the country in many different capacities. His distinguished military record includes achievements as a decorated combat veteran, former infantry officer, Airborne Ranger and Master Parachutist. Mr. McDaniel's military career spanned over two decades, during which he served as an infantryman and Special Operations Officer. Within the initial 10 years of his service, he frequently engaged in Airborne and Ranger assignments, while his latter 10 years were marked by his involvement in various Joint and Interagency roles within the Special Operations domain. Prior to entering the service, Mr. McDaniel graduated from the University of Wisconsin-Madison in Madison, Wisconsin, with a bachelor's degree in economics. In 2000, he received a master's degree in military arts and leadership from the U.S. Army Command and General Staff College in Fort Leavenworth, Kansas. In 2001, he received a Master of Business Administration from Baker University in Baldwin City, Kansas.

During his assignment at the Special Operations Command in Tampa, Florida, Mr. McDaniel began organizing hunting and fishing excursions during his free time for heroes recuperating at the James A. Haley Veterans' Hospital Polytrauma Rehabilitation Center. Witnessing the profound impact of this work on wounded Veterans while still on active duty, he recognized that serving them constituted a higher calling and a greater cause than furthering his military career. Despite having the potential to ascend beyond the rank of Lieutenant Colonel, he chose to redirect his focus toward aiding Veterans in their recovery from wartime experiences. He founded the Wounded Warriors in Action Foundation, Inc., also known as the WWIA, in 2007. Based in Apollo Beach, Florida, the WWIA is a National nonprofit dedicated to supporting combat-wounded Purple Heart recipients through therapeutic and adaptive outdoor sporting events and community engagement.

Mr. McDaniel's commitment to the organization and wildlife conservation led him to dedicate 410 acres of remote wilderness known as Camp Hackett in Northern Wisconsin to the WWIA, transforming it into a therapeutic retreat for Veterans. In response to a significant storm that toppled 12-century-old spruce trees, he and his team made the decision to harvest the fallen trees rather than allow them to go to waste. Despite the difficult task, they converted the spruce trees into 550 two-by-fours, which were used to construct American Disabilities Act (ADA) compliant modifications to the existing bunkhouses for Veterans, particularly those living with paralysis and mobility challenges. The WWIA's tagline, "Honor. Connect. Heal," succinctly encapsulates the core principles and values that the Foundation represents.

The WWIA has received numerous awards, and in 2023, the foundation was identified as a Top-Rated Nonprofit Organization by GreatNonprofits. The WWIA ranked first among 78 military charities in program performance, staff and volunteer support, and client satisfaction, per an independent survey conducted by a leading consortium of Veteran recreational programs. Mr. McDaniel's entrepreneurial spirit, inherited from a family with a legacy of business ventures, has been instrumental in fueling his passion for innovation and creation. He effectively harnessed this interest, coupled with his MBA qualifications, to drive the growth and expansion of the WWIA to the success that it is today. Striving for excellence in all his pursuits, Mr. McDaniel attributes his success to his determination and a commitment to continuous self-improvement.

Despite his professional accomplishments, Mr. McDaniel's greatest source of pride is being a single father to two young sons. For Mr. McDaniel, his achievements in his family life far outweigh any professional successes. Mr. McDaniel has always had a love of sport and respect for the outdoors, competing in wrestling, baseball, football and hockey from high school to his time in the military, as well as hunting and fishing. His goal as a father is to impart that same love and respect to his sons, and for anyone looking to enter his field, he would advise against quitting, as failure is simply another step in the process of success. 🌿🌿

Kenneth O. Preston

Senior Fellow
Association of the United States Army

Sergeant Major (Retired)
U.S. Army

MOUNT SAVAGE, MD UNITED STATES

For more than 35 years, Kenneth O. Preston found success as a command sergeant major, task commander and sergeant major of the U.S. Army. Prior to his retirement from the U.S. Armed Forces, he specialized in overseeing the administration of myriad policies and procedures regarding military training and the recruitment of military personnel. Mr. Preston also focused on advocating on behalf of U.S. troops to U.S. Army officers, and he frequently served as a personal adviser to the U.S. Army's chief of staff.

Between 1994 and 1995, Mr. Preston excelled as a deputy commandant at the U.S. Army Noncommissioned Officer Academy at Fort Knox. Throughout the following three years, he was appointed as a command sergeant major of the 3rd Battalion, 8th Cavalry Regiment, which is represented by the 1st Cavalry Division of the U.S. Army. Between 1998 and 1999, Mr. Preston worked in this capacity for the 3rd Brigade Combat Team of the aforementioned division.

After finding further success as a command sergeant major of the U.S. Army's 1st Armored Division in Bad Kreuznach, Germany, Mr. Preston was recruited as a command sergeant major for the Combined Task Force 7, which was an interim military formation that directed the U.S. Army's efforts in Baghdad, Iraq during the Iraq War. Between 2004 and 2011, he thrived as the 13th individual to be appointed as the sergeant major of the U.S. Army. During this period, Mr. Preston oversaw the training of U.S. troops in preparation for their deployment in support of Operation Enduring Freedom in Afghanistan and Operation Iraqi Freedom in Iraq.

Following his retirement, Mr. Preston prospered as the vice president of programs for noncommissioned officers and soldiers for the Association of the U.S. Army between 2013 and 2020. He had previously served as the president of Homes for Our Troops between 2012 and 2013. Mr. Preston currently contributes to Homes for Our Troops, which provides customized housing for injured veterans of the U.S. Armed Forces, as a board member.

In 2021, Mr. Preston was recruited as the director of the Eagle's Watch Foundation, which provides financial support for veterans of the U.S. Armed Forces. He has additionally excelled as a military adviser for Veterans United Home Loans for more than five years. Likewise, Mr. Preston currently serves as the director of the Institute for Veterans and Military Families and as a board member and director for the Army Historical Foundation. Between 2011 and 2006, he found further success as the co-chairperson of the U.S. Army Chief of Staff Retired Soldier Council.

Born in Mount Savage, Maryland, Mr. Preston earned an Associate of Arts in vocational education and instruction at the University of Louisville in 1989. While serving as the sergeant major of the U.S. Army, he simultaneously obtained a Bachelor of Science, Bachelor of Arts from Trident University International. Mr. Preston subsequently completed a Master of Business Administration at the aforementioned online university.

In recognition of his military service, Mr. Preston has been honored with a host of accolades on behalf of the U.S. Army, including a Distinguished Service Medal, a Legion of Merit, a Bronze Star Medal, a Meritorious Service Medal, a Commendation Medal, an Achievement Medal, a Good Conduct Medal, a Southwest Asia Service Medal and a Global War on Terrorism Service Medal. He has also been celebrated with a George Catlett Marshall Medal on behalf of the Association of the U.S. Army, which recognizes distinguished and selfless service, and was included in the 76th edition of Who's Who in America. The aforementioned nonprofit organization had previously distinguished Mr. Preston as a senior fellow in 2020.

Carol Roberts

Former Chairperson
Health Care District of Palm Beach County

Former Mayor
City of West Palm Beach

PALM BEACH GARDENS, FL UNITED STATES

Drawing on over three decades of experience, Carol Roberts distinguished herself through her work in various government service roles, through which she accumulated a wealth of expertise in health care, budgeting and fiscal planning. Prior to her retirement, she earned distinction in her position as an appointed member of the Health Care District of Palm Beach County Board of Commissioners, during which time she served as chairperson from 2013 to 2015. In this capacity, Ms. Roberts notably helped establish internal auditing procedures for the district, and held the role of first chair of the audit and compliance committee. Established to function as a safety net for the residents of Palm Beach County, the Health Care District was first advocated by Ms. Roberts during the late 1980s and was approved by voters in 1988.

Prior to her work at the Health Care District, Ms. Roberts found success as a commissioner of the city of West Palm Beach from 1975 to 1986 and then joined the Palm Beach County Commission in 1986. She was the first woman elected to the West Palm Beach commission in 1975. She served as mayor of the city between 1985 and 1986. Additionally, she had served as vice mayor of the city on two occasions from 1976 to 1977 and 1984 to 1985. She served in the Palm Beach County Commission from 1986 to 2002.

As a county commissioner, Ms. Roberts served as the chair of the county commission from 1987 through 1989. She served as chair of the National Association of Counties' transportation committee and also on the urban counties committee. As a county commissioner she was asked by the National Association of Counties to be part of a delegation to visit cities in China. This invitation was issued to the National Association of Counties by the Chinese government. She served as President of the Florida Association of Counties in 1997 through 1998.

Ms. Roberts also sat on the committee on intergovernmental relations for the state of Florida from 1996 until 1997, the chair of the women's division for the Palm Beach County Comprehensive Community Mental Health Center Board between 1978 and 1980, and a commissioner for the Palm Beach County Film and Television Commission. Other civic commitments to her credit include her work as the chairman of the marketing committee for the Solid Waste Authority, the chair of the artificial reef committee for Art in Public Places, a co-chair of the Water Resources Management Advisory Board, the vice-chair of the Intergovernmental Relations Committee of the Florida League of Cities, and a member of the Palm Beach Sports Authority, among many others.

Outside of her work in government service, Ms. Roberts dedicated herself to her local community as a member of the Jewish Federation of Palm Beach County. She also found success as the host of her radio program at Station WPBR from 1976 to 1983, during which time she served as the president of Sunshine Academy Press Inc. Furthermore, she functioned as a broker for VIP Management and Realty Inc. in 1980 and co-founded Denman Roberts & Ross in 1978.

Ms. Roberts first studied at Palm Beach Atlantic University, where she undertook coursework in 1972 and received a Distinguished Medal in 1986. Over the course of her subsequent career, she received numerous accolades, including recognition as the Leading Lady in Municipal Government by Network Connection in 1985, Woman of the Year by the Temple Beth El Sisterhood in 1986, and Most Superior and Dedicated County Commissioner by the Palm Beach Mid-County Council in 1997. She also earned induction into Florida's Hall of Fame in 1986, a Certificate of Appreciation by the Palm Beach County Criminal Justice Commission in 1996 and a framed Memento of Appreciation by the Health Care District of Palm Beach County Board of Commissioners in 2016.

Among her most cherished accomplishments, Ms. Roberts is particularly gratified to have lent her aid as a government servant for the people of Palm Beach County. In accounting for her success, she largely credits her passion for the profession and penchant for availing herself on behalf of others.

Richard R. Sklar II

Colonel (Retired)
U.S. Army

WILLIAMSBURG, VA UNITED STATES

For more than 20 years, Richard R. Sklar II served as a colonel in the U.S. Army. Widely renowned for his leadership skills, he regularly presided over infantry battalions consisting of hundreds of U.S. troops. Mr. Sklar also participated in numerous overseas conflicts throughout his military career such as the Vietnam War and frequently reported directly to the vice chief of staff of the U.S. Army while executing critical combat initiatives in various foreign nations.

During his childhood, Mr. Sklar initially intended to follow in his father's footsteps and pursue a formal education at the University of Kansas, where the latter individual had earned an undergraduate degree in architecture while garnering additional recognition as a prominent member of the aforementioned institution's football team. While attending high school, his family was contacted by a district representative, who asked if he harbored any interest in military service. Mr. Sklar subsequently enrolled in the Missouri Military Academy and completed numerous academic examinations with ease.

Following his graduation from the Missouri Military Academy in 1962, Mr. Sklar was appointed as a second lieutenant in the U.S. Army. During the late 1960s, he resumed his education at the University of Missouri's Robert J. Trulaske Sr. College of Business, where he obtained a Master of Business Administration. Toward the beginning of his military career, Mr. Sklar also completed coursework at the U.S. Army War College in Cumberland County, Pennsylvania.

While serving in the Vietnam War, Mr. Sklar notably risked his life to deliver communications equipment to a battalion that did not possess the correct equipment to execute the required offensive operation. The receiving battalion was located more than 100 meters away, and the battalion's base was obstructed by a large rice paddy, but he remained committed to his instructions. Mr. Sklar is extremely grateful to have survived a barrage of airstrikes from Vietnamese soldiers while crawling on his hands and knees to deliver the aforementioned equipment.

Following his retirement from the military, Mr. Sklar was recruited as a sales manager with AXA Equitable Life Insurance Corporation of Denver, Colorado. He subsequently found further success as a vice president with AXA Equitable Life in New York City, which is a subsidiary of AXA Equitable Holdings, Inc. During his tenure in the financial services industry, Mr. Sklar was selected to implement a series of strategic changes and improve the skill sets of myriad employees at a bank in Moscow, Russia. Under his leadership, the aforementioned bank experienced a substantial increase in annual revenue.

Mr. Sklar currently excels as a board member of the Cherry Creek School District 5 in Arapahoe County, Colorado. In addition to his firm commitment to his goals, he attributes a great deal of his success to the guidance of his mentors. During his military career, Mr. Sklar served alongside multiple highly celebrated military figures such as James Lee Dozier and Norman Schwarzkopf Jr., who was appointed commander of the U.S. Central Command throughout the Gulf War.

In the coming years, Mr. Sklar aims to focus on maintaining a healthy lifestyle while continuing to support the careers of his three children, all of whom have garnered success in their own respective fields. Due to the unpredictable nature of military professions, he advises aspiring military leaders to accept opportunities for professional growth that arise from unforeseen circumstances. In his spare time, Mr. Sklar relaxes by playing golf and football.

Pamela J.H. Slutz

Ambassador (Retired)
U.S. Department of State

President
The Mongolia Society

KERRVILLE, TX UNITED STATES

P amela J.H. Slutz served more than 30 years as a commissioned U.S. Foreign Service officer, including service at U.S. embassies and consulates in Asia and Africa and as a member of the U.S. Delegation to the Nuclear and Space Talks with the USSR from 1987 to 1989. Her distinguished career included two ambassadorships: to Mongolia from 2003 to 2006 and later to Burundi from 2009 to 2012. She counts among her major accomplishments the resettlement in the U.S of a dozen Chinese political dissidents and their families from Shanghai; the establishment of shelters for victims of domestic abuse in Mongolia; and compensation for Kenyan employees of the U.S. Embassy in Nairobi who were victims of the 1998 terrorist bombing of the embassy.

Passionate about public service and representing the American people overseas, Ms. Slutz found additional success in the nonprofit sector. Following her retirement from the U.S. Foreign Service, she served as the chairman of the North America-Mongolia Business Council until 2016, advocating on behalf of the interests of U.S. and Canadian companies invested in Mongolia. Since 2019, as president of The Mongolia Society, a nonprofit organization that promotes the study of Mongolia in all its facets through its publication series, annual scholarly conference and document/library service, Ms. Slutz has focused on building people-to-people and institutional relationships to support Mongolia's democratic transformation and to create a broader awareness in the United States of Mongolia and its importance in world affairs.

Ms. Slutz attended Hollins University in Roanoke, Virginia, earning a Bachelor of Arts in politics. She also garnered a Master of Arts in Southeast Asian studies from the University of Hawaii at Manoa, where she was the recipient of an East-West Center fellowship.

In recognition of her diplomatic achievements, Ms. Slutz received several Superior Performance Honor Awards from the U.S. Department of State, as well as the U.S. Presidential Rank Award of Meritorious Executive in 2011 for her work in Mongolia and Kenya. In recognition of her contributions to promoting people-to-people and institutional relationships between the U.S. and Mongolia, Ms. Slutz was also recognized by the president of Mongolia in 2015 with the Order of the Polar Star, the highest state award given to a non-Mongolian citizen.

Frances Colbert-Clements Terrell

Deaconess
Oakland Baptist Church

Congressional Staff Assistant (Retired)
U.S. House of Representatives

ALEXANDRIA, VA UNITED STATES

For more than 25 years, Frances Colbert-Clements Terrell found success as a congressional staff assistant for the U.S. House of Representatives in Washington, D.C. Prior to her retirement, she specialized in coordinating congressional hearings and attending congressional meetings, where she frequently documented key points into comprehensive transcripts. Ms. Terrell also focused on helping various state representatives develop and organize documentation for proposed legislation in relation to economic growth and small business funding.

In 1972, Ms. Terrell was recruited as a staff assistant for Jack Brooks, who served as a representative of the second and ninth congressional districts for the U.S. state of Texas. She worked in this capacity until 1976, at which point she was appointed as a staff assistant for multiple congressmen, including Parren Mitchell, who served as a representative of the seventh congressional district of the U.S. state of Maryland, and John Conyers, who served as a representative of several congressional districts within the U.S. state of Michigan. Ms. Terrell shared her administrative expertise with both of the aforementioned representatives until 1999, at which point she issued her retirement from her career with the U.S. House of Representatives.

Between 2006 and 2010, Ms. Terrell found further success as the owner of the Fran and Cal Travel Agency, which she established with the help of her husband, Calvin Terrell. She currently excels as a deaconess at the Oakland Baptist Church in Alexandria, Virginia. Ms. Terrell had previously completed her certification as a deaconess in 1996.

Since 2019, Ms. Terrell has contributed to the Seminary Hill Association as a board member and representative of Alexandria's West End region. She had previously been recruited as the president of the Seminary West Civic Association between 2011 and 2021. Likewise, Ms. Terrell continues to maintain active affiliations with the Alexandria Federation of Civic Associations, the Fort Ward and Seminary African American Descendants Society, the National Urban League and the National Association for the Advancement of Colored People (NAACP).

Born in the aforementioned city of Alexandria, Ms. Terrell originally intended to pursue a career as an educator. During the early 1960s, she completed undergraduate coursework at Hampton University, which inspired her to shift her focus toward business administration. Ms. Terrell's decision to accept her initial position with the U.S. House of Representatives was also influenced by her mother, who enjoyed her own prosperous career as an employee of the U.S. federal government.

Between 2009 and 2014, Ms. Terrell garnered widespread recognition for her instrumental role in the restoration of a historic cemetery within Alexandria's Fort Ward Park. The aforementioned cemetery contains the graves of myriad African Americans who relocated to Fort Ward following the end of the U.S. Civil War. Prior to Ms. Terrell's efforts, the city of Fort Ward had neglected to maintain the cemetery, a portion of which had been converted into a recreational area for dogs. Thanks to the Fort Ward and Seminary African American Descendants Society, the cemetery is now under new ownership and will continue to preserve the legacy of Fort Ward's original African American settlers.

In addition to her organizational skills, Ms. Terrell attributes a great deal of her success to her inclination toward increasingly challenging opportunities. She is particularly proud to have previously worked alongside several former presidents of the U.S. such as Bill Clinton. In the coming years. Ms. Terrell intends to continue contributing to the advancement of her local community.

William W. Wiseman II

Deputy Operations Manager (Retired)
SOC LLC

Sergeant Major (Retired)
U.S. Marine Corps

YUMA, AZ UNITED STATES

A security and defense specialist, William W. Wiseman II celebrates a long and successful career in military and defense contracting. Joining the U.S. Marine Corps in 1989, Mr. Wiseman rose to the rank of sergeant major by his retirement in 2015. During his service, he received an Associate of Science in general studies from the City University of Seattle, as well as military training in Emergency Response and Marine Air Ground Task Force Operations. He completed the Senior Enlisted Joint Professional Military Enlisted Course in 2007, the U.S. Marine Corps Senior Enlisted Professional Military Education Course in 2012 and the Field Grade Officers Winter Warfare Planning Course in 2014. In addition, he served as the director of a Leadership Academy within the U.S. Marine Corps.

Prior to his retirement, Mr. Wiseman began working with SOC LLC, a mission support provider serving both the U.S. government and commercial clients. As he transitioned from the service to a civilian, he became a Protective Security Specialist with the company in Baghdad, Iraq. In 2015, he moved to the position of Shift Leader, followed by a 2018 promotion to Protective Security Operations Chief in Somalia.

From 2019 to 2020, he served as the Deputy Operations Manager for Security for the embassy in Baghdad, Iraq.

Mr. Wiseman considers his most notable achievement to be returning home after four combat tours in Iraq. For his exemplary service, he was awarded the Meritorious Service Medal in 2012 as well as two Navy and Marine Corps Commendation Medals and three Navy and Marine Corps Achievement Medals. Contracted to the U.S. State Department, he is proud to have led over 600 security personnel at the U.S. Embassy in Baghdad, Iraq, during the New Year's attack in 2020. Due to Mr. Wiseman's fortification and defense efforts, when the embassy was breached by over 100 militia members on December 31, 2019, there were no casualties.

Looking to the future, Mr. Wiseman plans to remain in the security industry, and he still sees himself continuing in defense contracting in the next five to 10 years. For his professional achievements, he has been recognized with inclusion in the 76th edition of Who's Who in America. He hopes to be a person his granddaughter can look up to the way he looked up to his grandfather, a fellow Marine who served in WW II, Korea and Vietnam. Throughout his career, Mr. Wiseman was famous for quoting to his Marines and all who worked for him these immortal words, "The legacy you leave behind will be the history we inherit."

Neil N. Colicchio, Esq.

Attorney

The Law Office of Neil N. Colicchio

GROTON, MA UNITED STATES

F or more than 20 years, Neil N. Colicchio, Esq. has thrived as an attorney at the Law Office of Neil N. Colicchio. With more than 35 years of legal experience to his credit, he specializes in criminal law. Mr. Colicchio frequently litigates on behalf of suspects of various criminal offenses, particularly individuals who suffer from substance use disorder or other mental health conditions. He also focuses on ensuring the protection of his clients' civil rights during prosecution.

Between 1985 and 1987, Mr. Colicchio began his legal career as a staff attorney for the Committee for Public Counsel Services, which oversees the public defender system within his home state of Massachusetts. During this period, he simultaneously worked as a trial attorney in a part-time capacity. Mr. Colicchio subsequently found further success in this capacity at the Law Office of Joseph P. Marchese Jr., which has since closed, between 1987 and 1988 before the establishment of the Law Office of Neil N. Colicchio in Essex County, Massachusetts, where he worked as a solo practitioner for more than 10 years.

Between 2000 and 2001, Mr. Colicchio was appointed as the managing attorney at the Law Offices of H. Drew Romanovitz in Salem, Massachusetts. Throughout the following 15 years, he prospered as a solo practitioner at the aforementioned Essex County-based private practice. In 2018, Mr. Colicchio relocated the Law Office of Neil N. Colicchio to Worcester, Massachusetts, where he has since developed a widespread reputation for litigating on behalf of indigent defendants and helping his clients obtain mental health counseling services.

Alongside his responsibilities as an attorney, Mr. Colicchio currently excels as a board member for the Cable Television Advisory Committee of Worcester, Massachusetts. Likewise, he additionally serves as a board member for the Friends of the Worcester Senior Center. In order to stay up to date with the latest developments in his field, Mr. Colicchio continues to maintain an active affiliation with the Massachusetts Bar Association, the Worcester County Bar Association and the National Association for Public Defense.

Born in Medford, Massachusetts, Mr. Colicchio earned a Bachelor of Science in biology at Boston State College, which has since closed, in 1981. His subsequent decision to pursue a career as an attorney was chiefly inspired by his father, who enjoyed his own prosperous career as a legal professional who oversaw the recruitment of public defenders in the state of Massachusetts. In 1985, Mr. Colicchio obtained a Doctor of Jurisprudence from Suffolk University Law School.

Following the completion of his undergraduate degree, Mr. Colicchio was selected for the Mary E. Lynch Award, which recognizes academic excellence and extensive involvement in extracurricular affairs, on behalf of Boston State College. In 1985, he was honored with an American Jurisprudence Award in commercial law on behalf of Suffolk University Law School. Additionally, he has been selected for inclusion in the 76th edition of Who's Who in America. Alongside his family's support, Mr. Colicchio attributes a great deal of his success to the guidance of his former mentors.

In the coming years, Mr. Colicchio intends to gradually diminish his responsibilities at the Law Office of Neil N. Colicchio while preparing for his well-deserved retirement. He also aims to establish a statewide service that provides mental health counseling services to indigent defendants during criminal trials. Since his tenure with the Committee for Public Counsel Services played an instrumental role in the trajectory of his career, Mr. Colicchio advises aspiring attorneys to pursue opportunities with their local district attorney's office or public defender's office while completing their education.

Philip A. Greenberg

Family Attorney & Partner
Philip A. Greenberg, P.C.

NEW YORK, NY UNITED STATES

F or more than 20 years, Philip A. Greenberg has thrived as a family attorney and partner at Philip A. Greenberg, P.C. in New York City. With more than four decades of legal experience to his credit, he specializes in guiding his clients through challenging legal processes such as filing for divorce, drafting prenuptial agreements, appointing legal guardianship and obtaining child custody. Mr. Greenberg also regularly harnesses his exceptional litigation skills to negotiate favorable contractual terms for business agreements and partnerships, particularly involving commercial real estate.

In 1973, Mr. Greenberg began his legal career at Kamerman, Uncyk, Soniker and Klein P.C. After working as an associate for more than five years, he excelled as a partner at the aforementioned law firm, which was formerly known as Kamerman and Kamerman, between 1978 and 1982. Mr. Greenberg subsequently found further success as a partner at Segal and Greenberg LLP between 1982 and 1984.

Throughout the following 10 years, Mr. Greenberg prospered as a managing partner at Segal and Greenberg. Between 1993 and 1995, he served in this capacity with Bizar Martin and Taub LLP. Mr. Greenberg subsequently worked as a partner with Wallman, Gasman and McKnight, LLP, from 1995 until 2000, at which point he established Philip A. Greenberg, P.C.

Alongside his responsibilities as an attorney, Mr. Greenberg has contributed to the National Business Institute as a lecturer for more than 10 years. He had previously served in this capacity with the Sobelsohn School in New York City between 1988 and 2000. In order to stay up to date with the latest developments in his field, Mr. Greenberg continues to maintain active affiliations with the American Bar Association, the New York State Bar Association and Phi Alpha Delta Law Fraternity, International.

Between 2003 and 2005, Mr. Greenberg excelled as the president of the Masters and Wardens Association, which had initially appointed him as a secretary between 2000 and 2003. He had previously been recruited as a trustee and as the vice president of Congregation Emunath Israel, also known as the Chelsea Shul, between 1984 and 1999. In 2019, Mr. Greenberg garnered further recognition as a co-author of "Divorce Insights: Conversations with America's Leading Divorce Professionals."

Born in Brooklyn, New York, Mr. Greenberg's decision to pursue a career as an attorney was heavily influenced by his admiration for Abraham Lincoln. In 1970, he earned a Bachelor of Arts in political science and sociology from Brooklyn College, which is part of the City University of New York system. Mr. Greenberg subsequently completed a Doctor of Jurisprudence at New York University Law School in 1973.

Since 2016, Mr. Greenberg has consistently been distinguished as a "Super Lawyer" on behalf of SuperLawyers, which is owned by Thomson Reuters Corporation. He has also been honored in the 76th edition of Who's Who in America. In addition to his exceptional work ethic, he attributes a great deal of his success to his abstinence from drugs and alcohol. Mr. Greenberg also draws tremendous inspiration from his wife, who has enjoyed her own prosperous career as a realtor.

In the coming years, Mr. Greenberg intends to continue serving his clients while maintaining a healthy lifestyle. Since his close relationships with his clients have played a central role in his professional growth, he advises aspiring attorneys to treat their clients with the utmost kindness and respect. Throughout his career, Mr. Greenberg has treated each client with an equal degree of importance, regardless of the client's economic background.

Harry H. Kazakian

President & Chief Executive Officer

USA Express Legal & Investigative Services Inc.

WOODLAND HILLS, CA UNITED STATES

For more than 20 years, Harry H. Kazakian has thrived as the president, chief executive officer and founder of USA Express Legal & Investigative Services Inc. With more than three decades of experience as a claims adjuster to his credit, he focuses on investigating insurance claims on behalf of law firms, insurance companies and insurance policyholders to determine the extent of the insurance company's liability. Mr. Kazakian also specializes in helping law firms gather evidence for cases involving missing persons or allegations of fraud, personal injury or wrongful death.

Prior to the formation of USA Express Legal & Investigative Services, Mr. Kazakian was appointed as a high-exposure claims adjuster for the Automobile Club of Southern California, which is the Southern California affiliate of the American Automobile Association (AAA), in 1989, and he continued to serve in this capacity for more than 20 years. He had previously worked as an emergency medical technician for the Los Angeles County Emergency Medical Services Agency between 1982 and 1997. In 1981, Mr. Kazakian honed his expertise in critical care medicine while working in the emergency department of Children's Hospital Los Angeles.

Alongside his responsibilities at USA Express Legal & Investigative Services, Mr. Kazakian found further success as a board member for the California Association of Independent Insurance Adjusters between

2014 and 2016. He had previously been recruited as the governor of the San Fernando Valley District of the California Association of Licensed Investigators between 2004 and 2005. In order to stay up to date with the latest developments in his field, Mr. Kazakian continues to maintain active affiliations with the Association of British Investigators, the Consumer Attorneys of California, the California Association of Licensed Investigators, the World Association of Detectives, the Consumer Attorneys Association of Los Angeles and the National Council of Investigation and Security Services.

Throughout his career, Mr. Kazakian has contributed numerous articles to Forbes, particularly in relation to employee screening and various human resources issues. Thanks to his widespread reputation, he has shared his expertise at workshops, seminars and industry conferences across the United States. Likewise, Mr. Kazakian has additionally conducted training seminars for the Consumer Attorneys Association of Los Angeles as well as claims investigators at the Automobile Club of Southern California.

Born in Armenia, Mr. Kazakian's decision to pursue a career as a private investigator was heavily inspired by his affinity for puzzles and other challenging mental exercises. In 2001, he became a certified private investigator through the School of Private Investigations in Atlanta, Georgia. Mr. Kazakian and his team at USA Express Legal & Investigative Services have since helped multiple clients recover millions of dollars after achieving favorable verdicts or settlements.

In recognition of his contributions to the Consumer Attorneys Association of Los Angeles, Mr. Kazakian was honored with a commemorative plaque. He has also been celebrated with a commemorative plaque for his continuous support of the California Highway Patrol 11-99 Foundation, which provides scholarships and financial support to family members of employees of the California Highway Patrol. In addition to his exceptional work ethic, Mr. Kazakian attributes a great deal of his success to his transparent approach to his work and his close relationships with his clients. In the coming years, he intends to continue expanding his professional skill set while furthering his contributions to various nonprofit organizations.

Richard D. Michels, JD

State Attorney

LAKE CHARLES, LA UNITED STATES

Having demonstrated proficiency in all aspects of his area of expertise, Richard D. Michels, JD, found success throughout the span of his career in legal service. Now retired, he distinguished himself as a state attorney on behalf of the state of Louisiana from 1990 until 2018, during which time he specialized in paternity and child support enforcement. Holding more than four decades of experience, he previously served as an assistant district attorney for Calcasieu Parish, during which time he sharpened his talents in child support enforcement between 1984 and 1990. Throughout this period, he notably helped establish an intake process for women who needed help raising their children. During the initial stages of his professional journey, Mr. Michels served as the acting director of legal services for the state of Louisiana from 1981 to 1983.

Before embarking upon his career path, Mr. Michels worked in various roles as a hospital assistant and a personnel manager. In this role, he was responsible for hiring new employees and training them on safety requirements. Due to ongoing labor strikes at the time, he resolved to enter the field of legal service. After studying in Connecticut, New York, Massachusetts, and Italy, he attended the Salmon P. Chase College of Law at Northern Kentucky University, from which he received a Doctor of Jurisprudence in 1978. Following this accomplishment, Mr. Michels was licensed to practice law by the states of Kentucky and Louisiana. To remain aware of developments in his field, he also maintained affiliation with the Louisiana State Bar Association.

In accounting for his success, Mr. Michels largely credits his intrinsic sense of determination, as well as the efforts of his support team during his career. Moreover, he took a great deal of inspiration from his older brother, who encouraged him to pursue his education, become proficient in his profession and work selflessly on behalf of others. Among his most cherished accomplishments, he is most proud to have ensured excellent support and care for numerous children, to have developed his education in the Latin language, and to have consistently held high grades. Likewise, he is gratified to have passed the bar examination in Kentucky and Louisiana. To commemorate his achievements, he was included in the 76th edition of Who's Who in America.

Outside of his primary professional pursuits, Mr. Michels has remained active as a member of the Knights of Columbus, a fraternal Catholic order. He has also parlayed his knowledge of the field to others as an adviser, consultant and mentor for aspiring attorneys. Looking toward the future, Mr. Michels aspires to continue enjoying his retirement and quality time spent with his family, including three stepchildren, eight grandchildren and 18 great-grandchildren.

James Malachy Morris

Attorney at Law

MCLEAN, VA UNITED STATES

F or more than 45 years, James Malachy Morris, Attorney at Law, has found success as a practicing lawyer and as a chief legal officer for the U.S. Farm Credit Administration and the Farm Credit System Insurance Corporation. Throughout his career, he specialized in maintaining the aforementioned government-controlled corporation's compliance with the U.S. Farm Credit Administration, particularly in relation to the determination of insurance premiums and the methodologies in which the Farm Credit System Insurance Corporation collects insurance claims. Mr. Morris also focused on ensuring the Farm Credit System Insurance Corporation's fulfillment of its obligations toward the nationwide network of banks and lending institutions that comprise the Farm Credit System.

During the late 1970s, Mr. Morris began his legal career as an associate at Thelen LLP. He subsequently worked as a senior law clerk at the Supreme Court of Illinois before finding further success as an associate at Carter, Ledyard and Milburn between 1981 and 1983. Throughout the following five years, Mr. Morris excelled as a lawyer at his former private legal practice in New York City.

In 1987, Mr. Morris accepted a position as counsel to the U.S. Farm Credit Administration, where he thrived in this capacity for more than 15 years. Throughout the 1990s, he simultaneously served as an acting secretary and general counsel to the Farm Credit System Insurance Corporation. Between 2006 and 2013, Mr. Morris continued to prosper in the latter capacity at the Farm Credit System Insurance Corporation's headquarters in McLean, Virginia, where he additionally established a private legal practice.

After sharing his legal expertise at the aforementioned private practice for more than five years, Mr. Morris was appointed as counsel to the director of the Farm Credit System Insurance Corporation between 2018 and 2023. During this period, he simultaneously contributed to the Farm Credit Administration as counsel to the aforementioned regulatory agency's director. Mr. Morris currently serves as a lawyer at his aforementioned private practice in McLean, where he regularly provides legal assistance in relation to banking and regulatory law.

Alongside his primary professional responsibilities, Mr. Morris was simultaneously appointed as a consultant to Herbert Oppenheimer Nathan and Vandyk, which has since merged with Dentons HPRP, between 1985 and 2004. He has also been recruited in this capacity for the Pritzker Architecture Prize and the International Balzan Prize Foundation. Outside of his professional circles, Mr. Morris contributes to the Lansdowne Club, the Penn Club of New York and the Brown University Association of Class Leaders in various capacities.

Born in Champaign, Illinois, Mr. Morris initially pursued a formal education at Oxford University in England, where he completed undergraduate coursework during the early 1970s. Following his return to the U.S., he earned a Bachelor of Arts at Brown University. Mr. Morris eventually concluded his education in 1977, at which point he obtained a Doctor of Jurisprudence at the University of Pennsylvania Carey Law School.

In 2019, Mr. Morris was selected to serve as the chief marshal for the commencement procession of Brown University's graduating class. He had previously been celebrated with multiple accolades on behalf of the Farm Credit Insurance Corporation as well as the U.S. Farm Credit Administration. As an esteemed professional, he was selected for inclusion in the 76th edition of Who's Who in America. In order to stay up to date with the latest developments in his field, Mr. Morris continues to maintain active affiliations with the New York City Bar Association and the British Institute of International and Comparative Law.

Mark B. Rotenberg

Vice President of University Initiatives and Legal Affairs

Hillel International

WASHINGTON, DC UNITED STATES

Since 2017, Mark B. Rotenberg has thrived as the vice president of university initiatives and legal affairs for Hillel International. With more than 40 years of legal experience to his credit, he specializes in protecting the civil rights of Jewish college students across the United States. Mr. Rotenberg also focuses on ensuring the safety of Jewish college students and responding to acts of discrimination and antisemitism.

Prior to his recruitment at Hillel International, Mr. Rotenberg excelled as special counsel to Wilmer Cutler Pickering Hale and Dorr LLP between 2015 and 2017. He had previously found success as a vice president and general counsel at Johns Hopkins University after working in the latter capacity for the University of Minnesota for more than 20 years. Between 1989 and 1992, Mr. Rotenberg was appointed partner at Dorsey and Whitney LLP in Minneapolis, Minnesota.

Alongside his primary professional responsibilities, Mr. Rotenberg has simultaneously contributed to the American University Washington College of Law as an adjunct professor of law since 2020. He had previously served in this capacity at the University of Minnesota Law School during the early 1990s. In order to stay up to date with the latest developments in his field, Mr. Rotenberg continues to maintain active affiliations with numerous professional organizations, including the Minnesota Bar Association, the Hennepin County Bar Association, the American Society for Legal History, the American Law Institute and the Alumni Association of the Law School of Columbia University.

Born in Minneapolis, Mr. Rotenberg's decision to pursue a career as a lawyer was chiefly inspired by his father, who enjoyed his own prosperous career as an attorney for several decades. In 1976, he obtained a Bachelor of Arts in history and politics, magna cum laude, from Brandeis University in Waltham, Massachusetts. Mr. Rotenberg subsequently earned a Doctor of Jurisprudence from Columbia Law School, where he was additionally appointed as an editor of the Columbia Law Review between 1978 and 1979.

Throughout the following three years, Mr. Rotenberg earned a Doctor of Jurisprudence as well as a Master of Arts and a Master of Philosophy from the aforementioned New York-based institution. Between 1981 and 1984, he was recruited as an attorney adviser with the U.S. Department of Justice's Office of Legal Counsel. In 1985, Mr. Rotenberg found further success as the press coordinator for the re-election campaign of Donald Fraser, who had previously served as the mayor of Minneapolis between 1980 and 1984.

In recognition of his contributions to the University of Minnesota, Mr. Rotenberg was honored with a Certificate of Outstanding Service. He had previously been selected for the U.S. Attorney General's Special Commendation Award on behalf of the U.S. Department of Justice. In 2013, the former governor of Minnesota established "Mark Rotenberg Day" following Mr. Rotenberg's central role in the largest lawsuit involving a public university in the history of the U.S. higher education system.

In addition to the influence of his father, Mr. Rotenberg attributes a great deal of his success to the guidance of his former mentors and law professors at Columbia Law School. He is extremely proud to have displayed his exceptional litigation skills before the U.S. Supreme Court, the Minnesota Supreme Court and the U.S. Court of Appeals. In the coming years, Mr. Rotenberg intends to continue helping Jewish college students receive fair treatment from their peers through his position at Hillel International.

Jia Zhao

Principal (Retired)
Baker McKenzie

CHICAGO, IL UNITED STATES

For more than 20 years, Jia Zhao found success as a principal attorney and as a partner with Baker and McKenzie LLP. Prior to her retirement, she specialized in guiding large organizations from various industries through the myriad challenges of manufacturing, distributing and selling their products or services in foreign nations, particularly the People's Republic of China. Ms. Zhao also focused on helping her clients maintain compliance with regulations and sanctions in relation to international trade, specifically concerning product labeling, commercial contracts, promotional tactics and the importation and exportation of goods.

Between 1988 and 1994, Ms. Zhao served as a senior associate with Baker and McKenzie. She subsequently thrived as a partner at the aforementioned Chicago-based law firm between 1994 and 2012. Throughout the following five years, Ms. Zhao excelled as senior counsel at Baker and McKenzie before issuing her professional retirement in 2019.

Prior to her career with Baker and McKenzie, Ms. Zhao worked as a first secretary within the Department of Treaty and Law as well as the Department of American and Oceanic Affairs of the Ministry of Foreign Affairs of the People's Republic of China between 1984 and 1988. She had previously been recruited as a desk officer for the aforementioned Department of American and Oceanic Affairs between 1972 and 1980. Toward the end of this period, Ms. Zhao was simultaneously appointed as an interpreter for President Richard Nixon during the aforementioned former president's frequent visits to the People's Republic of China.

Alongside her primary responsibilities with the Ministry of Foreign Affairs of the People's Republic of China, Ms. Zhao also helped establish a legal practice that eventually fostered monumental international trade agreements between businesses based in the United States and the People's Republic of China. During her career with Baker and McKenzie, she simultaneously contributed to the Lurie Children's Hospital of Chicago Foundation as a board member between 1996 and 2019. In order to stay up to date with the latest developments in her field, Ms. Zhao continues to maintain active affiliations with the District of Columbia Bar, the Chicago Bar Association and the Illinois State Bar Association.

Born in Shanghai, Ms. Zhao obtained a Bachelor of Arts at Beijing Foreign Studies University in 1963. She subsequently worked as a teacher of English as a second language before her initial recruitment with the Ministry of Foreign Affairs of the People's Republic of China. Following her relocation to the United States in 1980, Ms. Zhao established her legal expertise while pursuing internships at multiple prominent law firms such as Paul, Weiss, Rifkind, Wharton and Garrison LLP, Baker and McKenzie, Pillsbury Winthrop Shaw Pittman LLP, Covington and Burling LLP and Arnold and Porter Kaye Scholer LLP. Toward the end of this period, she earned a Doctor of Jurisprudence at the Harvard Law School in 1983.

During her tenure with the Ministry of Foreign Affairs of the People's Republic of China, Ms. Zhao played an instrumental role in the establishment of a cooperative relationship between the United States and the People's Republic of China. She is also widely recognized among the first Chinese nationals to earn a Doctor of Jurisprudence in the United States. In recognition of her professional excellence, she has been included in the 76th edition of Who's Who in America. Since she did not initially anticipate her success as an attorney, Ms. Zhao advises aspiring attorneys to capitalize on sudden opportunities to advance their careers, particularly those that arise from unforeseen or inconvenient circumstances.

John D. Bowker

Director of Frequency Management (Retired)
The RCA Corporation

SUN CITY CENTER, FL UNITED STATES

F or more than 30 years, John D. Bowker found success within the RCA Corporation. Prior to his retirement, he played an instrumental role in the development of color television for mass consumption throughout the United States.

In 1953, Mr. Bowker accepted a position at RCA Laboratories, also known as David Sarnoff Research Center, in Princeton, New Jersey. He subsequently advanced to several leadership positions such as Director of Frequency Management while building his expertise under the tutelage of Raymond D. Kell, who is widely recognized as a pioneer of color television. During his tenure as Director of Frequency Management, Mr. Bowker regularly ensured the RCA Corporation's compliance with the U.S. Federal Communications Commission rules. He also served as the president of his local chapter of the Institute of Electrical and Electronics Engineers for one year.

Following his retirement from the RCA Corporation in 1987, Mr. Bowker found further success as an entrepreneur for a number of years. Throughout the 1990s, he traveled to all U.S. states while simultaneously composing and publishing a monthly column about AM radio stations in each U.S. state. During this period, Mr. Bowker identified and recorded the legal station identifications as broadcast by more than 4,000 U.S. AM radio stations.

Throughout the 2000s and the 2010s, Mr. Bowker also excelled as the founder of the Bowker eNEWS, a newsletter that accumulated more than 5,000 subscribers worldwide. Moreover, he additionally helped create an audiovisual book about the history of Sun City Center, which is a senior living community in Hillsborough County, Florida. Likewise, Mr. Bowker has contributed to the Sun City Center Men's Club, the Sun City Center Security Patrol, and, with his wife, volunteered for 20 years as nighttime dispatchers for the Sun City Center Emergency Ambulance Squad.

Mr. Bowker's interest in radio broadcasting emerged during his childhood when he uncovered his radio's ability to receive transmissions from dozens of cities throughout the United States and Canada. While attending high school in Princeton Junction, New Jersey, he helped create a radio station known as WWPH. In 1952, Mr. Bowker earned a Bachelor of Science in engineering physics from Middlebury College, where he simultaneously thrived as the founder of WRMC-FM, the radio station of the aforementioned Vermont-based institution.

In addition to the support of his wife, Mr. Bowker attributes a great deal of his success to the guidance of Raymond D. Kell, who was selected for the Stuart Ballantine Medal in 1948. In recognition of Mr. Bowker's contributions to Sun City Center, January 22nd was established as "John Bowker Day" in 2011 by the directors of the aforementioned senior living community. He has also been recognized for his achievements with inclusion in the 76th edition of Who's Who in America. In the coming years, he intends to further his involvement in the improvement of several services and facilities within Sun City Center while spending more time with his six grandchildren.

Alan G. Burghard Sr.

President & Owner
Reel Action Advisors Inc.

SEAL BEACH, CA UNITED STATES

Since 2015, Alan G. Burghard Sr. has thrived as the president and owner of Reel Action Advisors Inc. Widely renowned for his decades of military service, he specializes in educating actors, producers, screenwriters, and production crew members about realistic components of military training and combat tactics. Mr. Burghard also focuses on providing firearms training for actors and evaluating the accuracy of film and television storylines in relation to law enforcement or military operations.

In 2012, Mr. Burghard was recruited as a technical adviser for the television series "NCIS: Los Angeles." Throughout the following 10 years, he served in this capacity while frequently collaborating with producers, directors, and screenwriters to construct scenery and develop storylines for more than 200 episodes of the aforementioned television series. Mr. Burghard additionally participated in the composition of myriad scripts and dialogue sequences for "NCIS: Los Angeles" while continuously improving the series' sense of realism.

Toward the middle of his tenure with "NCIS: Los Angeles," Mr. Burghard simultaneously excelled as an actor in multiple episodes within the series' eighth, ninth and tenth seasons. During the COVID-19 pandemic, he was simultaneously appointed as a technical adviser for the television series "NCIS: Sydney" in a remote capacity. In 2023, Mr. Burghard advanced to the position of associate producer with "NCIS: Los Angeles" before shifting his attention toward Reel Action Advisors.

Alongside his responsibilities as a technical adviser, Mr. Burghard was featured in a documentary series concerning innovative treatments for traumatic brain injuries titled "Hyperbaric Miracles." In 2013, he contributed to a documentary film titled "Assaulted: Civil Rights Under Fire" as a technical adviser. Throughout his career, Mr. Burghard has also shared his technical expertise with aspiring filmmakers at Long Beach City College in Long Beach, California. In order to stay up to date with the latest developments in his field, he continues to maintain active affiliations with the Federal Law Enforcement Officers Association and the North Carolina Sheriffs' Association.

Born in Bay Shore, New York, Mr. Burghard served in the U.S. Marine Corps for more than 30 years. In 1979, he simultaneously earned a Bachelor of Arts in political science at Fairleigh Dickinson University. Mr. Burghard eventually concluded his education at Troy University, where he obtained a Master of Public Administration in 1989.

Toward the end of his tenure with the U.S. Armed Forces, Mr. Burghard advanced to the rank of lieutenant colonel and participated in the Iraq War as a commander before issuing his retirement from the military in 2007. Between 1984 and 2009, he simultaneously found further success as a special agent with the U.S. Naval Criminal Investigative Service. Mr. Burghard also worked as a stunt coordinator for numerous television series and films, including 1995's "The Feminine Touch."

In recognition of his military service, Mr. Burghard has been celebrated with numerous accolades, including a Bronze Star Medal and a Purple Heart. He is deeply honored to have safeguarded his entire military unit from severe harm during his participation in the Iraq War. Mr. Burghard is also proud of his recovery from a traumatic brain injury he sustained during his tenure with the U.S. Marine Corps. In 2017, "Hyperbaric Miracles" was selected for a Bronze Telly Award in the category of Non-Broadcast Production, General Health and Wellness.

In addition to an amicable and engaging personality, Mr. Burghard attributes a great deal of his success to his commitment to excellence. In the coming years, he intends to pursue a position as a technical consultant on another major television series. Mr. Burghard also aims to find further success as a consulting producer for a feature film.

Yancy L. Carrigan

On-Air Host & Music Director (Retired)
WESM

SALISBURY, MD UNITED STATES

For more than 30 years, Yancy L. Carrigan found success as a radio host with WESM, which is owned by the University of Maryland Eastern Shore. Prior to his retirement, he specialized in providing listeners with classic and contemporary music from a variety of genres, including jazz, R&B and blues. Mr. Carrigan also focused on managing a team of radio hosts, educating listeners about different recording artists and compiling daily playlists based on selections from hundreds of albums released by leading jazz and blues musicians.

In 1988, Mr. Carrigan began his career with WESM as a radio host in a volunteer capacity. He worked in this capacity for more than five years before accepting a position as a radio host in a part-time capacity with the aforementioned public radio station, which is an affiliate of National Public Radio, Public Radio Exchange, American Public Media and several other radio program providers. In 1997, Mr. Carrigan was appointed as a radio host with WESM in a full-time capacity.

Throughout the following 20 years, Mr. Carrigan served as the host of multiple radio shows on WESM, including "Blues Train," "Afternoon Jazz" and "Music from the Wax Museum," which features R&B music from the 1960s as well as the early 1990s. He also contributed to WESM as the music director between 1997 and 2020, at which point he issued his professional retirement. Between 2020 and 2022, Mr. Carrigan excelled as a radio host with WESM in a volunteer capacity. Alongside his primary responsibilities with WESM, he simultaneously found further success as a mobile disc jockey between 1990 and 2014.

Born in Salisbury, Maryland, Mr. Carrigan's decision to pursue a career as a radio host was chiefly inspired by his passion for jazz. During his childhood, he also accumulated a particularly large collection of records, which he frequently shared with his neighbors and classmates. In 1969, Mr. Carrigan earned a Bachelor of Business Administration at Morgan State University, formerly known as Morgan State College.

Prior to embarking on his professional path, Mr. Carrigan served in the U.S. Army between 1969 and 1973, during which period he gradually advanced to the rank of captain. He was subsequently recruited as a first-line supervisor with DuPont de Nemours, Inc., between 1973 and 1993. In order to stay up to date with the latest developments in the military community, Mr. Carrigan continues to maintain active affiliations with the Disabled American Veterans, the Veterans of Foreign Wars, the American Legion and the Military Order of the Purple Heart.

In recognition of his military service, Mr. Carrigan has been honored with a host of accolades on behalf of the U.S. Army. In 1972, he was celebrated with a Purple Heart. Thanks to his widespread reputation as a radio host, Mr. Carrigan has also been featured in multiple local newspapers and publications such as Delmarva Now, which is owned by Gannett Satellite Information Network, Inc.

In addition to his exceptionally patient approach to his work, Mr. Carrigan attributes a great deal of his success to his affinity for sharing his vast knowledge of music with younger generations. He is particularly proud to have been appointed as the host of "Music from the Wax Museum," which is widely recognized among WESM's most popular radio programs. In the coming years, Mr. Carrigan intends to continue enjoying his retirement while maintaining a healthy lifestyle.

Donald C. Clark Jr.

Co-Owner
Chicago Magic Lounge
GLENVIEW, IL UNITED STATES

S ince 2016, Donald C. Clark Jr. has thrived as the co-owner of the Chicago Magic Lounge, which is a nightlife venue featuring regular performances by renowned magicians and musicians in a sophisticated cabaret setting. In this capacity, he focuses on overseeing daily operations for the aforementioned venue and supervising a team of more than 20 in-house entertainers. Mr. Clark also specializes in recruiting guest performers from all over the world and promoting the Chicago Magic Lounge's unique blend of magic and entertainment on various digital marketing channels.

Alongside his primary responsibilities with the Chicago Magic Lounge, Mr. Clark simultaneously excelled as the acting president of the Chicago Theological Seminary between 2017 and 2018. He currently contributes to the aforementioned Christian seminary as the general counsel. For more than 20 years, Mr. Clark has additionally served as an advisory committee member for Hands of Peace, which facilitates educational interactions between children from the United States, Israel and Palestine. He has also contributed to the Adler Planetarium as a member of the board of trustees since 2006.

Prior to his appointment with the Chicago Magic Lounge, Mr. Clark was recruited as the general counsel as well as the nationwide special counsel for the United Church of Christ between 2001 and 2015. He had previously prospered as a founding partner of Clark and DeGrand, which has since closed, for more than 10 years after finding success as a litigation partner with McDermott Will and Emery during the late 1980s. Between 1979 and 1988, Mr. Clark established his legal expertise while working as a litigation partner for Isham, Lincoln and Beale, which has since closed.

During his tenure with the United Church of Christ, Mr. Clark simultaneously found further success as the chairperson of the board of trustees for the Chicago Theological Seminary between 2007 and 2013. Likewise, he had previously been recruited in this capacity for the Adler Planetarium during the early 2000s. Toward the end of his tenure with Clark and DeGrand, Mr. Clark accepted a position as the president of the Board of Education for West Northfield School District 31.

In 2021, Mr. Clark was appointed as an executive producer of a theatrical production titled "When Harry Met Rehab," which was performed at the Greenhouse Theater Center in Chicago, Illinois. He had previously served in this capacity for the feature film "Guest Artist" in 2019. Mr. Clark has since garnered further recognition as the author of "Summary Judgment," which recounts his central role in the reversal of a conviction for an alleged capital crime in Alabama.

Born in Petersburg, Virginia, Mr. Clark's decision to pursue a career as a lawyer was partially inspired by his father, who enjoyed his own prosperous career as a corporate attorney. In 1976, he earned a Bachelor of Arts in political economy at Williams College. Throughout the following three years, Mr. Clark completed a Doctor of Jurisprudence at Rutgers Law School.

In 2015, Mr. Clark was selected for the Arthur E. Armitage Senior Distinguished Alumni Award on behalf of Rutgers Law School. He had previously been celebrated with a Lifetime Achievement Award on behalf of Crain's Cleveland Business in 2014, at which point he was also honored with a Doctor of Letters on behalf of Chicago Theological Seminary. Following his designation as an Eagle Scout on behalf of the Boy Scouts of America, Mr. Clark was inducted into the aforementioned organization's Order of the Arrow in 1972.

In 2022, "When Harry Met Rehab" was selected for nomination for the Libby Adler Mages Award for New York at the Joseph Jefferson Awards for Equity. In addition to his family's support, Mr. Clark attributes a great deal of his success to his passion for storytelling. He is particularly proud to have harnessed his lauded communication skills to successfully argue the legalization of same sex marriage in the state of North Carolina. In the coming years, Mr. Clark intends to devote more attention toward the promotion of "When Harry Met Rehab," which will be performed at the Romulus Linney Courtyard Theatre at the Signature Center in New York City in 2024.

Renée S. Edelman

Senior Vice President
Edelman

NEW YORK, NY UNITED STATES

Drawing on more than 30 years of public relations experience, Renée S. Edelman has thrived as the senior vice president of special projects as well as an archivist at Edelman, which is part of J. Edelman Holdings, Inc., since 2021. In these capacities, she specializes in the recruitment of new employees from different ethnic backgrounds and furthering Edelman's reputation as an ardent proponent of diversity, equity and inclusion in the public relations sector. Ms. Edelman also focuses on maintaining close relationships with myriad news outlets and individual journalists in order to facilitate the favorable placement of content from various clients of the aforementioned public relations agency.

Prior to her appointment as the senior vice president of special projects, Ms. Edelman contributed to Edelman as the senior vice president of diversity and inclusion after serving as a senior media strategist for Edelman's technology accounts for more than 15 years. Between 1998 and 2003, she found further success as the executive vice president of the Zeno Group, which is part of J. Edelman Holdings. Ms. Edelman had previously worked in this capacity for Edelman's new media group between 1996 and 1998.

During the early 1990s, Ms. Edelman held numerous leadership positions with Edelman such as the senior vice president of technology accounts and the vice president of technology accounts. Between

1987 and 1989, she established her public relations expertise as an account supervisor in Edelman's new media group. Ms. Edelman had previously harnessed her communication skills to find success in the media industry. Between 1981 and 1985, she prospered as a reporter for the Central New Jersey Home News Tribune, which is owned by Gannet Co., Inc., after working as a news assistant for the New York Daily News, which is owned by the Tribune Publishing Company.

Alongside her primary professional responsibilities, Ms. Edelman has excelled as a board member at J. Edelman Holdings for more than 10 years. Likewise, she additionally serves in this capacity for the Museum of Public Relations in New York City and the Theater for the New City. Ms. Edelman had previously been appointed as a board member of the Children's Museum of Manhattan between 1994 and 2021. Moreover, she currently contributes to Phillips Exeter Academy in New Hampshire as a member of the Women's Leadership Council. For her professional excellence, she has been featured in the 76th edition of Who's Who in America.

Born in Chicago, Illinois, Ms. Edelman's decision to pursue a career in the public relations field was chiefly inspired by her father, Daniel Edelman, who established Edelman in 1952 and served as the chairperson for more than 60 years. In 1977, she obtained a Bachelor of Arts in English at Yale University. Throughout the following three years, Ms. Edelman completed her education at the Columbia University Graduate School of Journalism, earning a Master of Science in journalism.

An active affiliate of the Yale Club of New York City, Ms. Edelman attributes a great deal of her success to the mentorship of her parents, both of whom vehemently encouraged her to pursue her talent for creative writing. In the coming years, she intends to devote more attention to helping her younger colleagues build prosperous careers as public relations specialists. Since her vast knowledge of her industry has continuously played a central role in her professional growth, Ms. Edelman advises aspiring public relations executives to stay up to date with the latest public relations tools and techniques, particularly in relation to advanced technology.

Rory A. Palmieri

Translator

Reporter (Retired)

U.S. Department of Defense

BOWIE, MD UNITED STATES

With 40 years of expertise and certifications in seven languages, Rory A. Palmieri has set himself apart as an accomplished translator. He began his career as a student at Harvard University in Cambridge, Massachusetts, where he graduated magna cum laude with a Bachelor of Arts in English language and literature in 1976. While lecturing at Brown University in Providence, Rhode Island, from 1978 to 1983, Dr. Palmieri pursued a master's degree in English language and literature from Brown University, graduating in 1981. Shortly after, in 1984, he earned a Doctor of Philosophy in English language and literature, also from Brown University. Once he received his doctorate, Dr. Palmieri went to work as a translator and reporter for the U.S. Department of Defense in Washington, D.C., from 1985 to 1999. Since 1999, he has been self-employed as a translator.

Early on, Dr. Palmieri recognized his skill at learning languages, and he decided to pursue translation because of his interest in grammar, film and literature. Through a program in his high school, he learned French, going on to teach himself German and Latin. While pursuing his master's degree, he learned Old English. Subsequently, after he began working in the federal government, Dr. Palmieri found that he enjoyed having the freedom to move around departments and projects, and he realized the best way to have that opportunity was through learning another language. He has language expert certifications in Bulgarian, French, German, Modern Greek, Serbo-Croatian, Italian and Albanian, though he is proficient in nine languages and able to read 17. While working for the Department of Defense, he was trained in two languages, but the others he learned in his spare time. Previously, Dr. Palmieri was featured in the Marquis Who's Who Millennium Magazine, Marquis Who's Who Top Professionals, and the 76th edition of Who's Who in America. He is a member of the Modern Language Association (MLA).

Dr. Palmieri attributes his success to his passion for film and cinema, literature and language. An amateur filmmaker, Dr. Palmieri has made three films over the course of his life. His first, a short horror film, was broadcasted on a local TV station in Washington, D.C., during his senior year of high school. Additionally, in the 1990s, he compiled a team and filmed "The Poets from Planet X," a feature-length documentary about local bar Planet X's free-form poetry night. Afterward, he filmed a short comedy titled "Dick/Who." In the future, Dr. Palmieri plans to delve further into his interest in books and movies. He is working on a fiction book titled "Power and Revolution: Surveying and Tracking the Films of Miklós Jancsó," and hopes to see it published in the coming years.

Dr. Palmieri's advice for fellow or aspiring translators is to have a passion and pursue it, saying "You have to have a love for the work that you do to keep you motivated to do your best." Though Dr. Palmieri has struggled with his eyesight since 2002, he has not let that keep him from continuing to work. Currently, he is in the process of translating his fourth book and is teaching himself Hungarian.

Susan Hershberg Adelman, MD, FACS

Author & Artist

Pediatric Surgeon (Retired)

SOUTHFIELD, MI UNITED STATES

H aving distinguished herself across the span of more than three decades in the field of health care, Susan Hershberg Adelman, MD, FACS, hails from a multifaceted career path in medicine, artisanship and writing. Throughout the vast span of her professional journey, she served in private practice as a pediatric surgeon in the Detroit metropolitan area from 1971 until 2002, whereupon she retired. During this time, Dr. Adelman earned distinction for her impeccable leadership qualities, which saw her elected to numerous offices across the state, including as the first woman president of the Wayne County Medical Society and Michigan State Medical Society. Additionally, she held numerous roles within the American Medical Association (AMA), including as a member of the board of trustees and the Council of Medical Service, and as the president of the Henry Ford Hospital House Staff Association, the Organization of State Medical Association Presidents and the Detroit Academy of Medicine. Likewise dedicated to sharing her knowledge with others, she also served as a clinical associate professor of surgery at the University of Michigan for a time.

Throughout her career in health care, Dr. Adelman found success as the editor of the Detroit Medical News, a print publication, for over 15 years. She also wrote a popular column for AMNews for more than a decade. Well-regarded for her prolific scholarship in her area of expertise, she has written well-over 300 articles for journals, penned several scientific papers and contributed book chapters to works by her colleagues.

Having first aspired to become a geologist, Dr. Adelman studied the subject at the University of Michigan, from which she earned a Bachelor of Science in 1962. However, after heeding the suggestions of her husband, Martin, she reoriented toward the field of medicine. She pursued her studies at the Wayne State University School of Medicine, where she received a Doctor of Medicine in 1967. During this time, she helped co-found and ultimately chaired the Jeffries Community Health Center. Following her graduation, she undertook her internship and surgical residency at Henry Ford Hospital and later held a fellowship in pediatric surgery at the Children's Hospital of Michigan from 1972 until 1974. Well-qualified in her field, Dr. Adelman was certified by the American Board of Surgery and the American Board of Pediatric Surgery. She was licensed to practice in the state of Michigan.

Following her retirement from medical practice, Dr. Adelman pivoted her efforts toward the creation of art and silversmithing, and opened a small business, Hershberg Jewelry, to sell her paintings, sculptures and other crafts. Additionally, she has become a published author, having written "From Jerusalem to Delhi, through Persia," a meditation on the great attraction to India felt by Israelis and other Jews, as well as a meditation on her studies of the Hebrew, Arabic, Hindu and Buddhist philosophies, and the common themes tying those beliefs together. Other books written by Dr. Adelman include "After Saturday Comes Sunday," published in 2018, and "The Rebel: A Biography of Ram Jethmalani," released in 2014.

In accounting for her success, Dr. Adelman largely credits the love and support of both her parents and her husband, as well as the quality of her education and, ultimately, the providence of good luck in having been born in the United States, where she has had the opportunity to follow her dreams. As a testament to her professional achievements, Dr. Adelman has been included in the 76th edition of Who's Who in America. Looking toward the future, she aspires to continue writing for her blog and engage with the podcasting medium to reach a larger audience.

Karen M. Bussone

Nurse Practitioner (Retired)
OSF Saint Francis Medical Center

EAST PEORIA, IL UNITED STATES

For 40 years, Karen M. Bussone has served her community as a nurse practitioner. Ms. Bussone graduated in 1971 with a Bachelor of Arts in English education from Bradley University in Peoria, Illinois, going on to work as the assistant to the director at the University of Illinois School of Medicine Library in Peoria from 1972 to 1973 before becoming a teacher. Though she taught in the local school system for 10 years, she realized education was not the ideal place for her and sought a career with a larger scope of service. Having worked with homebound students, children with chronic conditions or long illness recovery times, she was inspired to pursue nursing and shortly after became a registered nurse in the state of Illinois, receiving an Associate of Science in nursing from Illinois Central College in East Peoria, Illinois, in 1983.

Ms. Bussone served her first nursing position in the medical-surgical unit of Saint Francis Medical Center, a teaching hospital in Peoria, working as a staff nurse from 1983 to 1988, when she moved to the hospital's critical care unit. In 1990, she became a critical care nurse at Saint Francis Medical Center, remaining in that capacity until 1998, when she graduated from the University of Illinois, Chicago, with a Master of Science in nursing.

In 1995, the Saint Francis Medical Center added the acronym OSF, representing the Order of Saint Francis, to the medical center's name.

At the rebranded OSF Saint Francis Medical Center, Ms. Bussone served as a nurse practitioner from 1998 until her retirement in 2022. She initially retired in 2018 but remained working for the hospital on an as-needed basis. Upon her official retirement in 2022, as she was walking down the hall of the hospital, a colleague took a picture of her and said, "And the legend leaves." Being a pioneer and the first adult nurse practitioner at OSF Saint Francis Medical Center was a significant accomplishment for Ms. Bussone, as she paved the way for more adult nurse practitioners to join the institution.

While Ms. Bussone spent many years with the OSF Saint Francis Medical Center, she also devoted her time to other hospitals and medical offices, working as a registered nurse in intensive care units, internal medicine offices, pulmonary offices and family practice clinics. In addition, she served as the assistant manager of the medical intensive care unit of a local hospital, attributing her years of success to her passion for helping others and her affinity for the profession.

A former member of the American College of Cardiology, the Society of Critical Care Medicine and the board of directors for the Moms Association at the University of Illinois, Ms. Bussone has demonstrated a passion for going above and beyond in her career. Further exemplifying this, she is a past president of her local chapter of the American Association of Critical Care Nurses.

Looking to the future, Ms. Bussone plans to enjoy her retirement and devote more time to her hobbies, which include playing the guitar, golf, traveling and spending time with her family, including her three granddaughters.

Patricia A.M. Cardillo, RN, LPN, LNC

Senior Registered Nurse
Rhode Island Hospital

JOHNSTON, RI UNITED STATES

F or more than 35 years, Patricia A.M. Cardillo, RN, LPN, LNC, has progressed as a senior registered nurse at Rhode Island Hospital. In her profession, she specializes in surgical services and frequently helps patients recover from life-threatening illnesses or injuries. Ms. Cardillo also oversees daily operations at Rhode Island Hospital's main operating room and advocates for patients requiring surgical intervention.

As an employee of Rhode Island Hospital, Ms. Cardillo held the positions of scrub technician, operating room nurse and operating room charge nurse. Prior to this period, Ms. Cardillo established her expertise in other areas, working in multiple departments, including psychiatric, telemetry, oncology and medical-surgical services, and she has also functioned as an OB-GYN office manager.

Throughout her career as a legal nurse consultant, Ms. Cardillo has been a consultant, working as a mediator between medical and legal professionals for cases involving medical malpractice. She assists attorneys with interpreting medical literature, medical records, hospital policies and surgical procedures. Ms. Cardillo has also helped numerous attorneys interview witnesses, assess damages and draft legal documents for medical cases.

Outside of her professional circles, Ms. Cardillo supports charitable organizations such as St. Jude Children's Research Hospital. She also contributes to the National Shrine of St. Jude in Chicago, Illinois. In order to stay up to date with the latest developments in her specialty areas, Ms. Cardillo continues to maintain an active affiliation with the Association of Operating Room Nurses.

A native of Rhode Island, Ms. Cardillo's decision to pursue a career in health care was chiefly inspired by her mother, who taught her the value of an exceptional work ethic at a young age. Her mother also showed her the critical roles that leadership and dedication can play in solving complex problems. After obtaining an associate degree from the Community College of Rhode Island, Ms. Cardillo earned a bachelor's degree in nursing and psychology from Rhode Island College.

Along with her firm dedication to her profession, Ms. Cardillo attributes a great deal of her success to her capacity to understand complex problems from the perspective of her patients. In the coming years, she intends to establish a legal nurse consulting service for health care providers. Since her genuine passion for her work has played an instrumental role in her professional growth, Ms. Cardillo advises aspiring nurses to prepare themselves to devote tremendous amounts of time and energy to the advancement of their careers. She also frequently encourages her younger colleagues to maintain their confidence in their own abilities while simultaneously heeding the guidance of their professors and supervisors. To commemorate her decades of excellence in nursing, Ms. Cardillo has been selected for inclusion in the 76th edition of Who's Who in America.

Kathryn G. Froiland-Deck

Oncology Nurse Educator (Retired)
GSK Oncology

HOUSTON, TX UNITED STATES

F or more than 40 years, Kathryn G. Froiland-Deck found success as a nurse as well as an educator for oncology nurses. Prior to her retirement, she specialized in helping fellow nurses understand how to provide effective patient care to patients with various forms of cancer. Ms. Froiland also focused on educating nurses about the physical and mental effects of cancer treatment, such as chemotherapy, and the importance of respecting the emotional needs of their patients and their families.

In 1979, Ms. Froiland was appointed as a staff nurse at M Health Fairview University of Minnesota. Throughout the 1980s, she gradually advanced to numerous leadership positions at the aforementioned Minneapolis-based hospital, such as charge nurse, station instructor and assistant head nurse. Between 1988 and 1989, Ms. Froiland excelled as an assistant head nurse at Methodist Hospital in St. Louis Park, Minnesota, before finding further success as a hospice nurse with the Mayo Foundation House in Rochester, Minnesota, between 1989 and 1991.

During the early 1990s, Ms. Froiland worked as a senior nursing instructor at the University of Texas MD Anderson Cancer Center. She subsequently accepted a position as a senior wound ostomy continence nurse at the aforementioned cancer center between 1995 and 2001, at which point she was promoted to director of the wound ostomy continence nurse education program. Between 2003 and 2015, Ms. Froiland thrived as an oncology clinical nurse educator with Tesaro/GSK Oncology, which is part of GSK plc. Throughout the following five years, she prospered as an oncology nurse educator with GSK Oncology before issuing her professional retirement in 2020.

Alongside her primary professional responsibilities, Ms. Froiland has contributed to the American Cancer Society in various volunteer capacities for more than 30 years. She currently devotes her volunteer time to her church, Zion Lutheran. Between 1995 and 2000, she served as the president and as a board member of the Houston chapter of the Oncology Nursing Society. In order to stay up to date with the latest developments in her field, Ms. Froiland-Deck maintains active affiliations with the Oncology Nursing Society, the Wound, Ostomy and Continence Nursing Society, and the Sigma Theta Tau International Honor Society of Nursing.

Prior to her recruitment at M Health Fairview University of Minnesota, Ms. Froiland-Deck earned a Bachelor of Science in nursing at St. Olaf College in Northfield, Minnesota. Her eventual decision to pursue a position as a nursing instructor was heavily inspired by her passion for helping her younger colleagues expand their professional skill sets. While working as a senior nursing instructor at the University of Texas MD Anderson Cancer Center, Ms. Froiland-Deck simultaneously completed a Master of Science in nursing at the Cizik School of Nursing at the University of Texas Health Science Center at Houston in 1994.

In 2002, Ms. Froiland-Deck was selected for a Distinguished Alumna Award on behalf of the Cizik School of Nursing at the University of Texas Health Science Center at Houston. She has also been included in the 76th edition of Who's Who in America and was honored as a Wound, Ostomy and Continence Nurse of the Year on behalf of the Wound, Ostomy and Continence Nursing Society. In addition to the support of her husband, Ms. Froiland-Deck attributes a great deal of her success to her mother, who taught her the importance of an exceptional work ethic at a young age. Since her close relationships with her colleagues and patients also played a central role in her professional growth, she advises that balance is essential. Making time for self-care activities to build resilience and maintain a positive attitude toward life's challenges will bring joy in the face of adversity.

Martha G. Garrett-Shaver, MD

Family Practice Physician
South Arkansas Family Care Center

MAGNOLIA, AR UNITED STATES

S ince 2018, Martha G. Garrett-Shaver, MD, has thrived as a family practice physician at the South Arkansas Family Care Center in El Dorado, Arkansas. With more than 20 years of health care experience to her credit, she specializes in family medicine and provides preventative care services to children, young adults and adults. Dr. Garrett-Shaver also regularly harnesses her expertise in obstetrics and gynecology to protect the health of expecting women and facilitate healthy childbirths.

Alongside her responsibilities at the South Arkansas Family Care Center, Dr. Garrett-Shaver currently serves as a family physician at South Arkansas Regional Hospital. She additionally supports numerous nonprofit organizations in relation to animal rescue and environmental conservation such as the National Wildlife Federation, Ocean Conservancy and Best Friends Animal Society. In order to stay up to date with the latest developments in her field, Dr. Garrett-Shaver continues to maintain an active affiliation with the American Academy of Family Physicians.

Born in Santa Monica, California, Dr. Garrett-Shaver initially began her professional career as a receptionist for a number of years. Fueled by her interest in science, she eventually pursued a formal education at Hendrix College, where she obtained a Bachelor of Arts in science in 1968. Dr. Garrett-Shaver subsequently accepted a position as a science teacher for middle school students before finding further success as a kindergarten teacher.

Following her success as an educator, Dr. Garrett-Shaver worked at a warehousing organization. She was subsequently recruited as a receptionist for an organization that provided a broad range of machinery for construction companies. Toward the late 1990s, Dr. Garrett-Shaver concluded her education at the University of Arkansas for Medical Sciences College of Medicine, where she earned a Doctor of Medicine in 2000. Throughout the following three years, she underwent residency training in family medicine at the University of Arkansas for Medical Sciences College of Medicine.

While completing the aforementioned residency, Dr. Garrett-Shaver delivered healthy newborns for myriad patients, which inspired her to develop her knowledge of obstetrics and gynecology. Her decision to pursue a career as a physician was also heavily influenced by her husband, who vehemently encouraged her to attend medical school and revisit her passion for science. Prior to her recruitment at the South Arkansas Family Care Center, Dr. Garrett-Shaver was appointed as the director of a residency program at the University of Arkansas for Medical Sciences College of Medicine.

In addition to her exceptional work ethic and her husband's support, Dr. Garrett-Shaver attributes a great deal of her success to her ability to form genuine relationships with her patients. She also draws tremendous inspiration from her father, who served in the U.S. Army as an air traffic control operator during World War II. Moreover, Dr. Garrett-Shaver is extremely proud to have completed her graduate degree while simultaneously caring for her two children.

In the coming years, Dr. Garrett-Shaver intends to continue serving her patients while devoting more time to her passions for scuba diving and animal rescue. Since her collaborative approach to her work has played a central role in the longevity of her career, she advises aspiring physicians to treat their colleagues with kindness and respect. Due to the increasing role of technology in the health care landscape, Dr. Garrett-Shaver also regularly encourages her younger colleagues to continue to prioritize patient care during their daily routines.

Dr. Shilpa N. Gowda

Physician
U.S. Department of Defense

LORTON, VA UNITED STATES

Between 2022 and 2023, Dr. Shilpa N. Gowda thrived as a physician with the Alexander T. Augusta Military Medical Center, which is owned by the U.S. Department of Defense (U.S. DoD). With more than 20 years of health care experience to her credit, she specializes in occupational medicine, and during her time with the U.S. DoD she regularly helped firefighters, police officers and members of the U.S. Armed Forces recover from severe injuries and illnesses. Dr. Gowda also focused on identifying unsafe working conditions and protecting her patients from excessive exposure to hazardous substances.

Prior to her recruitment at the Alexander T. Augusta Military Medical Center, Dr. Gowda excelled as the director of occupational employee health for the Veteran Affairs Southeast Louisiana Healthcare System between 2020 and 2022. She had previously worked as an attending physician at MaineGeneral Medical Center in Augusta, Maine. Between 2016 and 2017, Dr. Gowda prospered as a medical officer for the National Institute for Occupational Safety and Health in Cincinnati, Ohio.

Alongside her primary responsibilities as a physician, Dr. Gowda currently contributes to the American College of Occupational and Environmental Medicine (ACOEM) as a media representative of the environmental health section and as a member of an anti-racism task force. In 2023, she was part of the delegation from the ACOEM that went to Havana, Cuba, which was the first such delegation visit in approximately 30 years. During her tenure with the Veteran Affairs Southeast Louisiana Healthcare System, she simultaneously found further success as the education chairperson of the environmental medicine section of the American College of Occupational and Environmental Medicine. Dr. Gowda has also served as an adjunct professor at Tulane University. Between 2021 and 2022, the aforementioned Louisiana-based institution additionally recruited her as a consultant for the U.S. Department of Veterans Affairs.

Throughout her career, Dr. Gowda has contributed articles to multiple professional journals and publications, including the Journal of Occupational and Environmental Medicine, the Journal of Gastrointestinal Oncology and the World Journal of Surgery. Between 2018 and 2020, she was notably appointed as a board member and as a delegate for the New England chapter of the American College of Occupational and Environmental Medicine. Moreover, Dr. Gowda currently serves as a member of the planning committee of the American Occupational Health Conference, which is organized by the American College of Occupational and Environmental Medicine.

Born in Cincinnati, Ohio, Dr. Gowda's decision to pursue a career as a physician was chiefly inspired by her mother, who enjoyed her own prosperous career as an internist with the U.S. Department of Defense for more than 20 years. After obtaining a Bachelor of Science in neuroscience at Brown University in 2008, she earned a Doctor of Medicine at the aforementioned institution's Warren Alpert Medical School. Dr. Gowda subsequently underwent residency training in general surgery at Los Angeles General Medical Center between 2012 and 2013.

In 2014, Dr. Gowda completed an externship in general, tropical and occupational medicine at Bowring and Lady Curzon Hospital in Bangalore, India. Throughout the following two years, she pursued a fellowship in occupational and environmental medicine at the University of Washington's Department of Medicine. During this period, Dr. Gowda simultaneously obtained a Master of Public Health in environmental and occupational health sciences at the University of Washington School of Public Health.

In 2016, the University of Washington School of Public Health selected Dr. Gowda as the "Outstanding Master's Student of the Year." In 2023, she was awarded the "Top Occupational Medicine Physician of the Year" by the International Association of Top Professionals (IAOTP) at their annual gala in Manhattan. She attributes a great deal of her success to her persistence as well as her resilience and her ability to draw helpful insights from both positive and negative experiences. In the coming years, Dr. Gowda intends to further her involvement in charitable initiatives, particularly in relation to community health.

Alan C. Hartford, MD, PhD, FACR, FASTRO

Professor of Medicine
The Geisel School of Medicine at Dartmouth College

LYME, NH UNITED STATES

F or more than 20 years, Alan C. Hartford, MD, PhD, FACR, FAS-TRO, has thrived as an educator at the Geisel School of Medicine at Dartmouth College and as a physician and administrator at Dartmouth Hitchcock Medical Center. In the former capacity, he specializes in developing his students' knowledge of various forms of cancer, including brain, genitourinary, and head and neck cancers. Dr. Hartford also regularly harnesses his expertise in radiation oncology to hone his students' proficiency with the latest advancements in radiation therapy and other prevalent cancer treatments.

Between 2004 and 2010, Dr. Hartford began his career at Dartmouth College as an Assistant Professor of Medicine at the Geisel School of Medicine. Toward the middle of this period, he was simultaneously appointed as the Interim Chief of the Radiation Oncology Section at Dartmouth Hitchcock Medical Center, serving in that position for more than 10 years. Between 2010 and 2021, Dr. Hartford found further success as an Associate Professor of Medicine at the aforementioned medical institution, which promoted him to Professor of Medicine in 2021. Since 2016, he has additionally served as the Director of the Radiation Oncology Residency Program at Dartmouth Hitchcock Medical Center. An accomplished author, having published the novel First Days of August in 2015 under the pen name Alan Froning, he also teaches writing and literature at the Geisel School of Medicine.

Alongside his responsibilities as a professor and program director, Dr. Hartford excels as the current president of CARROS, the American College of Radiology's Council of Affiliated Regional Radiation Oncology Societies. Since 2015, he has also contributed to the Norris Cotton Cancer Center at Dartmouth Hitchcock Medical Center as the chairperson of the quality improvement committee for clinical cancer research. In order to stay up to date with the latest developments in his field, Dr. Hartford continues to maintain active affiliations with the American Society for Radiation Oncology, the American College of Radiology, the Radiological Society of North America, the New Hampshire Medical Society, the Vermont Medical Society, the Massachusetts Medical Society and the American Medical Association.

Throughout his career, Dr. Hartford has served as a principal investigator at Dartmouth of myriad clinical trials for the Radiation Therapy Oncology Group. Likewise, he has contributed articles to multiple professional journals and publications, including the International Journal of Radiation Oncology and Radiotherapy and Oncology. Since 2020, he has served as an Associate Editor of the journal Practical Radiation Oncology. Moreover, Dr. Hartford was appointed Chairperson of the American College of Radiology's Committee on Practical Parameters and Technical Standards between 2012 and 2019.

Born in Berkeley, California, Dr. Hartford obtained a Bachelor of Science in biological sciences, with distinction, as well as a Master of Arts in philosophy at Stanford University in 1983. Following a year of touring with the international goodwill organization Up With People in 1984, he resumed his education at Harvard Medical School, where he completed a Doctor of Medicine before pursuing a medical internship at Beth Israel Deaconess Hospital. Dr. Hartford subsequently underwent residency training and completed a fellowship in radiation oncology at Massachusetts General Hospital between 1993 and 1998.

Simultaneously, in 1997, Dr. Hartford earned a Doctor of Philosophy in political economy and government at the Harvard University John F. Kennedy School of Government. Between 1994 and 1998, he worked as a lecturer for medical students, medical residents and participants of various fellowship programs at Harvard Medical School. During this period, Dr. Hartford also contributed to Harvard Medical School as a member of its Admissions Committee.

In recognition of his contributions to the Geisel School of Medicine, Dr. Hartford has been honored with numerous accolades in relation to excellence in teaching and administrative leadership. A fellow of the American College of Radiology and of the American Society for Radiation Oncology, he has been included in New Hampshire Magazine's list of New Hampshire's Top Doctors on more than eight occasions and was featured in the 76th edition of Who's Who in America. Dr. Hartford has additionally been distinguished among America's Top Doctors on behalf of Castle Connolly for more than 10 consecutive years.

Maya D. Hennessey

Independent Consultant

SUN CITY, AZ UNITED STATES

Maya D. Hennessey began her career in behavioral health 45 years ago by advocating for gender-sensitive treatment approaches to improve outcomes for addicted women and their families. She provided hundreds of workshops on vital approaches to restore healthy families ravaged by the debilitating effects of oppression, poverty, trauma and addiction.

In the 1980s, Ms. Hennessey became a patient advocate for rape victims, supporting traumatized women through the rape kit collection and interviews by medical staff and police. She participated in a year-long lay ministry training and became an on-call chaplain. She also received certifications in neuro-linguistic programming, family systems and group dynamics.

Throughout her professional career, Ms. Hennessey developed cross-training and inter-agency collaboration to help leaders and stakeholders enact policies and approaches to restore healthy families. She created interactive skill-building exercises to train professionals on the impact of the combined issues of addiction, trauma, poverty, child abuse, sexual assault and domestic violence. As a contractual consultant for the Substance Abuse and Mental Health Services Administration's (SAMHSA) Center for Substance Abuse Treatment (CSAT), Ms. Hennessey cross-trained state directors of substance abuse and child welfare across the nation on Project SAFE, a successful Illinois evidence-based model.

From 1992 to 2004, Ms. Hennessey was notably employed by the Illinois Department of Human Services (IDHS), Division of Alcoholism and Substance Abuse (DASA), as the women's specialist. She continued to enhance and expand Project SAFE sites across Illinois. During her distinguished tenure, she was appointed to serve on numerous policy advisory, advocacy and workgroups, including the Illinois governor's forums and advisory councils, as well as two of former First Lady Hillary Clinton's subcommittees on addicted women and families. As the women's specialist, Ms. Hennessey served on the Illinois child welfare and substance abuse advisory council. She collaborated with Cook County Courts, the Family Justice Leadership Institute, the Illinois Coalition Against Domestic Violence and the Chicago City Council Subcommittee on Domestic Violence. She served as a coordinator of volunteers for the Midwestern states for the National Family Caregivers Association and served on Chicago Mayor Daley's Caregivers Advisory Council.

Ms. Hennessey wrote a book titled "If Only I'd Had This Caregiving Book," a guide to help family caregivers establish effective networks of support for both the caregiver and the patient. She also authored articles on women and addiction. She and William L. White co-authored an article on females driving under the influence of alcohol.

An alumnus of Northeastern Illinois University, in 1984, Ms. Hennessey earned a bachelor's degree in behavioral health, business, management and theology. As a professional member of the Illinois Alcohol and Drug Dependence Association (IADDA), she chaired the first women's issues committee of IADDA. She taught courses at Governors State University discussing such topics as women across the life cycle, infant mortality and addicted seniors. She and Project SAFE were featured in the 1999 PBS TV series on addiction titled "Close to Home" by Bill Moyers. She was recognized in 1991 with the Keith Keisey Award and has been featured in the 76th edition of Who's Who in America. In 2010, at the National SAMHSA Women's Conference, the Illinois Women's Advisory Council awarded Ms. Hennessey for her progressive advancement of gender-competent women's services. Moreover, she was named among the "women making a difference in the field of addiction" by Counselor Magazine in 2004. She continues to advocate for gender equality for women.

John Carroll Kennedy, MD

Pediatrician

Pediatrics in Brevard

ROCKLEDGE, FL UNITED STATES

For more than 20 years, John Carroll Kennedy, MD, has thrived as a pediatrician with Pediatrics in Brevard in Rockledge, Florida. With more than three decades of pediatric experience, he specializes in providing primary care services to infants, young children, adolescents and young adults. Dr. Kennedy also oversees clinical research and educates his patients about healthy lifestyle choices.

Prior to his recruitment with Pediatrics in Brevard, Dr. Kennedy excelled as a pediatrician at his former private practice in Ann Arbor, Michigan, between 1987 and 2000. During this period, he continuously broadened his professional skill set while collaborating with specialists from various branches of medicine such as obstetrics, gynecology and anesthesiology. Dr. Kennedy subsequently relocated to Florida, where he played an instrumental role in Pediatrics in Brevard's expansion to one of the largest pediatric practices in Central Florida.

Alongside his responsibilities as a pediatrician, Dr. Kennedy stays up to date with the latest developments in his field by maintaining active affiliations with several professional organizations, including the American Medical Association, the Florida Medical Association, the Central Florida Pediatric Society and the Brevard County Medical Society. He also frequently serves as a co-chief executive officer of Pediatrics in Brevard. In 2020, Dr. Kennedy harnessed his business acumen to help Pediatrics in Brevard secure a partnership with Privia Health, which is owned by the Brighton Health Group.

Dr. Kennedy's decision to pursue a career as a pediatrician was chiefly inspired by his fascination with science and his passion for helping others. He also wished to improve his capacity to care for his mother, who had developed a critical health condition following his father's death. Moreover, Dr. Kennedy was additionally influenced by the turbulent economy of the early 1970s, which showed him the importance of professional stability.

In 1976, Dr. Kennedy earned a Bachelor of Science at Furman University in Greenville, South Carolina. He subsequently obtained a Master of Science in immunology and parasitology from the University of Florida. Throughout the following five years, Dr. Kennedy completed a Doctor of Medicine at the University of Miami Leonard M. Miller School of Medicine. Between 1984 and 1987, he underwent residency training at Cincinnati Children's Hospital Medical Center.

Throughout his career, Dr. Kennedy has been selected for induction in multiple medical and academic honor societies, including Alpha Omega Alpha Honor Medical Society, the Phi Beta Kappa Society and the Honor Society of Phi Kappa Phi. He has also been distinguished as a fellow of the American Academy of Pediatrics. In addition to the support of his family and his genuine passion for helping children, Dr. Kennedy attributes a great deal of his success to his ability to withstand the heavy physical toll of his profession. While completing his medical degree, he engaged in intense physical training to prepare his mind and body for the lengthy shifts and rigorous testing of medical residency programs.

In the coming years, Dr. Kennedy aims to spend more time with his two children while preparing for his eventual retirement. He also intends to pursue further success as a virtual pediatrician in a part-time capacity. Since his exceptional interpersonal skills have continuously contributed to his professional growth, Dr. Kennedy advises aspiring pediatricians to develop their own methodologies for facilitating productive interactions with their colleagues, patients and employees.

Gary King

Substance Abuse Program Manager
Specialty Counseling and Consulting LLC

CHEYENNE, WY UNITED STATES

Since 2015, Gary King has thrived as a licensed addiction counselor with Specialty Counseling and Consulting LLC. With more than 20 years of mental health counseling experience to his credit, he focuses on helping adolescents, adults and prison inmates of various ages overcome addictions to a broad range of substances. Mr. King also regularly provides educational training to fellow addiction counselors and serves as a mentor to his younger colleagues.

Prior to his recruitment at Specialty Counseling and Consulting, Mr. King excelled as a mental health counselor with Southwest Wyoming Recovery Access Programs (SW-WRAP) between 2012 and 2015. He had previously worked in this capacity with Capstone Recovery Program LLC in Laramie, Wyoming, for more than five years. Alongside his responsibilities as an addiction counselor, Mr. King has found further success as the manager of the substance program at Specialty Counseling and Consulting since 2018.

Born in Telemac, Oregon, Mr. King enjoyed a prosperous career in the oil and gas industry in his home state of Wyoming over the course of several decades. During this period, he developed addictions to a variety of substances and completed numerous substance treatment programs. Mr. King's eventual recovery inspired him to pursue a second career as a mental health professional.

In 2003, Mr. King earned an Associate of Arts with a focus on psychology from Western Wyoming Community College in Rock Springs,

Wyoming. Toward the beginning of this period, he was simultaneously appointed as a residential staff member of Southwest Counseling Services' substance abuse service. Mr. King subsequently obtained a Bachelor of Science in psychology and a Bachelor of Science in gender and women's studies at the University of Wyoming in 2006.

Following these accomplishments, Mr. King was recruited as a seminar group facilitator at the University of Wyoming's Summer High School Institute between 2006 and 2011. During this period, he simultaneously earned a Master of Science in counseling with a focus in community counseling at the University of Wyoming School of Counseling, Leadership, Advocacy and Design. In 2011, Mr. King also completed the necessary provisional training to become a licensed professional counselor.

In order to stay up to date with the latest developments in his field, Mr. King has maintained an active affiliation with the American Society of Addiction Medicine since 2015. In addition to his passion for helping others, he attributes a great deal of his success to his extensive experience with addiction, which persisted for more than 25 years. During the early stages of his career as a mental health counselor, Mr. King worked alongside multiple substance abuse counselors who had previously guided him through his own recovery.

In the coming years, Mr. King intends to continue treating his patients while sharing his wealth of knowledge with his colleagues at Specialty Counseling and Consulting. Due to his tremendous respect and admiration for the work of addiction counselors, he is extremely proud to have helped elevate the careers of many former colleagues. In his spare time, Mr. King relaxes by exploring the geology of his natural environment and expanding his collection of local rocks. Since his empathic approach to his work has played a central role in the longevity of his career, he advises aspiring addiction counselors to speak to their patients with kindness and compassion, rather than becoming frustrated by the severity of their mental struggles.

Gail L. Lamoureux, BS, RN, PMH-BC

Care Manager
Humana Inc.

LARGO, FL UNITED STATES

For more than 10 years, Gail L. Lamoureux, BS, RN, PMH-BC, has thrived as a care manager for Humana Inc. With more than 40 years of health care experience to her credit, she specializes in collaborating with health care providers and caregivers to create personalized long-term health care treatment plans for elderly individuals. Ms. Lamoureux also focuses on understanding each patient's unique needs and preferences, maximizing the value of home health care, and educating seniors about medications and healthy lifestyle choices.

Prior to her recruitment at Humana in 2009, Ms. Lamoureux excelled as a nurse aide for a number of years. During this period, she frequently assisted elderly patients with daily activities while monitoring their health and keeping nurses up to date with each patient's well-being. Ms. Lamoureux had previously found success as a behavioral psychiatric mental health nurse and as a gerontological nurse, during which period she honed her expertise in helping elderly individuals adapt to the physical and mental effects of aging.

Alongside her responsibilities as a care manager, Ms. Lamoureux simultaneously serves as a clown in a part-time volunteer capacity. She also regularly harnesses her comedic prowess to entertain her patients at Humana and help patients with debilitating illnesses access the myriad health benefits of laughter. Moreover, Ms. Lamoureux has participated in several nationwide and regional events in relation to clowning such as the annual Southeast Clown Convention, which is organized by the South East Clown Association (SECA).

During the COVID-19 pandemic, Ms. Lamoureux delivered meals and other essential resources to elderly residents of her local community of Largo, Florida. She additionally provided meals for impoverished families. Channeling her vast experience with home health care, Ms. Lamoureux assisted many elderly members of her community in coordinating appointments with different health care specialists and seeking mental health counseling services during this period.

Born in Warwick, Rhode Island, Ms. Lamoureux's decision to pursue a career in health care was heavily inspired by her sister, who continues to enjoy her own prosperous career as a cardiac nurse. Likewise, her stepsister currently contributes to the Children's Hospital of Philadelphia in multiple capacities. In 1981, Ms. Lamoureux earned an associate degree in nursing. She subsequently completed a bachelor's degree in health care leadership.

Widely renowned for her unique brand of humor, Ms. Lamoureux has previously garnered recognition for her performances in several talent competitions at the Southeast Clown Convention. In addition to the guidance of her mentors, she attributes a great deal of her success to her ability to forge close relationships with her patients. Ms. Lamoureux is particularly proud to have helped one female patient overcome a severe case of agoraphobia to rekindle her passion for ballroom dancing and visit her daughters while they attended college.

In the coming years, Ms. Lamoureux intends to continue serving her patients at Humana while helping her patients overcome depression, anxiety and other mental health conditions without the use of pharmaceutical medications. She also aims to further her involvement in the South East Clown Association, particularly in relation to designing costumes and developing scripts for performances. Since her genuine passion for home health care has played an instrumental role in her professional growth, Ms. Lamoureux advises aspiring health care workers to pursue an area of health care that aligns with their personal interests and goals. In her spare time, she relaxes by composing scrapbooks to preserve fond memories of her loved ones.

Linda Sue Whisnant Malone, RN, BS, CPHQ, LNC

Director of Performance Improvement
NextMed Lithotripsy LLC

OAK ISLAND, NC UNITED STATES

Drawing on more than five decades of experience in her chosen field, Linda Sue Whisnant Malone, RN, BS, CPHQ, LNC, has earned distinction through her work as a health care professional. In addition to her service as the director of performance at NextMed Lithotripsy LLC, she has found success as a director at both Lithotripter's Inc. and the Highsmith-Rainey Specialty Hospital since 1992. In all of her roles, Ms. Malone is primarily responsible for assuring a high level of care on behalf of patients and assessing staff performance.

Prior to her current endeavors, Ms. Malone served in various roles throughout the health care industry. To wit, she functioned as the president of a paramedic service in Fayetteville, North Carolina, from 1982 until 1995. She also worked for more than a decade at the Cape Fear Valley Medical Center, where she rose from the level of a staff nurse in 1975 to the director of quality assurance in 1985. Previously, she had worked as a private duty nurse in New Jersey and as a nurse at the Heilbronn Elementary School in Germany from 1967 until 1968. In 2007, she was the director of nursing for the Wilson Health Department in Wilson, North Carolina.

Likewise dedicated to education, Ms. Malone has parlayed her knowledge of the field to students as a legal nurse consultant and lecturer on the subject of quality assessment and performance improvement. Moreover, she maintained involvement in 1995 as an instructor and health occupations judge at Fayetteville Technical Community College and as a nurse at the local Westover Middle School in 1979. An allied member of the American Lithotripsy Society from 1994 to 2004, she chaired the membership committee from 1995 to 1997 and the standards of care committee from 1995 to 2000. She further contributed to the North Carolina Quality Assurance Professionals as president from 1988 to 1989, the North Carolina chapter of the American Society for Healthcare Risk Management, and the North Carolina State Nurses Association.

Before venturing onto her vocational path, Ms. Malone sought a formal education at the Presbyterian Hospital School of Nursing, now the Novant Health Presbyterian Medical Center, from which she earned a diploma in nursing, with honors, in 1965. She later served her alma mater as the Sandhills alumni president in 1989. Earlier, she had graduated with honors from Crest High School in 1962 and been recognized by the SECAS Honor Society from 1962 to 1965 and the Beta Club Honor Society from 1960 to 1962. More than two decades later, Ms. Malone went on to obtain a Bachelor of Science from St. Joseph's College in 1986.

Well qualified in her field, Ms. Malone has been registered as a nurse in the states of Hawaii, New Jersey and North Carolina. Furthering her expertise, she is additionally certified as a professional in health care quality and received an EDAP certificate in training for prostatherpies in 1997. At the University of North Carolina at Chapel Hill, Ms. Malone achieved licensure as a legal nurse consultant and certificates in part one and part two infection control. She is the owner of Cape Fear Medical-Legal Consultant, LLC.

Among her most cherished accomplishments, Ms. Malone is simply proud to have saved the lives of so many patients, including that of young children. She is also gratified to have worked extensively with a variety of young mothers, many of whom went on to remain in contact long after she taught them how to care for their children. For her excellence, she has been featured in four editions of Who's Who of American Women, the fifth edition of Who's Who in American Nursing and the first edition of Who's Who of Emerging Leaders in America. In accounting for her success, Ms. Malone credits the words of her English teacher, "Nothing learned is ever lost." 🌿🌿

Rose C. Maly, MD, MSPH, FAAFP

Professor Emerita of Family Medicine
David Geffen School of Medicine
University of California, Los Angeles

LOS ANGELES, CA UNITED STATES

With nearly 50 years of experience to her name, Rose C. Maly, MD, MSPH, FAAFP, has demonstrated remarkable contributions to the fields of education and health care. After finishing her undergraduate schooling, Dr. Maly attended the University of California, Los Angeles School of Public Health, graduating with a Master of Science in public health. In 1976, she received a Doctor of Medicine from the University of California, Irvine, going on to complete a residency in family medicine at the University of California, Los Angeles (UCLA) David Geffen School of Medicine in 1979 and again in 1986. She became a geriatric medicine fellow with the David Geffen School of Medicine in 1994. Since 1994, she has taught at the David Geffen School of Medicine, first as an assistant professor and then as a full professor. For her service and contributions to the university, she was named professor emeritus.

Dr. Maly attributes her academic accomplishments to her mother's unwavering belief in the value of education for women. A refugee from communist Czechoslovakia and former German teacher, Dr. Maly's mother supported her intellectual growth from an early age. This support facilitated Dr. Maly's premature advancement in grade levels and encouraged her to pursue academic challenges. While in the first grade, her mother arranged for her to advance to the second grade based on her intellectual aptitude. Upon arriving on the first day of second grade, she was asked to undergo an IQ test, and following the test, she was promoted to the third grade. Dr. Maly is grateful for her mother's efforts, which she believes played a critical role in her ability to achieve her doctorate.

For her achievements, Dr. Maly has gained many accolades, including advancing to the position of George F. Kneller Chair in family medicine at the UCLA David Geffen School of Medicine and receiving a CMS Meaningful Use Stage 1 Certification. She is a fellow of the American Academy of Family Physicians and a member of the American Geriatrics Society.

Throughout her career, Dr. Maly has consistently emphasized the importance of the doctor-patient relationship, with a focus on empowering patients. Recognizing the inherent inequality in this relationship, she has sought to enable patients to communicate more effectively with their physicians. One of her earliest studies involved validating an instrument known as "patient-physician interactions," which has since been published and translated into multiple languages, including German, Dutch and Chinese. Attesting to its impact, the article has been cited over 300 times.

Although retired, Dr. Maly remains actively involved in the academic community at the UCLA David Geffen School of Medicine. She participates in faculty meetings and engages with residents and faculty members through meaningful conversations. Additionally, she provides mentorship to a select group of faculty members seeking to further their professional development.

Thakor G. Patel, MD, MACP, FRCP

Chairman
The Sevak Foundation Inc.

Chief Executive Officer
Russ & Associates LLC

FAIRFAX STATION, VA UNITED STATES

F or more than 10 years, Thakor G. Patel, MD, MACP, FRCP, has thrived as the chairman of the Sevak Project, Inc., which provides a broad range of essential health care and sanitation services to rural communities all over the world. With more than four decades of health care experience to his credit, he focuses on creating fundraising initiatives and forging close partnerships with donors. Dr. Patel also specializes in developing new methodologies for training residents of the aforementioned communities to identify symptoms of prevalent illnesses amongst fellow residents.

Alongside his responsibilities with the Sevak Project, Dr. Patel currently excels as the chief executive officer of Russ & Associates, LLC, and as an adjunct associate professor of medicine at Uniformed Services University of the Health Sciences in Bethesda, Maryland. He had previously contributed to the Department of Veteran Affairs as the director of numerous programs in relation to renal diseases, diabetes, gastrointestinal diseases, immunology and oncology. Dr. Patel has additionally held multiple leadership positions at Naval Medical Center Portsmouth such as the director of a nephrology fellowship program, the chairman of graduate medical education and the chief of medical staff.

Prior to his recruitment with the Department of Veteran Affairs, Dr. Patel served in the Medical Corps of the U.S. Navy between 1976 and 1998, during which period he advanced to the rank of captain. Between 1993 and 2016, he found further success as a staff nephrologist at Walter Reed National Military Medical Center. Toward the beginning of this period, Dr. Patel played a central role in the establishment of the Surface Warfare Medical Institute, which provides health care education and professional training to members of the U.S. Navy.

After obtaining a Bachelor of Medicine, Bachelor of Surgery from Baroda Medical College in Vadodara, India, Dr. Patel relocated to the United States, where he completed an internship in nephrology at the State University of New York Downstate Health Sciences University. In 1976, he pursued a fellowship in nephrology at the aforementioned New York-based medical institution. Dr. Patel subsequently furthered his medical expertise while serving as an internist and as a staff nephrologist in the U.S. Navy.

In 2002, Dr. Patel was honored with a Presidential Award and a "Friend of Friends" Award on behalf of the American Association of Physicians of Indian Origin. He has also been celebrated with a host of accolades in recognition of his military service, including a Legion of Merit, a Meritorious Service Medal, a Navy Commendation Medal, a Southwest Asia Service Medal and a Kuwait Liberation Medal. Moreover, Dr. Patel was selected for an Admiral Joel T. Boone Award on behalf of the Association of Military Surgeons of the United States in 1989.

A fellow of the Royal College of Physicians, Inc., Dr. Patel was notably distinguished as a Master of the American College of Physicians, Inc. He is incredibly proud to be the first veteran of the U.S. Navy to have been honored with the aforementioned accolade. In addition to the influence of his parents, Dr. Patel attributes a great deal of his success to his decades of service in the U.S. Navy and his extensive tenure with the Department of Veteran Affairs. Since his entrepreneurial personality has repeatedly contributed to his professional growth, he advises aspiring physicians to continuously hone their leadership skills throughout their careers.

Maria Magdalena B. Rabago, RN, BSN, BSMT, MA

Founder
Manawa Lea Health Services Inc.

AIEA, HI UNITED STATES

For nearly five decades, Maria Magdalena B. Rabago, RN, BSN, BSMT, MA, has committed herself to health care and administration. After receiving a Bachelor of Science in nursing and a Bachelor of Science in medical technology, Ms. Rabago attended Central Michigan University in Mount Pleasant, Michigan, earning a master's degree in management, supervision and health care administration in 1984. Currently, she is in the process of receiving a doctorate.

Coming from a long line of successful and hardworking individuals, Ms. Rabago draws inspiration from her mother and grandmother, both successful entrepreneurs in their home country of the Philippines. In 1927, Ms. Rabago's grandfather immigrated to the United States and worked at Pearl Harbor in Hawaii. Continuing a legacy of industriousness, Ms. Rabago founded Manawa Lea House Services Inc., a home health care service company, in 1997. As the eldest child in her family, she helped her mother, a single parent, take care of her four siblings and, as a result, developed principles of empathy and responsibility. Since childhood, she has been working to improve the lives of others, a desire that manifested in the founding of Manawa Lea. Ms. Rabago first became involved in her profession out of a desire to care for disabled children, but she has also worked in homes for the elderly and mentally ill.

In 1983, Ms. Rabago received the Rising Young American Award, the first of many awards, including the Albert Nelson Marquis Lifetime Achievement Award and a feature in Who's Who of Professional Women. For her accomplishments in health care, Ms. Rabago was invited to attend a White House dinner with President George W. Bush in 2004. After traveling to Washington D.C., she and her family toured Europe to celebrate her and her husband's 25th wedding anniversary. Ms. Rabago's husband, Aurelio Jr., is a retired U. S. Navy veteran who operates a farm in Hawaii, and their three children have also found success in medicine and administration. She remains close with her younger siblings, who live in San Diego, California.

In the future, Ms. Rabago hopes to take a step back from the business and is looking forward to retiring when she finds the right person to continue her work at Manawa Lea and uphold her legacy. Education is important to Ms. Rabago, and she hopes to continue helping others by providing scholarships through her company, but her greatest goal in retirement is to spend more time with her family and attend to her health. In recognition of her exceptional professional achievements, she has been featured in the 76th edition of Who's Who in America.

Ernest S. Reeh, DDS, MS, PhD

Owner & Dentist

River Valley Endodontics

STILLWATER, MN UNITED STATES

For more than 30 years, Ernest S. Reeh, DDS, MS, PhD, has thrived as a dentist and as the owner of River Valley Endodontics in Stillwater, Minnesota. In this capacity, he specializes in diagnosing, preventing, and treating various diseases affecting dental pulp. Dr. Reeh also focuses on creating a relaxing environment for his patients and providing actionable advice about improving their oral health.

Alongside his responsibilities at River Valley Endodontics, Dr. Reeh currently serves as a consultant for the dental division of 3M as well as Carestream Dental, which is owned by Onex Corporation. He previously found further success as a faculty member at the University of Minnesota School of Dentistry. In order to stay up to date with the latest developments in his field, Dr. Reeh additionally maintains active affiliations with the American Association of Endodontists and the American Board of Endodontics.

Throughout his career, Dr. Reeh has contributed articles to numerous professional journals and publications, including the Journal of Endodontics, the Journal of Prosthetic Dentistry, and Biochemical and Biophysical Research Communications. Likewise, he has shared his expertise at academic institutions, industry conferences and symposiums all over the world. Dr. Reeh has also garnered widespread recognition as the owner of two patents in relation to innovative dental technology.

Dr. Reeh's decision to pursue a career in dentistry was heavily inspired by the exceptional dexterity he developed while repairing watches, model cars and airplanes throughout his childhood. After obtaining a Bachelor of Science in chemistry with a minor in business from the University of Calgary, he earned a Doctor of Dental Surgery at the University of Alberta Faculty of Medicine and Dentistry. Dr. Reeh subsequently began his dental career as a general dentist in Edmonton, Alberta, Canada.

While working as a general dentist, Dr. Reeh simultaneously underwent additional training in endodontics at the University of Minnesota School of Dentistry. Following the establishment of River Valley Endodontics in 1987, he resumed his education at the aforementioned Minneapolis-based institution, where he earned a Master of Science in material science. In 1993, Dr. Reeh concluded his education with a Doctor of Philosophy in biophysics and a minor in engineering at the University of Minnesota College of Biological Sciences.

Upon completing a Doctor of Dental Surgery, Dr. Reeh was selected for the James McCutcheon Honor Award on behalf of the University of Alberta Faculty of Medicine and Dentistry. He has also been honored with several accolades for his master's thesis, which has been cited in the research of myriad fellow dentists. A fellow of the American Association of Endodontists, Dr. Reeh has previously been distinguished as a "Top Dentist" in the endodontics category on behalf of Mpls. St. Paul Magazine. He has also been selected for inclusion in the 76th edition of Who's Who in America.

Dr. Reeh attributes a great deal of his success to his persistence, which enabled him to complete his dental degree despite the lack of support he received from certain professors. In the coming years, he intends to continue serving his patients while furthering his research efforts and pursuing a position as an educator in a part-time capacity. Since the continuous expansion of his professional skill set has played an instrumental role in the longevity of his career, Dr. Reeh vehemently advises aspiring dentists to anticipate significant industry-wide changes by consistently familiarizing themselves with the most advanced dental tools, techniques and research.

Julia Davis Rhodes, RN

Team Leader (Retired)
Piedmont Physicians Neurosurgery Athens

ATHENS, GA UNITED STATES

For more than 35 years, Julia Davis Rhodes, RN, found success as a surgical nurse at multiple health care organizations across her home state of Georgia. Prior to her retirement, she specialized in assisting physicians during surgical procedures and providing them with the necessary equipment for each operation. Ms. Rhodes also focused on creating a calm and orderly working environment for her colleagues and maintaining her team's access to the most up-to-date medical equipment and devices.

In 1964, Ms. Rhodes began her career in health care at Piedmont Atlanta Hospital, where she worked as an operating room nurse until 1965. Throughout the following five years, she excelled as a registered nurse at Athens General and Colorectal Surgeons, P.C. Ms. Rhodes subsequently thrived as a registered nurse and as a surgical assistant to Dr. James Green between 1970 and 1976.

During the late 1970s and the early 1980s, Ms. Rhodes found further success as a registered nurse for a local obstetrician and gynecologist. She was appointed as a team leader within Piedmont Physicians Neurosurgery Athens, part of Piedmont Athens Regional Medical Center, between 1985 and 2003. Due to her leadership skills, Ms. Rhodes was frequently referred to as "The General" by her colleagues at the aforementioned hospital. Following her retirement, she provided various essential health care services to a number of patients who had Alzheimer's disease in a part-time capacity for more than 15 years.

Ms. Rhodes currently serves as a registered nurse for a single elderly patient with the aforementioned degenerative illness. Alongside her responsibilities as a registered nurse, she has contributed to Beech Haven Church in Athens, Georgia, in numerous volunteer capacities since 2008. Ms. Rhodes also regularly supports several local charitable organizations in relation to animal rescue and wounded military veterans.

Born in Willacooche, Georgia, Ms. Rhodes' decision to pursue a career as a surgical nurse was heavily influenced by her profound admiration for a nurse who worked for her former pediatrician. She frequently recalls her fascination with the aforementioned nurse's elegant appearance, most notably her flight cap, white uniform and matching white shoes. In 1964, Ms. Rhodes obtained a diploma in nursing at Piedmont Atlanta Hospital. She subsequently earned a certification as a registered nurse while working as an operating room nurse at the aforementioned Atlanta-based hospital. As a highly accomplished professional, Ms. Rhodes has been selected for inclusion in the 76th edition of Who's Who in America.

In addition to her Baptist faith, Ms. Rhodes attributes a great deal of her success to her husband, who understood the indispensable nature of her profession. Throughout her career, she also drew tremendous inspiration from her mother, who taught her the value of an exceptional work ethic at a young age. Ms. Rhodes is additionally extremely grateful to have been mentored by Dr. James Green, who helped her understand the role of a surgical nurse in critical procedures such as an emergency appendectomy.

In the coming years, Ms. Rhodes intends to continue caring for patients with degenerative illnesses while maintaining her own health. She also aims to further her involvement in community organizations as well as Beech Haven Church. Since her personal connection to her work played a central role in the longevity of her career, Ms. Rhodes vehemently advises aspiring health care practitioners to pursue an area of medicine that aligns with their values and goals. In her spare time, she relaxes by reading, sewing and traveling to different cities across the United States.

Gary S. Roubin, MD, PhD

Interventional Cardiology and Vascular Consultant
Excision Medical Inc.

JACKSON, WY UNITED STATES

Having accrued over four decades of inimitable experience in the field of interventional cardiology, Gary S. Roubin, MD, PhD, has distinguished himself as a leader and internationally recognized luminary of his profession. Well-regarded for his pioneering efforts in developing the first FDA-approved coronary stent, his work has largely resided in the areas of carotid stenting, large bore vascular closure technology and the creation of embolic protection devices. Singularly dedicated to promoting the best outcomes in patient health care through his prowess as an inventor, Dr. Roubin notably holds more than 10 patents for device technology and innovative treatment techniques in both the United States and Europe.

During the course of his prolific career in the field, Dr. Roubin has earned distinction as a board-level executive of various biotechnology companies, including InspireMD, Excision Medical Inc. and Essential Medical Inc., the latter of which was successful in bringing a large bore vascular close device to the health care market. Previously, Dr. Roubin served in positions of high leadership at the University of Alabama at Birmingham, for which he was the chief of interventional cardiology, and Lenox Hill Hospital, where he presided over the cardiology department and worked as the chief of service for the cardiac and vascular programs.

Well-regarded for his deep and comprehensive research in multivessel coronary disease, peripheral vascular and carotid disease, Dr. Roubin's name has appeared as the co-author to over 280 papers and articles in peer-reviewed journals. His first book, "The First Balloon Expandable Coronary Stent: An Expedition that Changed Cardiovascular Medicine," concerns his technical innovations and commitment to scientific development, as well as the pioneering work performed by Andreas Gruentzig, a German radiologist and cardiologist who developed the first angioplasty for the treatment of narrowed arteries.

Dr. Roubin's performance in the field was largely born of his academic journey, which began at the University of Queensland's School of Veterinary Science. Following his graduation in 1970, he attended the university's medical school, where he attained a Doctor of Medicine in 1975. He proceeded to undertake residencies in internal medicine at Royal Prince Alfred Hospital and cardiology training at the Hallstrom Institute of Cardiology of Sydney University. Dr. Roubin subsequently attended Sydney University, from which he earned a Doctor of Philosophy in cardiovascular physiology in 1983.

Dr. Roubin concluded his academic efforts with postdoctoral research at Emory University, after which he developed his balloon expandable stent and served as the director of research at the Andreas Gruentzig Cardiovascular Center of Emory University. Continuing his tenure in education, he next maintained involvement as a professor of medicine and radiology at the University of Alabama Hospital. To remain aware of developments in the field, Dr. Roubin has been inducted as a fellow of both the American College of Cardiology and the Royal Australian College of Physicians, and has held memberships with the American Heart Association (AHA), the Society for Cardiac Angiography and Intervention, the Society for Vascular Medicine and Biology and the Society of Interventional Radiology, among others.

Celebrated for his contributions to the field, Dr. Roubin has earned numerous accolades throughout the course of his career. Among them, he received a Lifetime Achievement Award from the International Symposium on Endovascular Therapy in 2018, has been listed for over 25 years among the Best Doctors and Best Cardiologists in America, and attained the Eugene Drake Award for contributions to cardiovascular medicine from the AHA's Annual Scientific Sessions in 2008. Moreover, he was invited to serve as a visiting professor at Xiamen University during the same year.

In accounting for his success, Dr. Roubin largely credits the providence of good fortune. He has been honored with inclusion in the 76th edition of Who's Who in America. Looking toward the future, Dr. Roubin plans to sustain his commitment to spreading the use of innovative cardiac and vascular devices to patient care worldwide.

Gilbert O. Sanders, PhD

Psychologist
Sanders Psychological Services
CHOCTAW, OK UNITED STATES

F or more than 20 years, Gilbert O. Sanders, PhD, has thrived as a psychologist and as the owner of Sanders Psychological Services. With more than five decades of psychological experience to his credit, he specializes in conducting neuropsychological evaluations for victims of severe head injuries, particularly veterans of the U.S. armed forces. Dr. Sanders also focuses on determining the specific locations of traumatic brain injuries and assessing the relationship between different types of injuries and changes in mood or behavior.

Prior to the establishment of Sanders Psychological Services, Dr. Sanders excelled as a psychologist with the U.S. Public Health Service for more than 10 years. During this period, he was appointed to numerous leadership positions, including the director of a substance abuse rehabilitation program for the U.S. Federal Bureau of Prisons. Dr. Sanders had previously worked as a psychologist with the U.S. Army Research Institute for the Behavioral and Social Sciences.

Toward the end of his tenure with the U.S. Public Health Service, Dr. Sanders served as a substance abuse adviser for the U.S. District Court for the District of Alaska as well as the Indian Health Service in Sitka, Alaska. He was subsequently recruited as a psychologist for the U.S. Division of Immigration Health Services. During this period, Dr. Sanders helped oversee a substance abuse rehabilitation program at the El Centro Detention Facility in El Centro, California.

Alongside his responsibilities at Sanders Psychological Services, Dr. Sanders found further success as the chief of behavioral sciences for the U.S. Department of the Air Force Office of Special Investigations during the early 2000s. Under his leadership, the aforementioned federal law enforcement agency established a rehabilitation center for U.S. military veterans based in Germany. Dr. Sanders also returned to El Centro, California, to provide mental health counseling services to members of the U.S. Navy, particularly a flight demonstration squadron known as the Blue Angels.

In 2017, Dr. Sanders was elected president of the American Psychological Association. He currently contributes to the aforementioned organization as a council representative. In order to stay up to date with the latest developments in his field, Dr. Sanders continues to maintain active affiliations with the Oklahoma Psychological Association, the National Academy of Neuropsychology, the American Association for Marriage and Family Therapy, and the Commissioned Officers Association of the U.S. Public Health Service, which had previously appointed him as a board member.

After completing undergraduate coursework in history, Dr. Sanders served in the Vietnam War as a member of the U.S. Air Force. During the early 1970s, he helped oversee a substance abuse program for fellow military veterans, which inspired him to pursue a career as a psychologist. Between 1972 and 1975, Dr. Sanders earned a Doctor of Philosophy in mental health counseling from the University of Tulsa. He subsequently found further success as a member of the U.S. Army for more than 15 years before his initial recruitment with the U.S. Public Health Service.

In 2014, Dr. Sanders was selected for a Gold Medal for Lifetime Achievement on behalf of the American Psychological Foundation and the American Psychological Association. He has also been honored with a Karl F. Heiser Presidential Award for Advocacy on behalf of the latter organization and has been included in the 76th edition of Who's Who in America. In the coming years, Dr. Sanders intends to further his involvement in charitable initiatives through Tinker Chapel at Tinker Air Force Base, where he has been distinguished as a Knight of the Order of the Holy Sepulchre.

Raymond L. Smith, MD, FACS

Chief of Wound Care and Hyperbaric Medicine
Reading Hospital

Assistant Professor of Surgery
Drexel University College of Medicine

WYOMISSING, PA UNITED STATES

F or more than 15 years, Raymond L. Smith, MD, FACS, has thrived as the chief of the wound care and hyperbaric medicine division of Reading Hospital, which is part of the Tower Health system. With more than 45 years of surgical experience to his credit, he specializes in performing reconstructive surgery to help his patients recover from severe injuries of the hand or fingers. Dr. Smith also frequently harnesses his expertise in hyperbaric oxygen therapy to facilitate the healing of particularly complex or hazardous wounds as well as the development of new blood vessels while decreasing the risk of infection.

Alongside his primary responsibilities at Reading Hospital, Dr. Smith additionally contributed to the aforementioned hospital's wound care center at Reading Hospital as a medical director in 2016. Since 2022, he has simultaneously excelled as an assistant professor of surgery for the department of surgery of the Drexel University College of Medicine at Tower Health since 2022. In order to stay up to date with the latest developments in his field, Dr. Smith continues to maintain active affiliations with a host of professional organizations, including the American College of Surgeons, the American Society of Plastic Surgeons, the Undersea Hyperbaric Medical Society, the Berks County Medical Society, the Lipoplasty Society North America, the Pennsylvania Medical Society, the Northeastern Society Plastic Surgeons and the American Association of Hand Surgery.

In 1976, Dr. Smith began his medical career as a staff member at multiple hospitals within his home state of Pennsylvania such as Reading Hospital, the Community General Hospital, which has since closed, and St. Joseph Medical Center, which is part of the Pennsylvania State University Health System (Penn State Health). While working in these capacities, he simultaneously established his former private practice, which was known as Raymond L. Smith M.D. P.C. in 1981. Throughout the following 20 years, Dr. Smith continued to share his expertise through his private practice and the aforementioned hospitals. Between 1983 and 1989, he found further success as the chief of the plastic surgery section of Penn State Health St. Joseph Medical Center.

Outside of his professional circles, Dr. Smith frequently contributes to the Republican National Committee. Likewise, he maintains an active affiliation with the Republican Majority Fund. Moreover, Dr. Smith also supports the Advent Lutheran Church in East York, Pennsylvania, in various volunteer capacities. He has been a member of the American Legion since December 2023.

Born in Norristown, Pennsylvania, Dr. Smith's decision to pursue a career as a plastic surgeon was heavily inspired by his profound admiration for his own family's physician. After obtaining a Bachelor of Science at Ursinus College in 1962, he earned a Doctor of Medicine at the Lewis Katz School of Medicine at Temple University in 1966. Dr. Smith subsequently served in the U.S. Air Force Medical Service Corps, where he gradually advanced to the rank of captain.

Between 1969 and 1973, Dr. Smith underwent residency training in general surgery at the Graduate Hospital of the University of Pennsylvania, now known as Penn Medicine Rittenhouse. Toward the end of this period, he was appointed as the chief resident of the general surgery residency program at Geisinger Medical Center, which has since been acquired by Kaiser Foundation Health Plan, Inc. Throughout the following three years, Dr. Smith pursued a second residency in plastic surgery at Penn State Health Milton S. Hershey Medical Center.

In 2018, the Berks County Medical Society honored Dr. Smith with a 50-Year Achievement Award. He has been recognized for his achievements with inclusion in the 76th edition of Who's Who in America. As a fellow of the American College of Surgeons, he has also been distinguished as a lifetime member of the aforementioned organization as well as the American Society of Plastic Surgeons. In addition to his knowledge of human anatomy, Dr. Smith attributes a great deal of his success to the support of his wife, who has served as a nurse for many years. Since his transparent approach to his work has consistently played a central role in his professional growth, Dr. Smith advises aspiring surgeons to treat their patients with the utmost kindness and respect.

Clark Springgate, MD, PhD

Chief Medical Officer
Springgate Biotechnology Consultants

GUILFORD, CT UNITED STATES

For more than 20 years, Clark Springgate, MD, PhD, has thrived as the chief medical officer of oncology and immunology clinical development and regulatory affairs with Springgate Biotechnology Consultants. In this capacity, he specializes in overseeing clinical trials for pharmaceutical medications as well as gene therapies, vaccines, allergenics and other biologics for the treatment of cancer and various autoimmune diseases. Dr. Springgate also focuses on helping major pharmaceutical organizations develop new forms of cancer treatments derived from living cells or organisms.

Prior to the establishment of Springgate Biotechnology Consultants, Dr. Springgate excelled as the chief medical officer of oncology clinical development and regulatory affairs for GlycoGenesys, Inc., in Boston, Massachusetts, between 1999 and 2003. He had previously found success as the founder and director of the clinical research center at the University of Connecticut School of Medicine after serving as the vice president of clinical and regulatory affairs and as the chief medical officer of immunology and oncology for the National Medical Research Corporation in Hartford, Connecticut, between 1994 and 1995. During the early 1990s, Dr. Springgate prospered as a medical director, senior scientific and regulatory consultant and the vice president of product development for the Clinical Research Center.

Alongside his primary professional responsibilities, Dr. Springgate regularly shares his expertise with pharmaceutical organizations and clinical laboratories in an independent consultant capacity. Throughout his career, Dr. Springgate has also contributed articles to numerous professional journals and publications, including Cancer Research, Archives of Biochemistry and Biophysics, and the Journal of Immunology.

Born in Champaign, Illinois, Dr. Springgate earned a Bachelor of Arts in biology at Boston University before completing a predoctoral fellowship at Boston College, where he subsequently obtained a Doctor of Philosophy in biochemistry and molecular biology in 1972. Between 1971 and 1975, he was appointed as a clinical research fellow, visiting scientist and postdoctoral fellow with the Fox Chase Cancer Center, the Temple University Health System and the University of Pennsylvania Perelman School of Medicine. In 1976, Dr. Springgate completed a postdoctoral fellowship in oncology and leukemia at the University of Pennsylvania.

Following these accomplishments, Dr. Springgate earned a Doctor of Medicine, with honors, at the University of Miami Miller School of Medicine in 1983. He subsequently underwent residency training at Tulane Medical Center, which is part of the Tulane University School of Medicine, before pursuing a fellowship in clinical pathology at the aforementioned New Orleans-based institution. Between 1983 and 1985, Dr. Springgate pursued a second postgraduate fellowship in immunohematology at Tulane Medical Center.

In addition to his firm commitment to his professional goals, Dr. Springgate attributes a great deal of his success to the influence of his parents, both of whom taught him the value of an exceptional work ethic at a young age. He also draws tremendous inspiration from his loving wife, Diane Louise Rotnam, PhD, who served as a faculty member at Yale Medical School for more than 20 years and was previously appointed as a board member of the American Board of Clinical Social Workers. Since his vast knowledge of his field has played an instrumental role in his professional growth, Dr. Springgate advises aspiring clinical researchers to consistently stay up to date with the latest developments in their specialty areas, both in the U.S. and abroad.

Sharon T. Stauffer

Executive Director

Positive Choices Pregnancy Resource Center

BIRMINGHAM, AL UNITED STATES

S ince 2019, Sharon T. Stauffer has thrived as the executive director of the Positive Choices Pregnancy Resource Center in Birmingham, Alabama. In this capacity, she focuses on overseeing the implementation of various medical, educational and support services for young men and women in relation to unplanned pregnancies or sexual health. Ms. Stauffer also specializes in helping pregnant women navigate the myriad challenges of terminating their pregnancies or coordinating adoptions for unborn infants.

Prior to her appointment as the executive director, Ms. Stauffer excelled as the office manager of the Positive Choices Pregnancy Resource Center, which was formerly known as Sav-A-Life East, Inc., for a number of years. She had originally begun her tenure at the aforementioned faith-based organization as a counselor in a volunteer capacity between 2014 and 2016. Ms. Stauffer had previously found success as a financial officer in the department of radiology research at the University of Alabama at Birmingham for more than 30 years.

Alongside her responsibilities at the Positive Choices Pregnancy Resource Center, Ms. Stauffer simultaneously served as the president of the Trussville Noon Rotary Club between 2022 and 2023. She currently contributes to Rotary International as the assistant governor of Zone 13 of District 6860, which encompasses more than 50 Rotary clubs across Northern Alabama. In order to stay up to date with the latest developments in her local community, Ms. Stauffer additionally maintains an active affiliation with the Trussville Area Chamber of Commerce. Likewise, she also contributes to Leadership Trussville, which provides professional development and leadership building services to young professionals, as a mentor in a volunteer capacity.

Born in Birmingham, Alabama, Ms. Stauffer initially began her professional career with the Blue Cross Blue Shield Association during the early 1980s. She also worked as a teacher at a local middle school. In 1984, Ms. Stauffer accepted a position at the University of Alabama at Birmingham, where she also completed undergraduate coursework in business administration and management. While honing her administrative skills at the University of Alabama at Birmingham, she eventually resumed her education at Faulkner University in Montgomery, Alabama, where she obtained a Bachelor of Science, with honors, in business administration and management in 1997.

Ms. Stauffer's subsequent decision to pursue her initial position at the Positive Choices Pregnancy Resource Center was heavily inspired by her own experience as the mother of an adopted daughter. During her tenure with the Positive Choices Pregnancy Resource Center, she played an instrumental role in the expansion of the aforementioned organization's online presence and overall utilization of technology in order to increase the accessibility of their services for young adults. Ms. Stauffer was promoted to the position of executive director following the retirement of the previous executive director of Positive Choices Pregnancy Resource Center.

Outside of her professional circles, Ms. Stauffer regularly participates in charitable initiatives in a volunteer capacity through her local church. She also maintains an active affiliation with the National Institute of Family and Life Advocates, which is part of the National Pro-Life Religious Council. In addition to her genuine passion for her work, Ms. Stauffer attributes a great deal of her success to her firm commitment to her professional goals. In the coming years, she intends to continue expanding the customer base of the Positive Choices Pregnancy Resource Center while simultaneously sharing her expertise with the adoption process in an independent consultant capacity.

Dr. Frank J. Vozos

President & Chief Executive Officer (Retired)
Monmouth Medical Center

OCEANPORT, NJ UNITED STATES

For more than 40 years, Dr. Frank J. Vozos found success as a general surgeon, educator, and health care executive. Prior to his retirement, he focused on overseeing daily operations at multiple hospitals throughout the United States East Coast and managing each facility's financial health. Dr. Vozos also specialized in honing his students' proficiency with various noninvasive surgical procedures, particularly involving prominent laparoscopic techniques.

Between 1979 and 1998, Dr. Vozos thrived as a general surgeon at Monmouth Medical Center, which is part of the RWJBarnabas Health System. Toward the end of this period, he was simultaneously appointed president of the medical and dental staff at the aforementioned New Jersey-based medical center. Dr. Vozos subsequently prospered as the president and chief executive officer of Monmouth Medical Center and as the director of the general surgery residency program for more than 20 years before issuing his professional retirement in 2020.

Alongside his responsibilities at Monmouth Medical Center, Dr. Vozos simultaneously excelled as a clinical associate professor of surgery at the Drexel University College of Medicine between 1993 and 2016. During the 2010s, he was additionally recruited as the executive director of the SBH Health System. Dr. Vozos had previously found further success as a member of the boards of trustees for the SBH Health System and the RWJBarnabas Health System between 1995 and 1999.

Throughout his career, Dr. Vozos has served as a board member for a host of health care centers and nonprofit organizations, including the American Red Cross, the Muscular Dystrophy Association and the Encompass Health Rehabilitation Hospital of Tinton Falls. Between 1992 and 1995, he additionally contributed to RWJBarnabas Health System as the chairperson of the credentials committee for Monmouth Medical Center. Thanks to his widespread reputation, Dr. Vozos has shared his surgical expertise and innovative research at conferences, symposiums and other industry events across the United States.

After obtaining a Bachelor of Arts in biology at West Virginia University, Dr. Vozos earned a Doctor of Medicine at the National and Kapodistrian University of Athens' School of Medicine in Greece. Between 1796 and 1979, he underwent residency training in general surgery at Monmouth Medical Center. Toward the end of this period, Dr. Vozos was appointed as the chief resident of the aforementioned medical center's general surgery program.

In 2021, Dr. Vozos was celebrated with a Lifetime Achievement Award on behalf of the RWJBarnabas Health System. He had previously been honored with a Distinguished Service Award on behalf of the New Jersey Hospital Association, a Citizen of the Year Award on behalf of the Lakewood Chamber of Commerce, and an accolade in relation to hospital partnerships on behalf of the New Jersey Primary Care Association. Moreover, Dr. Vozos has been distinguished as a fellow of several professional organizations, including the American College of Surgeons, the Southeastern Surgical Congress, the New Jersey Society of Thoracic Surgeons and the New Jersey chapter of the American College of Surgeons. He has also been honored for his accomplishments in the 76th edition of Who's Who in America.

In addition to his close relationships with his colleagues, Dr. Vozos attributes a great deal of his success to the perpetual expansion of his professional skill set. In the coming years, he intends to spend more time with his children and three grandchildren. Due to the collaborative nature of his former profession, Dr. Vozos advises aspiring surgeons to treat their colleagues with the utmost kindness and respect.

Johanna Devon

Author

Principal Real Estate Broker & Owner
Devon Home Realty LLC

BROAD RUN, VA UNITED STATES

For more than 20 years, Johanna Devon has prospered as the principal real estate broker and owner of Devon Home Realty, LLC. With more than 40 years of real estate experience to her credit, she specializes in helping her clients navigate the myriad complexities associated with purchasing land for the development of residential or commercial real estate. Ms. Devon also regularly harnesses her lauded negotiation skills to lower the final price of her clients' desired purchases and prevent her clients from overpaying for real estate due to market fluctuations or limited inventory.

Prior to the formation of Devon Home Realty and Florida House of Brokers, Ms. Devon thrived as an associate real estate broker with Northern Virginia Homes. During the 1970s and the early 1980s, Ms. Devon found success as a diagnostic radiologist for more than 10 years.

Alongside her responsibilities as a principal real estate broker, Ms. Devon has volunteered at the Hylton Performing Arts Center in Prince William County, Virginia, as an usher and a greeter. She also frequently participates in charitable initiatives on behalf of several local ministries. Likewise, Ms. Devon additionally supports numerous food banks, clothing banks and youth programs throughout her home state of Virginia.

A native of Pennsylvania, Ms. Devon completed coursework in radiology at the Conemaugh School of Radiologic Technology, which is part of the Conemaugh Health System, after attending the Portage Area Junior-Senior High School. She subsequently worked as a radiology technologist at a hospital in Maryland before completing additional coursework in diagnostic ultrasound at the Georgetown University Department of Radiology in Washington, D.C. While working in diagnostic ultrasound, Ms. Devon simultaneously became a licensed real estate agent in Virginia in 1982.

Throughout her career, Ms. Devon has been distinguished as a "Top Producer" on multiple occasions. She has also been celebrated amongst the "Top Five in Northern Virginia" in the category of residential and commercial real estate sales. Moreover, Ms. Devon has additionally been honored with numerous accolades in relation to gross revenue and real estate sales volume.

In 2011, Ms. Devon garnered further recognition as the author of a suspense novel titled "What Goes Around..." Released through Author-House, the aforementioned work of fiction chronicles the tumultuous and abusive relationship between a married couple as well as both spouses' struggles with mental health. She is currently working on her first children's book. In addition to her commitment to her professional goals, Ms. Devon attributes a great deal of her success to her ability to adapt to unforeseen fluctuations in the local or global real estate market.

In the coming years, Ms. Devon intends to devote more attention to providing mentorship to new real estate agents, specifically in relation to the key differences between selling land and understanding land use. Likewise, she also aims to educate agents on the aspects of land acquisition and development. Since her innovative mindset has continuously played a central role in her professional growth, Ms. Devon advises aspiring real estate agents to accustom themselves to developing strategies for fulfilling their clients' needs rather than implementing the same sales tactics as their industry peers.

Maurice J. Jordan

Real Estate Broker
Coldwell Banker Commercial

LOS ANGELES, CA UNITED STATES

With successful careers in both the culinary field and real estate, Maurice J. Jordan has proven himself a man who can wear many hats. While working as a dishwasher in the Boston Naval Shipyard as a teenager, Mr. Jordan thrived in the kitchen and fell in love with the environment and the people working in it. He worked as a second cook and broiler cook at the Locke-Ober Café in Boston, Massachusetts, from 1973 to 1974 while attending the School of Culinary Arts, Vocational, in Boston, Massachusetts. After graduating in 1974, he went on to work as the second cook at Cafe L' Orange in Concord, Massachusetts, until 1975 and as a rounds cook at Union Oyster House in Boston, Massachusetts, from 1975 to 1976. In 1976, Mr. Jordan graduated from the John Robert Powers School of Modeling and relocated to California shortly after. While in California, he worked in various positions and restaurants, including as the executive chef of Smuggler's Inn in Fresno, California, from 1992 to 1993, a private home chef in Oakhurst, California, from 1992 to 1996, and as the executive sous chef of Hillcrest Country Club in Los Angeles, California, from 1999 to 2003.

From 2004 to 2005, Mr. Jordan worked as a chef at the University of California Los Angeles in Los Angeles, California, while transitioning his career from the culinary arts to real estate. His first real estate position was with the Reliance Network and RE/MAX Commercial, where he worked as a sales agent from 2004 to 2006. From 2006 to 2007, Mr. Jordan was a sales associate with Coldwell Banker Premier Team Realty before going on to work as the general manager and broker associate for Coldwell Banker Commercial Wilshire Properties from 2007 to 2011. In 2011, he was named a senior associate at NAI Capital Commercial, Inc., in Los Angeles, California. Mr. Jordan has worked as a real estate broker for Coldwell Banker Commercial since 2011 and as a property manager at SNT Property Management, LLC, where he has managed six buildings, 70 units and 154 tenants since 2017. Mr. Jordan has won awards for both his work in culinary arts and real estate, such as the Excellence Award as Sous Chef and Banquet Chef from Marriott International, Inc., and the Coldwell Banker Sterling Award. He has also been featured in the 76th edition of Who's Who in America.

An avid runner, Mr. Jordan has completed many races, including the Pasadena 5K Run, Maui Marathon, Disney Half Marathon, Santa Monica 10K Clean the Bay Run, LA Marathon and Boston Marathon. Mr. Jordan is a member of the American Culinary Federation and Toastmasters International, which he served as president of Fox Talkz Toastmasters from 2010 to 2012. Previously, he was featured in Marquis Who's Who in America. He attributes his success to his hard work, dedication and discipline. In the future, he hopes to continue his work as a property manager.

Shellie Young, PA, MCNE, CLHMS, CIARP

Global Real Estate Adviser

Premier Sotheby's International Realty

BRADENTON, FL UNITED STATES

F or more than 10 years, Shellie Young, PA, MCNE, CLHMS, CIARP, has thrived as a realtor sales associate with Premier Sotheby's International Realty, which is part of the Sotheby's International Realty network. With more than 20 years of real estate experience to her credit, she specializes in guiding her clients through the complexities of purchasing or selling luxury real estate and waterfront properties within Florida's Gulf Coast. Ms. Young also focuses on forging close relationships with her clients and promoting her expertise to her target audience through a broad range of digital and print marketing initiatives.

Prior to her recruitment at Premier Sotheby's International Realty, Ms. Young was appointed as a realtor associate for the Miami Real Estate Team, which is part of Home and Business Realty, Inc., between 2009 and 2011. She had previously served in this capacity for Fortune International Realty for more than five years. Between 1997 and 2001, Ms. Young worked as a proprietor at the Wilder Farm Inn in Waitsfield, Vermont, after building her leadership skills as the general manager of numerous restaurants in New York City and Los Angeles throughout the 1990s.

Alongside her responsibilities as a realtor sales associate, Ms. Young currently excels as a producer and host of an exclusive segment of a reality television series titled "The American Dream," which can be viewed on multiple streaming platforms and television networks. Previously, Ms. Young was featured on a 2018 edition of HGTV's "Beach

House." She also supports numerous nonprofit organizations, including Habitat for Humanity International and Guiding Eyes for the Blind, which provides trained guide dogs for visually impaired individuals. In order to stay up to date with the latest developments in her field, Ms. Young continues to maintain active affiliations with the National Association of Realtors, the International Association of Certified Real Estate Professionals and the Worldwide Women's Association.

Raised in Beverly Hills, California, Ms. Young developed an appreciation for the architecture of luxury homes during her childhood. She eventually expanded her knowledge of the global real estate market while living in several major cities around the world, including Los Angeles, New York City, Milan and Miami. After finding success in the hospitality industry for a number of years, Ms. Young became a licensed realtor in 2004.

In recognition of her exceptional sales record, Ms. Young was selected for inclusion into Premier Sotheby's International Realty's Club 1744 in 2023. She had previously been designated as a certified luxury home marketing specialist on behalf of the Institute for Luxury Home Marketing, where she has also been inducted into the Million Dollar Guild. Throughout her career, Ms. Young has additionally been featured in myriad local publications such as Sarasota Scene Magazine, the Tampa Bay Business Journal and Forbes Magazine. Moreover, Ms. Young has been acknowledged in RealTrends among the Top 1.5% in Real Estate.

In addition to her exceptional organizational skills, Ms. Young attributes a great deal of her success to her genuine compassion for her clients. In order to devote the same level of attention to each client, she upholds strict limitations regarding the number of listings she accepts. Ms. Young is particularly proud to have facilitated the sales of multiple residential properties valued at more than $5 million.

In the coming years, Ms. Young intends to continue helping her clients navigate the life-changing decision of buying or selling a home. She also aims to further her contributions to animal rescue organizations. Since her empathic approach to her work has played an instrumental role in her professional growth, Ms. Young advises aspiring realtors to treat their clients with tremendous kindness and respect.

Lin Morel, MA, DSS

Chief Executive Officer
Beyond Words Group Inc.

DOWNINGTOWN, PA UNITED STATES

Prompted by a desire to make the world a better place, Lin Morel, MA, DSS, has dedicated her life to helping others. She received her first of many qualifications in 1969, earning a Bachelor of Arts in psychology from Fairleigh Dickinson University in Teaneck, New Jersey. Years later, she graduated from the University of Santa Monica in Santa Monica, California, in 1994 with a Master of Arts in applied psychology. Dr. Morel went on to study at Peace Theological Seminary and College of Philosophy in Los Angeles, California, receiving a master's degree in applied theology in 1997 and a Doctor of Spiritual Science in 2001. In addition to her degrees, she has completed a victim assistance training program and the Alchemy Leadership Training Program with the Annenberg Foundation. A passionate practitioner of martial arts since 1965, Dr. Morel is a fifth-degree black belt with certifications to teach tai chi and qigong.

Spending nearly two decades of volunteering for domestic violence causes and leading nonprofit organizations, Dr. Morel's life of service includes assisting people in need as a nondenominational ordained minister and spiritual director. She has been working directly with C-level company executives and individuals interested in improving the world, including entrepreneurs, documentary filmmakers and scientists across the globe. Her reach extends to Italy, Australia, Scotland, England, France and Canada. Since she founded Lin Morel & Associates, now Beyond Words Group, Inc., in 1984, she has relied solely on word-of-mouth promotion.

Having experienced abuse and hardship throughout her life, Dr. Morel is empathetic to the ordeals of others and seeks to lessen their suffering through talk therapy and philanthropic endeavors. When she initially entered college, she studied pre-medicine with an economics scholarship but changed paths upon realizing that being a medical doctor would preclude her from interacting freely with others, listening to their struggles and encouraging them to find the solutions within themselves to tackle their challenges. At Beyond Words Group, Inc., Dr. Morel offers services such as personal development coaching, relationship counseling and career guidance, helping clients overcome adversity through a combination of psychology, theology and martial arts principles. In addition to her work with Beyond Words Group, Inc., Dr. Morel has developed multiple successful martial arts businesses, including cofounding the Academy of Asian Arts in 1976 and the Academy of Martial Arts in 1983.

For her work, Dr. Morel has received the Lifetime Achievement Award for 2023 by the International Association of Top Professionals (IAOTP), a commendation for community impact from A Window Between Worlds (AWBW) and International Coach of the Year. As a martial artist, she is a national karate champion, a state and national silver medalist with the Amateur Athletic Union, and a two-time gold medalist at the Garden State Open Karate Championships. Dr. Morel is the author of eight books, including her bestselling 2014 book, "Soul Lifts: From Bumps to Brilliance" and "The Grace of Love," published by Inspired Vizions Publishing in 2022.

A civic leader, Dr. Morel is a founding member of the Evolutionary Business Council, a task force participant at the Center for Collective Wisdom in Los Angeles, and a former board member at A Window Between Worlds in Venice, California. Dr. Morel considers herself to be a minister, spiritual director and martial artist, and strives to continue on her current path, helping others find their strength.

Kurt Franklin Stone, BA, MAHL, DD

Founding Rabbi

Bet Chaverim Congregation

BOCA RATON, FL UNITED STATES

For more than 30 years, Kurt Franklin Stone, BA, MAHL, DD, has thrived as the founding rabbi of Congregation Bet Chaverim, Inc. in Coral Springs, Florida. In this capacity, he specializes in educating members of the local Jewish community about the principles of Judaism and regularly provides various spiritual leadership and prayer services. Mr. Stone also frequently performs readings from the Torah, and he serves as a mentor to young members of the aforementioned Jewish center.

Alongside his responsibilities as a rabbi, Mr. Stone has been appointed as a member of the institutional review board for Advarra, Inc. since 2013. In this capacity, he focuses on translating medical terminology and procedures into layman's terms. Mr. Stone had previously excelled in this capacity for a nonprofit medical center known as the Cleveland Clinic between 1995 and 2003. Toward the beginning of this period, he was simultaneously recruited as the director of the Sholem Aleichem Foundation in New York City.

Mr. Stone has additionally found success as an adjunct professor at Florida Atlantic University and Florida International University, where he taught numerous courses in relation to history, international relations, literature and cinema. Widely renowned for his unique political perspectives, he has garnered further recognition as the author of 2010's "The Jews of Capitol Hill: A Compendium of Jewish Congressional

Members" and 2000's "The Congressional Minyan: The Jews of Capitol Hill." Likewise, Mr. Stone has also shared his expertise in political and Jewish history as the author of more than 900 political essays.

Prior to his appointment at Congregation Bet Chaverim, Mr. Stone worked as a rabbi at Temple Beth Torah in Tamarac, Florida, between 1983 and 1990. He had previously channeled his creative spirit to compose and perform in a theatrical production titled "An Evening with Sholem Aleichem" during the 1970s. Mr. Stone has since performed in the aforementioned show more than 400 times on multiple continents. In order to stay up to date with the latest developments in his field, he continues to maintain an active affiliation with the Central Conference of American Rabbis.

Born in Hollywood, California, Mr. Stone's interest in politics inspired him to pursue an internship with the U.S. Senate in 1969. He subsequently earned a Bachelor of Arts in American history, philosophy and political science at Adlai E. Stevenson College at the University of California, Santa Cruz, in 1971. Mr. Stone eventually resumed his education at Hebrew Union College – Jewish Institute of Religion, which is part of New York University, where he obtained a Master of Arts in Hebrew letters in 1979. He eventually returned to the aforementioned New York City-based institution to complete a Doctor of Divinity in 2005.

In 2004, Mr. Stone was selected for an Excellence in Teaching Award on behalf of Florida Atlantic University. He had previously been honored with a Lion of Judah Award on behalf of B'nai B'rith International in 1986. In addition to the personality he inherited from his parents, Mr. Stone attributes a great deal of his success to his tremendous respect for the knowledge and wisdom of his mentors and colleagues.

In the coming years, Mr. Stone intends to maintain his responsibilities at Congregation Bet Chaverim while sharing his political insights through his personal blog, "The K.F. Stone Weekly." Since his enthusiastic working style has played a vital role in his professional growth, he advises aspiring rabbis to approach their profession with the curiosity of a young child. Throughout his career, Mr. Stone has dedicated significant time and attention to understanding new perspectives of Judaism and politics.

Sally A. Campbell

Owner & President (Retired)

S.A. Campbell

TRAVELERS REST, SC UNITED STATES

F
or more than 30 years, Sally A. Campbell found success as the president and as the owner of S.A. Campbell, which provided air quality analysis services for industrial sites across the U.S. and in the Caribbean. She specialized in helping her clients maintain compliance with various federal and statewide regulations in relation to air pollution and obtaining emissions permits.

Alongside her primary professional responsibilities, Dr. Campbell has channeled her environmental expertise to serve as a visiting professor at Johns Hopkins University. Likewise, she has additionally contributed to Dartmouth College's Geisel School of Medicine as a professor and toxicologist. In order to stay up to date with the latest developments in her field, Dr. Campbell maintains active affiliations with the Air and Waste Management Association, the American Physical Society and the American Association for the Advancement of Science.

Prior to the establishment of S.A. Campbell, Dr. Campbell thrived as the technical director of atmospheric services for the Lockheed Martin Corporation between 1979 and 1986. Toward the end of this period, she simultaneously provided organizational development services for a variety of federal and statewide social service agencies. During the 1970s, Dr. Campbell served on the opening faculty at the University of the District of Columbia, formerly Federal City College.

A fellow of the American Institute of Chemists, Dr. Campbell was previously appointed as the chairperson of ASTM International, formerly known as the American Society for Testing and Materials. During her tenure as an affiliate of the Air and Waste Management Association, she also played an instrumental role in the formation of the aforementioned organization's ethics committee. Toward the beginning of her professional career, Dr. Campbell additionally contributed to the passage of the Clean Air Act as a lobbyist.

Dr. Campbell's initial interest in science was chiefly inspired by her father, who vehemently encouraged her to pursue her fascination with chemistry and physics. In 1964, she earned a bachelor's degree in physical chemistry from Wellesley College in Massachusetts before obtaining a master's degree in physical chemistry at Harvard University. Dr. Campbell subsequently completed a Doctor of Philosophy in atmospheric and nuclear chemistry at the University of Maryland in 1977. She eventually concluded her education at the Carey Business School at Johns Hopkins University, earning a master's degree in management and organizational development in 1983.

Since her retirement, Dr. Campbell has found further success as a stamp collector and seller. She has also helped establish a new program at her local church in relation to diversity, equity and inclusion. In addition to her persistence, Dr. Campbell attributes a great deal of her success to the guidance of her father, who enjoyed a prosperous career as a lawyer, and her grandfather, who garnered widespread recognition throughout his local community as an educator and entrepreneur.

In the coming years, Dr. Campbell intends to devote more attention to organizing her stamp collection, which currently amounts to more than two million stamps. She also aims to further her involvement in the eradication of racial discrimination in her hometown. Since her exceptional work ethic continuously contributed to her professional growth, Dr. Campbell advises aspiring environmental scientists to pursue their goals with the utmost determination.

Thomas R. Freeman, MS, BCBA, LBA-NY, LBA-MA

Senior Vice President for Research and Dissemination
ABA Technologies, Inc.
MELBOURNE, FL UNITED STATES

An accomplished behavioral analyst, Thomas R. Freeman, MS, BCBA, LBA-NY, LBA-MA, began working in mental health care in 1979, when he was hired as a direct care staff member at the Walter E. Fernald State School in Waltham, Massachusetts. From 1979 to 1995, he rose to assistant psychologist and later staff psychologist, providing care for those with developmental disabilities. Prior to his work at the state school, Mr. Freeman worked for nine years as a certified instructor of professional crisis management, the act of physically containing a violent individual in a way that is safe for both parties. After receiving a Master of Science in applied behavior analysis from the Florida Institute of Technology in Melbourne, Florida, in 2000, Mr. Freeman became a board-certified behavior analyst and served as the district behavior analyst for the Agency for Persons with Disabilities in Volusia County, Florida, until 2010. Since 2000, Mr. Freeman has worked for ABA Technologies, Inc., an online educational institution headquartered out of Melbourne, Florida. Beginning as vice president, Mr. Freeman is now the senior vice president for research and dissemination.

Mr. Freeman is working on a book that focuses on the coordination of behavior analysis services with medication management services and anticipates its publication within the next five years. Following this endeavor, he intends to embark on writing another book that explores the topic of behavior analysis versus eugenics, emphasizing the clear distinction between the two and how behavioral analysis negates the illegitimate science of eugenics. He remains committed to promoting the field of behavior analysis by delivering presentations on this subject.

In addition to his work helping human beings, Mr. Freeman is passionate about animal welfare and behavior, having taken part in multiple research projects studying dolphins and orangutans. He initially joined the North Pacific Humpback Whale Project, a conservation initiative by the University of Hawaii Kewalo Basin Marine Mammal Laboratory, as a volunteer but quickly rose to become a liaison and then chief director. Mr. Freeman met his wife, a conservation biologist with a degree from the Yale School of the Environment, while volunteering for the Wild Orangutan Research Project in Kalimantan Tengah, Indonesia.

Mr. Freeman is the coauthor of "Grief and Developmental Disabilities: Considerations for Disenfranchised Populations," published in Social Justice in Loss and Grief in 2016, and "Ethical Considerations for Applied Behavior Analysis," published in Applied Behavior Analysis in 2007. For his contributions to the Walter E. Fernald State School, he was awarded the Governor's Pride and Performance Award by the state of Massachusetts. While in graduate school, he won the Outstanding Graduate Student Award for Academic Excellence from the Florida Institute of Technology. His other achievements include the Albert Nelson Marquis Lifetime Achievement Award and features in Marquis Who's Who Industry Leader and Marquis Who's Who in America.

Mr. Freeman takes great pride in his work as a behavioral analyst, particularly in his teaching accomplishments. Possessing a superb ability to impart the concepts and principles of behavior analysis and their practical application in real-world scenarios, he excels in clarifying intricate material, thus aiding students in their comprehension and application of the subject matter. His teaching style has garnered positive reception from both students and other professionals in his field.

In his personal life, Mr. Freeman is an accomplished musician, playing the guitar in several bands over the years. Now, he enjoys photography and photo documentation. The most important guiding principle in Mr. Freeman's life has been the golden rule: "Treat others the way you want to be treated."

Mona Dickson Jensen, PhD, MBA

Biochemist
Jensen Craft Enterprises Inc.

HAMPSTEAD, NH UNITED STATES

When Mona Dickson Jensen, PhD, MBA, graduated from the Massachusetts Institute of Technology (MIT) in 1966 with a Bachelor of Science, only 22 out of 950 students were women. Since then, Dr. Jensen has established herself as one of the foremost scientists in her field, pioneering research on environmental control and cell culture. As a child, Dr. Jensen had an affinity for mathematics and sciences. She attributes her interest in the subjects to her mother, a math teacher who had pursued a PhD. Though Dr. Jensen's mother put her education on hold because of her pregnancy and the beginning of World War II, she instilled a love of the sciences in her daughter.

After graduating from MIT, Dr. Jensen went on to receive a Doctor of Philosophy from Cornell University in 1973. While working on her doctorate, she began working as a senior scientist at Instrumentation Laboratory in Lexington, Massachusetts, where she remained until 1996, rising to project manager, then reagent systems applications manager, then senior research and development manager. During this time, she received a Master of Business Administration from Babson College in 1983. When she left Instrumentation Laboratory in 1996, she had reached scientific support/applications manager in the laboratory's clinical chemistry strategic business unit. From 1996 to 1998, Dr. Jensen worked as the research and development manager at a startup company in Boston, Massachusetts, before moving on to work at IDEXX Laboratory Inc. in Westbrook, Maine, from 2001 to 2012. At IDEXX Laboratory, Dr. Jensen began as a research scientist but quickly moved to research and development manager and then to manager of the veterinary clinical chemistry research and development department. She is the co-founder and president of Jensen Craft Enterprises Inc., in Hampstead, New Hampshire, which was formed in 1998, and remains an integral part of the company.

Along with her career achievements, Dr. Jensen was a member of the adjunct faculty at W. Alton Jones Cell Science Center in Lake Placid, New York, from 1974 to 1976, a special reviewer In Vitro from 1980 to 1981, and a proposal reviewer for the National Science Foundation (NSF) from 1983 to 1986. She has served as a subcommunications adviser to the National Committee for Clinical Laboratory Standards since 1991. Dr. Jensen is a contributing author to "Cell Culture and Its Application," released in 1977, and "Practical Tissue Culture Applications," released in 1979, as well as a contributor of articles to multiple professional journals. A grantee of the World Health Organization from 1980 to 1981 and holder of two patents, Dr. Jensen is extremely active in her field, having developed numerous clinical assay reagents in general chemistry, immunochemistry and coagulation and developed reagent analytical systems in human and veterinary medicine.

Previously, Dr. Jensen received the Albert Nelson Marquis Lifetime Achievement Award and has been featured in Who's Who in the World, Marquis Who's Who Top Professionals and the 76th edition of Who's Who in America. She is a member of the Daughters of the American Revolution, the American Chemical Society, the American Association for Clinical Chemistry, the American Philatelic Society, the Pilgrim Edward Doty Society and Beta Gamma Sigma. Dr. Jensen would like to be remembered by her peers as someone who achieved success in corporate America at a time when women were only beginning to have chances to do so.

Behrooz Kamgar-Parsi, PhD

Research Scientist

Navy Center for Applied Research in Artificial Intelligence

SILVER SPRING, MD UNITED STATES

F or more than 30 years, Behrooz Kamgar-Parsi, PhD, has thrived as a research scientist at the Navy Center for Applied Research in Artificial Intelligence, which is part of the information technology division of the U.S. Naval Research Laboratory in Washington, D.C. In this capacity, he specializes in developing and enhancing vision systems for autonomous aerial vehicles. Dr. Kamgar-Parsi also regularly harnesses his expertise in pattern recognition to improve the abilities of various autonomous and intelligent systems to process and analyze specific details of different objects.

Prior to his recruitment at the Navy Center for Applied Research in Artificial Intelligence, Dr. Kamgar-Parsi excelled as an assistant professor of computer science at George Mason University in Fairfax County, Virginia. Between 1985 and 1988, he prospered as a research scientist at the computer vision laboratory at the University of Maryland's Robotics Center. Dr. Kamgar-Parsi had previously found success as a visiting scientist at the National Institutes of Health's Center for Information Technology throughout the early 1980s.

Alongside his primary professional responsibilities, Dr. Kamgar-Parsi has contributed more than 70 articles to a host of professional journals and publications, including Biological Cybernetics, Computer Vision and Image Understanding, Nuclear Medicine Communications, and the Institute of Electrical and Electronics Engineers' (IEEE) Transactions on Image Processing, which is published on behalf of the IEEE Signal Processing Society. Likewise, he has previously served as an associate editor of Pattern Recognition Letters, which is published on behalf of the International Association for Pattern Recognition. In order to stay up to date with the latest developments in his field, Dr. Kamgar-Parsi continues to maintain active affiliations with IEEE and SPIE – The International Society for Optical Engineering (SPIE), which was formerly known as the Society of Photo-Optical Instrumentation Engineers.

Born in Shiraz, Iran, Dr. Kamgar-Parsi earned a Bachelor of Science in physics at the University of Tehran in 1968. He subsequently relocated to the United States in 1972. Throughout the following five years, Dr. Kamgar-Parsi completed a Doctor of Philosophy in physics at the Catholic University of America in Washington, D.C. Between 1978 and 1981, he was recruited as a patient researcher with the National Institutes of Health, where he conducted research in relation to various sleep disorders.

Thanks to his widespread reputation, Dr. Kamgar-Parsi has shared his innovative research at conferences all over the world, including IEEE's International Conference on Imaging Processing, the Biometric Consortium Conference, and IEEE's annual Conference on Computer Vision and Pattern Recognition. He has also garnered acclaim as the owner of multiple U.S. patents in relation to his specialty areas. In 2010, Dr. Kamgar-Parsi was recognized by the U.S. Department of Homeland Security for his invention of an advanced facial recognition system.

In addition to his genuine passion for his work, Dr. Kamgar-Parsi attributes a great deal of his success to the exceptional diversity of his scientific research. Due to the competitive nature of his profession, he advises aspiring research scientists to embrace the accomplishments of their colleagues, rather than becoming intimidated by their global reputations and vast experience. In his spare time, Dr. Kamgar-Parsi relaxes by playing chess, and he continues to maintain an active affiliation with the U.S. Chess Federation. In the coming years, he intends to further his research in the visual capabilities of artificial intelligence while spending more time with his three children.

Lawrence Bernard Kool, PhD

Senior Scientist
GE Aerospace Research

CLIFTON PARK, NY UNITED STATES

F or more than 20 years, Lawrence Bernard Kool, PhD, has thrived as a senior scientist at the General Electric Company's (GE) Global Research Center in Niskayuna, New York. With more than four decades of experience as a professional chemist to his credit, he specializes in altering the chemistry of metal compounds and other advanced materials to improve the performance and efficiency of aircraft engines. Dr. Kool also focuses on developing new processes to minimize chemical waste and recover chemical elements from used aerospace equipment.

Prior to his appointment with the GE Global Research Center, Dr. Kool excelled as a senior research scientist with GE's Superabrasives Division, which has since been acquired by Sandvik Tooling, during the late 1990s. Between 19988 and 1995, he worked as an assistant professor of inorganic and organic chemistry for the department of chemistry at the Morrissey College of Arts and Sciences at Boston College, where he simultaneously served as a mentor for more than 15 graduate students. Dr. Kool began his scientific career as a research chemist at KMS Fusion, which has since closed, between 1976 and 1982.

Alongside his responsibilities as a senior scientist, Dr. Kool has contributed articles to numerous professional journals and publications. He has also garnered further recognition as the owner of more than 75 patents in relation to organometallic chemistry and advanced materials. In order to stay up to date with the latest developments in his field, Dr. Kool continues to maintain an active affiliation with the American Chemical Society. He had previously contributed to the American Metallurgical Society in various capacities.

Dr. Kool's initial interest in science was chiefly inspired by his father, who enjoyed a prosperous career as a physician. In 1974, he obtained a Bachelor of Science in chemistry at the University of Michigan. Following his tenure at KMS Fusion, Dr. Kool resumed his education at the University of Massachusetts Amherst, where he earned a Doctor of Philosophy in organic chemistry, inorganic chemistry and organometallic chemistry in 1986. Toward the end of this period, he simultaneously contributed to Sandia National Laboratories in Livermore, California as a consultant.

After completing his doctorate, Dr. Kool relocated to Bavaria, Germany, to complete a second Doctor of Philosophy at the University of Bayreuth. Following his return to the United States, he pursued a postdoctoral fellowship in chemistry at Harvard University between 1987 and 1989. During this period, Dr. Kool additionally served as an educator at the aforementioned Ivy League institution.

In addition to his vast knowledge of the chemical makeup of advanced materials, Dr. Kool attributes a great deal of his success to his persistence, which continuously fueled him to pursue increasingly complex projects throughout his career. He is particularly proud to have developed a methodology for removing critical chemical elements from used gas turbines. Dr. Kool also acknowledges the crucial role of collaboration throughout his career as well as the importance of familiarizing himself with the newest advancements in his specialty areas.

In the coming years, Dr. Kool intends to devote more attention to submitting proposals for projects in relation to increasing sustainability in the aerospace industry. Since his highly specific skill set directly contributed to the longevity of his career, he advises aspiring scientists to choose an area of science that closely aligns with their individual interests and goals. Dr. Kool is also extremely grateful to have helped improve an industry that serves millions of people on a daily basis.

Nhora Lalinde, PhD

Senior Associate Director (Retired)
Pfizer Inc.

NORTH HALEDON, NJ UNITED STATES

F or more than 20 years, Nhora Lalinde, PhD, found success in leadership positions with numerous divisions of Pfizer Inc. Prior to her retirement, she specialized in facilitating compliance with various corporate and departmental policies and regulatory guidelines. Dr. Lalinde also focused on ensuring the safety of new pharmaceuticals as well as the accuracy of public information regarding the results of clinical trials.

In 1994, Dr. Lalinde began her career at Pfizer as a manager of regulatory safety for the aforementioned pharmaceutical company's animal health division. After working in this capacity for a number of years, she advanced to become a manager of compliance for Pfizer's Latin American locations from 1996 until 2001. Throughout the following five years, Dr. Lalinde thrived as a senior manager of quality and process standards. During this period, she oversaw the training of more than 20 staff members at a new call center for Pfizer in Mumbai, India.

Between 2005 and 2010, Dr. Lalinde excelled as an associate director of quality and process standards for Pfizer's medical communications division. In this capacity, she developed and implemented a series of quality management processes for the disclosure of completed and upcoming clinical trials on Clinicaltrials.gov. Dr. Lalinde also developed a comprehensive readiness plan in the event of an unannounced regulatory audit from the U.S. Food and Drug Administration. She subsequently found further success as a senior associate director from 2010 until 2016, at which point she issued her retirement from her career in the pharmaceutical industry.

Alongside her primary professional responsibilities, Dr. Lalinde has contributed articles to several professional journals and publications, including the Journal of Medicinal Chemistry and Medicinal Research Reviews. She has also garnered widespread recognition as the owner of four patents in relation to the composition of pharmaceutical analgesics and anesthetics. In order to stay up to date with the latest developments in her field, Dr. Lalinde continues to maintain an active affiliation with the American Medical Association.

Born in Bogota, Colombia, Dr. Lalinde's decision to pursue a career in the pharmaceutical industry was heavily influenced by her desire to provide a stable lifestyle for her two children. During the early 1970s, she earned a bachelor's degree as well as a master's degree. Dr. Lalinde eventually concluded her education at the City University of New York, where she obtained a Doctor of Philosophy in organic chemistry in 1981.

Throughout her career, Dr. Lalinde has been honored with numerous accolades in recognition of her innovative research in the field of medicinal chemistry. As a highly accomplished professional, she has been featured in the 76th edition of Who's Who in America. In addition to her determination and firm commitment to her professional goals, she attributes a great deal of her success to the support of her children. While completing her undergraduate and graduate degrees, Dr. Lalinde's devotion to her two children continuously inspired her to strive for excellence and serve as a role model for other single parents and immigrants.

In the coming years, Dr. Lalinde intends to spend more time with her three grandchildren while exercising her passion for international travel. She also aims to continue harnessing her knowledge of the stock market to grow her personal wealth. Since her perseverance played a central role in the longevity of her career, Dr. Lalinde advises aspiring medicinal chemists to remain confident in their skills and to develop a strong work ethic while completing their education.

Roger T. Richards, PhD

Physicist (Retired)

U.S. Naval Undersea Warfare Center

MYSTIC, CT UNITED STATES

For more than 25 years, Roger T. Richards, PhD, found success as a physicist with the U.S. Naval Undersea Warfare Center. Prior to his retirement, he specialized in researching the propagation of sound generated by various forms of marine and oceanographic military equipment. Dr. Richards also focused on improving the U.S. Navy's sonar capabilities, specifically in relation to the detection of underwater ballistic missiles or other hazardous objects.

Between 1976 and 1980, Dr. Richards excelled as a staff associate at The Pennsylvania State University Applied Research Laboratory. He was subsequently recruited as a technical staff member of the marine systems division of Rockwell International, which has since closed, throughout the early 1980s. Between 1984 and 1987, Dr. Richards prospered as a senior scientist for Raytheon BBM Technologies, which is owned by RTX Corporation.

Throughout the late 1980s and the early 1990s, Dr. Richards was appointed as a physicist at the U.S. Naval Undersea Warfare Center in New London, Connecticut. Between 1996 and 2013, he thrived as a physicist at the U.S. Naval Undersea Warfare Center's Newport division in Rhode Island before issuing his professional retirement. During his tenure with the U.S. Naval Undersea Warfare Center, Dr. Richards was selected to travel to St. Petersburg, Russia, to help develop acoustic technology alongside several renowned scientists from the Russian Academy of Sciences.

Alongside his primary professional responsibilities, Dr. Richards contributed to the U.S. Coast Guard Research and Development Center as an engineer in a consultant capacity between 1982 and 1984. During this period, he simultaneously served as the founding corporate director of the United States Othello Association. Dr. Richards had previously been appointed vice chairperson of the Nittany Grotto chapter of the National Speleological Society. Between 1973 and 1974, he was recruited to the executive board of directors of The Pennsylvania State University Alumni Association.

Following his retirement, Dr. Richards served as a member of the board of trustees for the Mystic and Noank Library in Groton, Connecticut, between 2015 and 2021. Since 2007, he has contributed to American Mensa as the coordinator of the Southern Connecticut chapter. In order to stay up to date with the latest developments in his field, Dr. Richards continues to maintain active affiliations with the Acoustical Society of America, the National Speleological Society, the American Institute of Aeronautics and Astronautics, and the American Institute of Physics.

Born in Akron, Ohio, Dr. Richards obtained a Bachelor of Science in physics at Westminster College in New Wilmington, Pennsylvania, in 1964. He subsequently earned a Master of Science in physics at Ohio University, where he simultaneously worked as a graduate assistant and as the director of the physics library. Between 1968 and 1971, Dr. Richards was recruited as an associate engineer for the transducer library and the acoustics department for the General Dynamics Corporation. While working as a staff associate at The Pennsylvania State University, he completed a Doctor of Philosophy in acoustics at the aforementioned Philadelphia-based institution in 1980.

In 2001, Dr. Richards was recognized with an accolade in relation to excellence in the field of developmental engineering on behalf of the Naval Sea Systems Command. In addition to his exceptional work ethic, he attributes a great deal of his success to his scientific curiosity and firm commitment to his professional goals. In the coming years, Dr. Richards intends to further his involvement in the preservation of multiple historic buildings throughout his home state of Connecticut.

Dr. James K. Selkirk

Chairman (Retired)
Interagency Testing Commission
U.S. Environmental Protection Agency

CHAPEL HILL, NC UNITED STATES

F or more than 35 years, Dr. James K. Selkirk found success as a biochemist as well as an educator and laboratory director for multiple research organizations within the National Institutes of Health. Prior to his retirement, he specialized in the identification of chemical substances with the ability to facilitate the development of cancer in human beings. Dr. Selkirk also focused on creating chemical reactions to uncover new derivatives of chemical and biological carcinogens.

Between 1975 and 1985, Dr. Selkirk was appointed senior staff scientist and leader of a chemical carcinogenesis unit within the biology division of Oak Ridge National Laboratory in Tennessee. He subsequently worked as the chief of the carcinogenesis and toxicology evaluation branch for a nationwide toxicology program of the National Institute of Environmental Health Sciences, which is part of the National Institutes of Health, toward the late 1980s. Between 1989 and 1992, Dr. Selkirk excelled as the associate director of the National Institute of Environmental Health Sciences' division of toxicology research and testing.

Throughout the following five years, Dr. Selkirk thrived as the chief of a carcinogen mechanism group with the National Institute of Environmental Health Sciences. Between 1997 and 2000, he contributed to the aforementioned organization as the special assistant to the science director of technology development. Dr. Selkirk subsequently prospered as the deputy director of the National Center for Toxicogenomics, which is part of the National Institute of Environmental Health Sciences, between 2000 and 2009, at which point he issued his professional retirement.

Alongside his responsibilities at Oak Ridge National Laboratory, Dr. Selkirk was simultaneously recruited as an adjunct professor at the Oak Ridge Institute for Science and Education, which is part of the University of Tennessee Knoxville, between 1975 and 1985. Toward the middle of this period, he additionally served as a member of the National Academy of Science's committee on pyrenes and analogs and as a member of the National Institutes of Health's breast cancer task force. During the beginning of his tenure with the National Institute of Environmental Health Sciences, Dr. Selkirk was appointed chairperson of the U.S. Environmental Protection Agency's Interagency Testing Commission.

Throughout his career, Dr. Selkirk has contributed articles to a host of professional journals and publications, including Cancer Letters, Carcinogenesis and BioTechniques: the International Journal of Life Science Methods. He also accepted a position as an editorial board member of Carcinogenesis between 1984 and 1987 and between 1991 and 1993. Between 1981 and 1986, Dr. Selkirk served in this capacity for Cancer Research.

Born in the Bronx, New York, Dr. Selkirk served in the U.S. Army Chemical Corps between 1959 and 1961 before earning a Bachelor of Science in environmental chemistry at the State University of New York (SUNY) College of Environmental Science and Forestry as well as a Bachelor of Science in chemistry at Syracuse University in 1964. Throughout the following five years, he completed a Doctor of Philosophy in biochemistry at SUNY Upstate Medical University. Between 1969 and 1972, Dr. Selkirk pursued a postdoctoral fellowship at the McArdle Laboratory for Cancer Research, which is part of the Wisconsin Institute for Medical Research. He was subsequently recruited as a staff fellow at the National Cancer Institute, which is part of the National Institutes of Health.

In 2016, Dr. Selkirk was included in the ninth edition of the "2000 Outstanding Intellectuals of the 21st Century." In addition to his passion for science, he attributes a great deal of his success to his tendency to implement unorthodox research methodologies into his work. Due to the connection between various environmental hazards and the development of cancer, Dr. Selkirk advises aspiring biochemists to focus their initial research projects on the biochemistry of individual hazards such as water pollution, radiation or chemicals in consumer products.

Priyalal Wijewarnasuriya, PhD

Project Scientist
Teledyne Scientific and Imaging LLC

MOORPARK, CA UNITED STATES

Since 2019, Priyalal Wijewarnasuriya, PhD, has thrived as a project scientist with Teledyne Scientific and Imaging LLC, which is owned by Teledyne Technologies. With more than 20 years of experience with infrared technology to his credit, he focuses on the design and improvement of infrared sensors and cameras for a broad range of tactical and security applications. Dr. Wijewarnasuriya also specializes in designing infrared technology for space exploration, specifically in relation to the detection of exoplanets, asteroids and other substellar objects.

Prior to his recruitment with Teledyne Scientific and Imaging, Dr. Wijewarnasuriya worked as a technical staff member with the Rockwell Science Center, LLC in Thousand Oaks, California. During this period, he played a central role in demonstrating the functionality of a new line of infrared focal plane arrays for the U.S. Army Combat Capabilities Development Command Army Research Laboratory. Dr. Wijewarnasuriya had previously served as a scientist for the U.S. Army for more than 15 years.

Alongside his responsibilities with Teledyne Scientific and Imaging, Dr. Wijewarnasuriya currently excels as a board member for SPIE, the international society for optics and photonics, which was formerly known as the Society of Photographic Instrumentation Engineers. Since 2009, he has contributed to the aforementioned organization as a member of the program committees for numerous annual conferences, including SPIE Photonic Devices and Applications, SPIE Defense, Security and Sensing, and SPIE NanoScience and Engineering. Likewise, Dr. Wijewarnasuriya has found further success as the organizer of SPIE's annual sensors and imaging conference for more than 10 years.

Throughout his career, Dr. Wijewarnasuriya has contributed more than 300 articles to a host of professional journals and publications, including the Journal of Electronic Materials, Infrared Physics and Technology and the Journal of Vacuum Science and Technology. He has also been recruited as a co-author of chapters for multiple textbooks, including 2015's "Graphene – New Trends and Developments" and 2020's "Nanorods and Nanocomposites." Thanks to his widespread reputation, Dr. Wijewarnasuriya has shared his research at conferences all over the world. In 2010, he was appointed technical conference chairperson for SPIE Defense, Security and Sensing.

Born in Sri Lanka, Dr. Wijewarnasuriya's decision to pursue a career as a physicist was heavily inspired by his interest in mathematics. In 1981, he earned a bachelor's degree in physics at the University of Colombo. Dr. Wijewarnasuriya subsequently relocated to the United States to obtain a master's degree in semiconductor physics at the Illinois Institute of Technology. He eventually concluded his education at the University of Illinois Chicago, where he completed a Doctor of Philosophy in semiconductor physics in 1991.

In 2021, Dr. Wijewarnasuriya garnered further recognition as the owner of a patent for a new methodology for generating wavelength thermophotovoltaic power. He had previously been honored by the U.S. Army for his research in relation to the dislocation reduction of mercury, cadmium and telluride materials. In addition to his dedication to his profession, Dr. Wijewarnasuriya attributes a great deal of his success to his father, who vehemently encouraged him to pursue his passions for science and technology in the United States.

In the coming years, Dr. Wijewarnasuriya intends to continue developing infrared devices for the U.S. Armed Forces as well as numerous government agencies such as the National Aeronautics and Space Administration (NASA) and the European Space Agency. He also aims to eventually settle into his retirement. Since the guidance of his mentors directly contributed to the longevity of his career, Dr. Wijewarnasuriya advises aspiring physicists to heed the teachings and personal advice of their professors before embarking on their professional paths. 🌿🌿

Amina S. Woods, PhD

Principal Investigator & Laboratory Director
National Institute on Drug Abuse

PIKESVILLE, MD UNITED STATES

F or more than 50 years, Amina S. Woods, PhD, has found success as a principal scientific investigator, laboratory director
and educator. In the former capacities, she focuses on studying the role of interactions between different brain receptors
in the development of mental illness and traumatic brain injuries. Dr.
Woods also specializes in creating new methodologies for mapping
the interior dimensions of the human brain and designing therapeutic
chemical compounds for alleviating substance use disorder and other
neurological conditions.

After working as a laboratory scientist at the clinical chemistry
laboratory of the University of Maryland Medical Center during the
late 1970s, Dr. Woods was recruited as a laboratory coordinator and
supervisor for the Johns Hopkins University School of Medicine's
division of clinical pharmacology. She served in this capacity for more
than five years before advancing to become a research associate for
the oncology and immunology department of the aforementioned
Baltimore-based institution between 1993 and 1997. Dr. Woods subsequently found further success as a research associate for the Johns
Hopkins University School of Medicine's department of pharmacology
and molecular sciences, where she eventually thrived as an adjunct
assistant professor for more than five years.

In 2006, Dr. Woods was promoted to adjunct associate professor
at the aforementioned department of pharmacology and molecular

sciences. Between 2010 and 2013, she simultaneously excelled as a visiting professor at Taipei Medical University in New Taipei, Taiwan. Dr. Woods currently contributes to the Johns Hopkins University School of Medicine's department of pharmacology and molecular sciences as an adjunct professor. Between 1999 and 2021, she found further success as the director of a structural biology unit within the National Institute on Drug Abuse's Intramural Research Program, which is part of the National Institutes of Health.

Alongside her primary professional responsibilities, Dr. Woods has served as an executive advisory board member for the department of pediatrics and the division of neonatology at the University of Maryland School of Medicine since 2016. She has also contributed articles to numerous professional journals and publications such as the Social History of Medicine, the European Journal of Anesthesiology, and the Journal of Receptors and Signal Transduction. Likewise, Dr. Woods was recruited as an editorial board member of the Journal of the American Society for Mass Spectrometry between 2007 and 2012.

Dr. Woods' decision to pursue a career as a scientist was chiefly inspired by her initial interest in chemistry. In 1972, she earned a Bachelor of Science in chemistry at Loyola University in 1972 while working as a chemistry associate at the clinical chemistry laboratory of the Johns Hopkins Hospital. Dr. Woods subsequently obtained a Master of Science in pathology at the University of Maryland School of Medicine in 1975.

Between 1973 and 1975, Dr. Woods was simultaneously appointed as the supervisor of the enzymology laboratory at the University of Maryland Medical Center. During the early 1990s, she resumed her education at the Johns Hopkins University School of Medicine, where she earned a Doctor of Philosophy in pharmacology. Dr. Woods subsequently pursued a postdoctoral fellowship in the oncology and immunology department at the Johns Hopkins University School of Medicine.

In 2023, the American Society for Mass Spectrometry selected Dr. Woods for the Al Yergey Mass Spectrometry Scientist Award. She has also garnered recognition as the owner of multiple patents in relation to her expertise. Dr. Woods is particularly proud to have helped discover a new methodology for preventing the death of neuronal cells in individuals with traumatic brain injuries. Since the guidance of her mentors continuously contributed to her professional growth, she advises aspiring research chemists to devote significant attention to the teachings and professional advice of their professors. 🌿🌿

J.E. "Jack" Zimmerman, PG, CPG

Environmental Adviser
Precision NDT LLC

MIDLAND, TX UNITED STATES

For more than 20 years, J.E. "Jack" Zimmerman, PG, CPG, has found success as a geologist, project manager and environmental adviser. In these capacities, he specializes in overseeing assessments of subsurface geological conditions for organizations within the oil and gas industry. Mr. Zimmerman also focuses on helping his clients maintain compliance with federal and statewide environmental regulations and implementing essential safety protocols for field crews.

In 2002, Mr. Zimmerman was recruited as a senior project leader with the fuel systems and services group at Weston Solutions, Inc., where he participated in the maintenance and repair of active fuel pipelines at the U.S. Air Force Center for Environmental Excellence. He subsequently excelled as a geologist with the Science Applications International Corporation between 2003 and 2005, during which period he provided technical support to the Chevron Corporation's Environmental Management Company. Throughout the following five years, Mr. Zimmerman thrived as a senior geologist with the environmental consulting services group of Tetra Tech, Inc.

Between 2014 and 2015, Mr. Zimmerman prospered as a project manager and geologist with Terracon Consultants, Inc., before finding further success as a geologist with eTech Environmental & Safety Solutions Inc. He was subsequently appointed as a senior geologist and project manager with American Safety Services, Inc., where he worked between 2015 and 2023. During this period, Mr. Zimmerman helped several prominent oil and gas companies maintain compliance with regulatory bodies across multiple U.S. states, including the Railroad Commission of Texas and the oil conservation division of the New Mexico Energy, Minerals and Natural Resources Department. Since 2023, he has served as an environmental adviser for Precision NDT, LLC, in Midland, Texas.

Prior to embarking on his professional path, Mr. Zimmerman was distinguished as an Eagle Scout with the Boy Scouts of America. He had previously been recognized with numerous merit badges in relation to science, engineering and environmental conservation through the aforementioned organization, which inspired him to pursue a career as a geologist. In 1980, Mr. Zimmerman obtained a Bachelor of Science in geography at Pennsylvania Western University, Clarion.

Toward the late 1980s, Mr. Zimmerman resumed his education at the aforementioned Pennsylvania-based institution, where he earned a Bachelor of Science in geology. He eventually concluded his education in 1991, at which point he obtained a Master of Arts in environmental geography at Kansas State University. While completing his graduate degree, Mr. Zimmerman simultaneously worked as a graduate teaching assistant.

Alongside his responsibilities as an environmental adviser, Mr. Zimmerman continues to maintain active affiliations with the Society of Sigma Gamma Epsilon and Gamma Theta Epsilon. In addition to the guidance of his mentors, he attributes a great deal of his success to the consistent expansion of his perpetual skill set. Mr. Zimmerman also credits his reputation for composing particularly detailed reports to his exceptional writing skills, which he initially developed while completing his undergraduate degree.

In the coming years, Mr. Zimmerman intends to settle into retirement while devoting more time to his passion for golf. He is extremely proud to have obtained the necessary credentials to practice geology in several U.S. states. Due to the collaborative nature of his profession, Mr. Zimmerman advises aspiring geologists to heed the teachings of their mentors while treating their colleagues with kindness and respect.

Ian Amor

Founder
The Pack Mindset

OLATHE, KS UNITED STATES

Since 2020, Ian Amor has thrived as the founder of The Pack Mindset, which helps working professionals transition into new careers as entrepreneurs. In this capacity, he specializes in providing aspiring entrepreneurs with various resources in relation to professional development, education and interpersonal communication. Mr. Amor also focuses on expanding the online presence of the aforementioned nonprofit organization through numerous digital marketing channels and building his clients' knowledge of essential entrepreneurial skills such as leadership and professional networking.

Alongside his responsibilities with The Pack Mindset, Mr. Amor has excelled as a quality assurance tester for Keywords Studios Montreal in Quebec, Canada, for more than five years. Likewise, he currently serves as an arcade technical support specialist for Amusement Connect, LLC, for which he regularly assembles arcade cabinets and provides configuration and support services for local wireless networks within Kansas City, Missouri. Between 2019 and 2021, Mr. Amor found further success as a test center administrator for United Training in Overland Park, Kansas, which offers a broad range of online courses in relation to information technology.

Prior to the establishment of The Pack Mindset, Mr. Amor worked as an attendant for the city of Overland Park between 2018 and 2019. During this period, he simultaneously contributed to Johnson County Community College as a vending associate in a part-time capacity. Mr.

Amor had previously been appointed as a supervisor for Amazon. com's fulfillment center in Lenexa, Kansas, where he played a central role in the recruitment and training of new employees.

Born in Kansas City, Missouri, Mr. Amor initially developed his trademark worth ethic while serving in the Kansas Army National Guard, which is a component of the Army National Guard and the Kansas National Guard. During this period, he notably achieved a score of 91 percent on the Armed Services Vocational Aptitude Battery, which was developed by the U.S. Department of Defense. Following his exit from the military, Mr. Amor earned an Associate of Arts and Sciences in software development at Johnson County Community College, where he was included in his graduating class's honor roll. Between 2019 and 2020, he completed additional coursework in information technology at the New Horizons Computer Learning Center in Englewood, Colorado.

Throughout his career at The Pack Mindset, Mr. Amor has been featured in multiple local publications, including VoyageKC. His decision to establish The Pack Mindset was chiefly inspired by his dissatisfaction with his previous positions, most of which neglected to recognize his diverse skill set and provided few opportunities for professional development. Mr. Amor was also influenced by the encouragement he received from a previous supervisor, who selected him for an important position and enabled him to develop his expertise in his desired areas.

Outside of his professional circles, Mr. Amor frequently supports several nonprofit organizations in relation to environmental conservation and animal welfare, including Defenders of Wildlife. In addition to his tremendous confidence in his own talents, he attributes a great deal of his success to his vast professional network. Mr. Amor also credits the growth of The Pack Mindset to his notable communication skills, which enable him to understand the unique challenges of working professionals from various backgrounds and industries. Since many of his clients chose to pursue entrepreneurship as older adults, he advises aspiring entrepreneurs to dismiss the idea of placing a deadline on their goals and to refrain from comparing their career trajectories with those of their friends or relatives.

Philip Samuel Fraulino
Telecommunications Industry Executive (Retired)
U.S. Department of State

SILVER SPRING, MD UNITED STATES

For more than 20 years, Philip Samuel Fraulino found success as a technical information specialist and as a telecommunications technician with the U.S. Department of State in Washington, D.C. Prior to his retirement, he focused on identifying and repairing short circuits within the telecommunications equipment of the aforementioned department of the U.S. federal government. Mr. Fraulino also regularly provided technical support services to government employees and continuously improved the U.S. Department of State's capabilities for communicating with various U.S. embassies and consulates, as well as foreign governments and international organizations.

In 1977, Mr. Fraulino was appointed senior library assistant for the New Jersey Department of Human Services' Commission for the Blind and Visually Impaired. After serving in this capacity for a number of years, he thrived as a librarian and as a library technician for the National Oceanic and Atmospheric Administration, which is part of the U.S. Department of Commerce, between 1980 and 1987. Throughout the following two decades, Mr. Fraulino excelled in his aforementioned positions with the U.S. Department of State before issuing his professional retirement in 2010.

Alongside his responsibilities as a librarian and library technician, Mr. Fraulino was simultaneously recruited as the chairman of the public advisory transit committee for the municipality of Princeton, New Jersey, between 1983 and 1987. He also maintained active affiliations with numerous professional organizations throughout his career such as the Association for Information Science and Technology, the Rail

Passengers Association and the Office of Strategic Services Society (OSS), Inc., which honors the historic contributions of the U.S. Office of Strategic Services to the advancement of the U.S.'s intelligence efforts during World War II. Furthermore, Mr. Fraulino currently contributes to the Evangelical Lutheran Church in America in various volunteer capacities.

Born in Hartford, Connecticut, Mr. Fraulino's decision to pursue a career in library sciences was chiefly inspired by his tenure with the Library for the Blind and Handicapped, where he coordinated the reproduction of myriad books into braille. Following this appointment, he earned a Bachelor of Arts at Upsala College, which has since closed, in 1974. Mr. Fraulino subsequently obtained a Master of Arts in English at Seton Hall University, where he simultaneously served as the vice president of the Seton Hall Graduate Student Association. While working for the New Jersey Department of Human Services' Commission for the Blind and Visually Impaired, he concluded his education at the City University of New York, where he completed a Master of Library Sciences in 1984.

In recognition of his contributions to the U.S. Department of State, Mr. Fraulino was celebrated with a Franklin Award in 1999 and 2000. He was also selected for an Extra Mile Award on behalf of the U.S. Department of State in 2001, 2003 and 2008. Following his retirement, Mr. Fraulino was additionally celebrated with a commemorative plaque and an American flag.

In addition to his vast professional skill set, Mr. Fraulino attributes a great deal of his success to his father, who enjoyed his own prosperous career as an employee of the aforementioned OSS, which is recognized as the predecessor of the U.S. Central Intelligence Agency. In the coming years, he intends to maintain a healthy lifestyle while furthering his involvement in his local community. Since his technical expertise played an instrumental role in his professional growth, Mr. Fraulino advises aspiring technology and electronics professionals to continuously expand their knowledge of their specialty areas throughout their careers.

DISCLAIMER

The information submitted to Marquis Who's Who Ventures LLC ("the Company") is obtained primarily from those profiled themselves. Although every effort has been made to verify the information submitted, the Company makes no warranty or representation as to the accuracy, reliability, or currency of the data provided, and accepts no responsibility for errors, factual or otherwise. Furthermore, the Company will not be held responsible for any damage or loss suffered by any person or entity arising from the use of this information, including identity theft or any other misuse of identity or information, to the fullest extent permitted by law.

By using the information we provide in our publications, you agree to indemnify and hold harmless, and at the Company's request, defend, the Company, its parents, subsidiaries and affiliates, as well as the directors, officers, shareholders, employees, agents and owners from and against any and all claims, proceedings, damages, injuries, liabilities, losses, costs and expenses (including reasonable attorneys' fees) arising out of your acts or omissions.

Printed in the USA
CPSIA information can be obtained
at www.ICGtesting.com
LVHW020851190724
785273LV00008B/22

9 780837 978154